The
Library
Web

The Library Web

JULIE M. STILL, EDITOR

Information Today, Inc.
Medford, NJ
1997

Copyright© 1997 by: Information Today, Inc.
143 Old Marlton Pike
Medford, NJ 08055

Printed in the United States of America.

Library of Congress Cataloging-in-Publication Data

The library web / Julie M. Still, editor.
        p.   cm.
    Includes index.
    ISBN 1-57387-034-X
    1. Library information networks. 2. World Wide Web (Information retrieval system) 3. Library information networks—United States.
4. Web sites—Design. 5. Web sites—United States—Design.
I. Still, Julie.
Z674.75.L53 1007
025.04—dc21   97-12454
                                                      CIP

Price: $39.50

Editor: Diane Zelley
Cover Design: Jeanne Wachter

Contents

ACKNOWLEDGMENTS

The editor would like to acknowledge the assistance and support of Gary Golden, Theo Haynes, and John Maxymuk of Rutgers, Frank Campbell of the University of Pennsylvania, and the good people of Information Today, Inc. Those who contributed chapters to this book have my thanks for their hard work and commitment to the project.

"Step into My Parlor..."

Julie M. Still

Paul Robeson Library
Rutgers University, Camden
still@camden.rutgers.edu
http://www.libraries.rutgers.edu/rulib/abtlib/camlib

There are a variety of challenges involved in designing and creating a library page or site on the World Wide Web; it is an activity that requires a great deal of planning and work. One key element to remember is that very few activities in libraries take place in a vacuum: what one person does impacts another. One department taking on a new role or responsibilities may infringe on the "turf" of another department which may or may not welcome the newcomer. This is especially true with something as public as a Web page, which is open to all and an official representation of the parent institution. Advance knowledge of some of the possible pleasures and pitfalls may help make the process easier for those just starting out.

WHY HAVE A WEB PAGE?

Creating a Web page almost seems to be a trend, and, unfortunately, many personal Web pages are of limited interest beyond the designer's immediate circle of friends. After all, how many cat pictures can any one person be expected to look at? The design and maintenance of a Web page or site takes personnel and time, and some thought should go into whether or not such a project is warranted. However, when individuals, groups, or institutions have compiled or created resources that are likely to be of interest to the general public or to a specific population, they may want to investigate placing these resources on a Web page, especially if a noticeable percentage of the target users are known to have access to the Internet in general and graphical browsers in particular.

Libraries have always sought to reach their public in a variety of ways and to offer access to library materials as widely as possible. As soon as library catalogs were automated, people started talking about remote access. As soon as CD-ROM databases became available, there was talk of LANs and multiple access. As part of the profession, librarians have always tried to make information resources available to as many people as possible and to ensure they were being used effectively and fully. The Internet has provided one more avenue for doing that.

Initially the World Wide Web had an exotic quality, fully appreciable only to those with graphical browsers and advanced Internet access. However, graphical browsers are much more common now than they used to be, and the Web is available through many commercial Internet providers and services. Thus, the time and effort needed to produce a Web page is likely to have a much greater return now than just a few years ago. In some of the case studies in this book, an individual discovered the Web, created a page, and then introduced it to the library at large. In others there was a conscious group decision to create a page, and either an individual or a committee was assigned the task of design and, in some cases, actual production.

WHAT SHOULD BE ON THE PAGE?

Once a library has decided to investigate having a Web page, the first question should be "What should be on it?" Having a clear vision, or at least a wish list, at the start will save a lot of time later on. Initial plans always change during the process but a shared idea of priorities is an excellent starting point. Many traditional libraries would put access to the library catalog in their list of top priorities because this is usually one of, if not the most, used tools in the library. There may be other databases, either commercially or locally produced, that the library may want to make available. Staff lists with "mailto" links, subject-oriented guides to resources, and electronic forms, such as for ILL, are also popular. In some cases the list of items the library wants to make available is completely different.

The types of resources made available will also depend on the type of library involved. Corporate libraries will want to use their Web pages for advertising as well as for providing information to the general public. Special libraries will want to review the needs of their primary population. Some Web sites are accessible only to those affiliated with the parent institution. Public libraries may want to present community information on their Web site, or tie in with a city Web site if one is already in existence. Creating a Web site before others in the area or at the institution allows the library to play a leadership role and to take the initiative in creating connections with other departments or offices.

PERSONAL EXPERIENCES

At the Camden, New Jersey, campus of Rutgers University where I work, most of traditional library resources were already on the Rutgers University Libraries Web page. Rutgers University has three campuses; the largest is at New Brunswick, with smaller locations at Newark and Camden. The catalog, numerous databases, and other resources such as subject-related guides were on the system-wide page representing all three campuses. While the idea of having a page for the Camden library was intriguing, the other librarians and I did not want to duplicate what was already there, nor did we want to create a page just for the sake of having a page. We also wanted to make sure a campus-specific page would be used. The library itself has several Internet terminals, and there are computer labs on campus which allow Web access. Few Camden students live on campus; however, we have a high percentage of commuter students as well as visitors from other educational institutions in the area. Of these students and visitors, anecdotal evidence suggests that a noticeable percentage of the campus's community has dial-in access. Judging from the number of questions at the Reference Desk and in educational sessions on the procedure for getting Web access from home, a number of those who dial-in want or have graphical browsers. Thus, there was an audience for locally oriented materials on the Web.

Informal discussions among the librarians led to a list of things, specific to the Paul Robeson Library, that would be useful to have on a Web page. Our wish list included directions to campus, a list of departments and librarians with "mailto" links, a map of the building, library guides and handouts, a link to the catalog and other materials on the system-wide page, and a list of locally-oriented Internet resources; this would overlap with the list of New Jersey resources on the system-wide page but would also include other local libraries and some Philadelphia sites. Since a large percentage of our students are transfer students and, like most academic libraries, the most intensive basic library instruction is in the freshman English course, we knew we were missing many, or most, of our students. Thus, we wanted to put some instructional materials, a research tutorial, as well as electronic versions of our handouts, on the Web. Michael Engle's site at Cornell was an inspiration for this. However, we decided to start with something much more basic and then expand it after seeing how it was used and what refinements and additions might be needed. As an example of our needs, we have a local interest database, created by one of out librarians using ProCite, but this valuable resource is housed on the hard drive of one PC and is accessible to only one person at a time. The user interface is also different from any other database in the library and can be uncomfortable for users. If possible we wanted to make this resource available on the Web, not only for the convenience of the campus community but for our colleagues at other institutions and the local area in general.

WHO WILL DO THE WORK?

This is an important question and less facetious than it might appear. There are two parts to Web production. One is design which involves planning the look of each page and deciding what should link to where. The second part is the actual HTML programming; HTML is hypertext markup language, the coding used to create Web pages. In some of the chapters in this book the actual production was done in-house, usually by one person who is self-taught in HTML or who had taken a short instruction session on it. In other chapters, the library used departments or offices whose mission and responsibility are to do HMTL programming for the parent institution. Still others used student workers. Then there are two chapters written from the vantage point of professional Web designers hired to work within a library or library-related setting. There are pluses and minuses to each situation. If one person creates the Web page, he or she is likely to be nominated to maintain it. The drawbacks here is that this can be a time-consuming process and, unless written into the job description, may not count towards promotion or tenure and may not be included in other evaluative measures.

A GRANT AT RUTGERS IN CAMDEN

Through the Office of Undergraduate Education, I applied for a university grant to place instructional materials on the Web. The grant was accepted, although the award was a third of what was requested. We used the money to pay students to do some of the actual HTML programming, and my first mistake was in assuming I could find a student to do Web work for little more money than we paid shelvers. Actually, we ended up paying almost double the regular student rate.

Three students eventually worked on the Web site for us. The first, Dan Canna, set up the basic page, using a design mapped out by John Maxymuk, author of *Using Desktop Publishing to Create Newsletters, Handouts and Web Pages: A How-To-Do-It Manual for Librarians* (NY: Neal Schuman, 1996); he is also the librarian who would assume maintenance of the site once it was established. All of the librarians would review the work and then make suggestions for change. Most of the information placed on the Web, such as directions to campus, already existed in text form. The student added this to the Web and created links from the main page, as well as set up "mailto" links on the directory pages. He also took the "local resources" bookmark file on the reference desk terminals and created a "local resources" page. Most of the general information had been set up when this student graduated. A second student, Hassell Anderson, was hired. He made some modifications on the basic design and worked on the instructional information we wanted to include. One problem we had run into was the translation of library guides in WordPerfect to HTML. Some translation programs were suggested but we did not locate one we found really useful; this seems to be a common conclusion, judging from the experience of chapter authors. An experienced HTML programmer put the proper codes into an ASCII version of one guide to demonstrate what would be involved in manually adding the HTML codes. Using this as a template and HTML Assistant, a HTML creation/editor program, to speed up the process, I translated roughly half the guides. As I worked I noticed that many of the guides referred to databases available on the system-wide network, or to resources now available on the Web. Making links to these resources is now an item on our "refinements" list. The work was not difficult but quickly became tedious. Since there was a template to follow we decided to "borrow" a student, David Bigge from the circulation department, to translate the other guides. As his other primary duty was shelf-reading, he was eager for an alternate task.

LEARNING HTML

Some people have a natural knack for computers while others seem to short circuit them just by walking into the room. HTML is one more variation of this. Some people pick up all the nuances very quickly; others struggle. Even if the institution has a Webmaster or an office that does HTML programming, it is always a good idea to have some idea what can and cannot be done and a grasp of the basics. I had done some HTML work at a previous job but had forgotten most of it by the time I received the grant at Rutgers. Doing the "grunt" work on some of the library guides helped refresh my memory and made me aware of how I would want to enhance the materials we were making available. Hassell Anderson, who was also working with another campus department on a Web page, made some excellent suggestions. I had created a subject guide to periodical indexes available in the Paul Robeson Library, noting what format they were available in—paper, CD-ROM, or campus network. If they were in more than one format, I listed the most technologically advanced. I wanted to put this in the research tutorial section of our Web page, with direct connections to the databases on the network. Hassell suggested using a table format which made the information much easier to grasp than simply copying the print format.

Hiring someone, especially a student, who knows more than you do about something can be intimidating. However, I learned quite a bit from working with the grant students. I have gone back and reviewed their work using the "View" function in Netscape to see what coding they used to do particular things. Like the authors of many of the other chapters, I have also used this function to see how other Web designers have created various aspects of Web pages or documents.

Many organizations, academic institutions as well as library associations and library schools, offer programs or classes on HTML programming. Those who learn best in groups might want to investigate such options in their area. For those who learn best on their own, there are also several good books on the subject.

WHAT ARE THE ORGANIZATION OR COMMITTEE REQUIREMENTS?

Naturally if the Web page is going to represent someone other than its creator, some form of approval may be required before making the site public. This may be as simple as asking the boss and/or the director if everything looks okay. If others at the organization will be teaching or using the Web site, there should be input from them as well. At Rutgers, all of the librarians reviewed the Web page at various stages of development. It was not always possible to come to a consensus and sometimes we went back and forth on the use of some icons and wording. Although this may have been frustrating to the students who had to code and recode things, it helped make the Web site more of a group effort. All of the librarians contributed guides and handouts they had created to be added to the instruction section. The director reviewed the page on a regular basis as well. During the development stage, it was kept on a common network drive, accessible from the reference desk and all the librarians' offices, but not from the public terminals. As revisions were made they were loaded onto the common drive. This made it much easier for everyone to keep track of what was going on with the Web site.

The institution does have some general Web guidelines for pages that would carry the Rutgers name. The library system has a more formal structure. The Library INFO Advisory Committee (LIAC) reviews all prospective library-related Web pages and offers suggestions for improvement. Only select people have "write" access to the system-wide library Web page so it is impossible to link a site or page to the system-wide page without getting some form of approval. These controls ensure that library-related materials have some degree of consistency or are appropriate for inclusion on the larger page. It is also an opportunity to get feedback and suggestions from people who are seeing the work for the first time. Fresh eyes can catch glitches or see possibilities that others often cannot. The committee review process also lets representatives from each campus see what colleagues on other campuses are doing. It allows us to learn from each other and for new innovations and ideas to filter from one campus to another in a systematic way.

Having an oversight system can, in some ways, spoil the fun because someone else makes the final decision on page content. However, that spells out a key difference between personal pages and institutional pages. On a personal page, for the most part, the page creator can choose the content, color scheme or background, and the arrangement of material. On an institutional page there are likely to be limitations. Before getting started it might be a good idea to find out what guidelines or restrictions are in place and how stringently they are enforced. Knowing that a horizontal "button bar" is required on all pages before starting to design the site will save the trouble of having to go back and put it in later. Knowing that there is a written requirement that no one abides by it can be even more valuable.

WHERE WILL THE INFORMATION BE LOCATED?

This is the Internet equivalent of "access vs ownership." If the institution has its own server or "write" access to someone else's, it is more convenient for those involved in the page creation. However, the staff will have to understand the way the particular server works, and there are also financial considerations. Using space on someone else's server without direct access means that, while it eliminates dealing with the technical problems, it limits the ability to get things loaded or updated as quickly as desired. If a commercial Internet service's server is used, there should be some concern about the amount of time it takes to get revisions made and what sort of technical support is available. If possible, those involved in the page should get references from those who already have information on the server and ask about the reliability of the system and the response time for revisions and technical problems. Even if the library staff does not have its own server, or if there is an in-house expert, it is a good idea for someone on the staff to have some familiarity with HTML and Web production. This allows everyone involved to know the possibilities and realities of what can and cannot be done and how long it should reasonably expect to take.

HOW WILL THE PAGE BE MARKETED?

Once the page or resource is in place, those who created the page can just sit back and see if people stumble across it. Mostly likely they will have a target audience in mind and will want to let that audience know the information is available. Different chapters in this book discuss different means used to market their pages. If information is placed on an existing site in a noticeable way, there may not be a need to do much marketing. However, if the site stands alone, flyers and/or e-mail, demonstrations, announcements in print publications, inclusions on standard Web search engines, or all of the above will get the word out. In a public setting the staff may want to work with community groups and the local media to market the site. Some special libraries, who serve limited populations, may want to announce their site only to their target audience. Whatever marketing technique is employed, it will likely need to be repeated when revisions or new resources become available on the site.

Keeping track of who uses the Web page and how often is important. "Counters" are available that will show how often the page is accessed; however, that could indicate repeated use by a small group or an individual (a proud mother, for example, showing all her friends). Usually a server will show the domain address of those accessing the site, although it may or may not be possible to find out what individuals are using the information. This would show if the target population is using your Web page. If this happens, those involved in creating the Web page can rest, at least momentarily, on their laurels. If not, they can try to find who is using it and what for and why the target population is not using it.

WHO WILL MAINTAIN THE PAGE?

Chances are, the staff that created the page will maintain it—something that should be considered before taking the project on. This will involve making revisions, checking links to make sure they are still operative, or installing software that will check links, as well as adding new information as it becomes available. Those who created all of the information then will either need to keep track of it themselves or ask others to take responsibility for particular sections. If others provided information, they need to indicate needed revisions. This would include items like new editions of works listed on bibliographies or guides, changes in hours, phone numbers, staff or Internet addresses, as well as additions to the information already provided. The creation of an oversight committee or Web guidelines for the institution may be a good idea, as it would provide a policy to refer to in case of disagreement among the staff.

Setting up and maintaining a Web page or site, like any new library service, involves an ongoing commitment of staff time and computer space. It should be carefully thought out and planned. Since the Internet, and with it the World Wide Web, continue to enmesh themselves in everyday life, it is likely that all libraries will be investigating the possibility of providing information via these new avenues. The chapters in this book may assist librarians in deciding how to go about planning a new Web presence or revising an existing site.

ACADEMIC LIBRARY WEB SITES

Chapter 1

U-SEARCH: THE UNIVERSITY OF SASKATCHEWAN LIBRARY WEB

David Fox

Head, Systems Department
University of Saskatchewan Libraries
fox@sklib.usask.ca
http://library.usask.ca

U-SEARCH was created in the spring of 1994 as part of a $1.7 million library system upgrade which included installation of a new INNOPAC system. The principal goal of U-SEARCH was to integrate, through a single user interface, all electronic information services of the University of Saskatchewan (U. of S.) libraries. A secondary goal was to provide access to resources on the Internet. U-SEARCH has gone through three distinct development phases to arrive at where it is today:

- Phase 1: April 94—March 95: First tentative steps
- Phase 2: April 95—January 96: Systematic redesign; introduction of the graphical version
- Phase 3: February 96 to date: Expansion and involvement of subject specialists

PHASE 1: DOUGLYNX AND LYNX

In late 1993 and early 1994 the library staff and I were dimly aware of this new thing called the World Wide Web, and we thought that that it might be the platform on which to build a "front-end" to our library systems. However, we had some concerns that the Web was radically different from anything our users (and library staff) had been accustomed to. How would they react to this strange new tool? Would they even be able to operate the mouse!

Another concern was with system security, reliability, and accessibility. None of the Web browsers we evaluated early in 1994—MOSAIC, Cello, DOSLynx—was robust enough for our liking. What we wanted for our OPAC stations was something simple, user-friendly, and totally bullet-proof. We also placed a high priority on being able to access our DOS-based CD-ROM network from the OPAC stations. This ruled out using Lynx, which is a UNIX program. We also ruled out using X-terminals as OPAC stations although they were secure and relatively inexpensive. Instead we opted for higher cost PCs equipped with hard disks for running the CD-ROM software and floppy disks to download search results.

What we finally settled on for the first version of U-SEARCH was a hybrid system based on a locally developed DOSLynx look-alike program known as DougLynx (so named because it was written by Library programmer/analyst Doug MacDonald) running on the OPAC stations, plus a Lynx version running on a DEC Alpha system for dial-in and Web access.

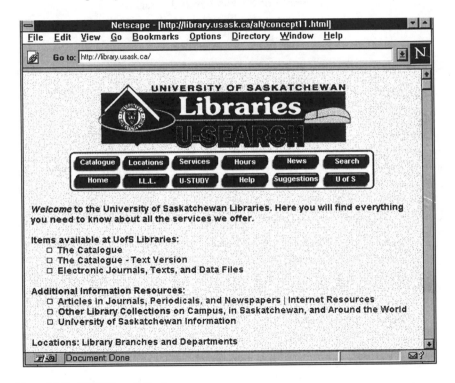

Figure 1.1 The U-SEARCH page in DougLynx

THE OPAC STATIONS

DougLynx ran on fifty-seven OPAC stations. These were IBM Valuepoint 486/33 machines with 8 MB RAM, 100 MB hard disks, and 1.44 MB floppy drives. Basic security measures for the public workstations included password-ing the system configuration setup and disabling the ability to boot from the floppy drive. The DougLynx files were stored on the hard disk of each machine; the master copy was maintained on a DEC Infoserver. Each morning when the machines were turned on, a file verification and update process was run. Because no printers were provided, the library encouraged users to download search results to diskette and sold formatted diskettes for this purpose.

DougLynx achieved the objective of tying together all the library's electronic services, including fifty-two locally mounted databases running on four unrelated servers. DougLynx provided access to local information pages (library hours, borrowing regulations, etc.), gopher connections to e-journals and data services, and telnet access to remote library catalogues. It also provided a secure, familiar looking, text-based, menu style user interface that OPAC users adapted to with very little training. The Lynx version of U-SEARCH available to Web and dial-in users provided access to all electronic resources except the CD-ROM applications.

DougLynx was not a true Web browser because it did not run HTTP protocol. That limitation was not a concern during its first year of operation. However, as the demand grew to be able to link to remote sites and documents on the Web, it was clear that it was time to move to Phase 2 of our Web development.

PHASE 2: U-SEARCH II

In April 1995 Director of Libraries Frank Winter appointed a seven-person committee to coordinate the ongoing development of U-SEARCH. The committee was carefully selected to include a balance of technical expertise and representation from major library interest groups such as Reference and Collection Development. The head of the systems department acts as the chair of the committee and the WebSite manager.

From the outset, U-SEARCH II development followed a systematic approach including the adoption of objectives and design principles.

Primary Objectives

- to serve as an access tool for our students, faculty, and staff
- to instruct and inform

Secondary Objectives

- to promote U. of S. libraries and their services
- to encourage widespread utilization
- to ensure ongoing institutional support
- to showcase U. of S. libraries' ability to manage and apply emerging technologies and information
- to highlight and demonstrate our expertise as librarians in managing information in traditional and emerging formats

Design Principles

U-SEARCH should be

- clear, simple, user-friendly

- accurate, up-to-date
- flexible, evolving
- organized by discipline
- offered as a full graphical interface eventually
- integrate local, regional and Internet resources

The focus of the U-SEARCH II Committee has been to revitalize the basic design of U-SEARCH, and to establish a structure within which other library subject specialists could contribute to the ongoing development. Design enhancements initiated by the committee included a complete review of the U-SEARCH page layout, commissioning the design of a logo and buttons, and incorporation of a "suggestion box" and comments forms. To encourage the participation of library subject specialists in the development of U-SEARCH, templates have been designed for subject and branch pages, a style guide was developed (see below), and a training page was created with links to an HTML tutorial and utilities for checking HTML code and verifying links.

U-SEARCH Style Guidelines

- Stay with the fonts, background and buttons used in the templates.
- Strive for clarity and simplicity of design. Cluttered pages are diffi-cult to read.
- Avoid using large graphics or many graphics as this slows down load-ing, especially over a modem.
- Don't release pages under construction. Do your development and testing first and then mount or replace a page with the tested version.
- Include the last date updated and a "comments to."
- If information exists on another page (e.g., library hours) link to it rather than having multiple copies which each require maintenance.
- Remove template headings with nothing on them.

In the summer of 1995 the U-SEARCH II Committee organized focus group meetings with faculty and students to obtain their reactions to our work. A number of design changes resulted from these meetings. Much useful feedback from users has also been gained from the U-SEARCH suggestion box and comments forms.

THE WIN95/NETSCAPE PROTOTYPE

The library systems staff selected Windows 95 and Netscape as the soft-ware platform for the graphical U-SEARCH workstation development, and in January 1996 seven OPAC stations in four branches were converted from DougLynx to the new "prototype."

The same security strategy is employed on the Windows 95 stations as was used with the DougLynx stations: passwording the system configuration and disabling booting from the floppy drive and daily file verification and updating from the server. In addition, library programmers have attempted to make

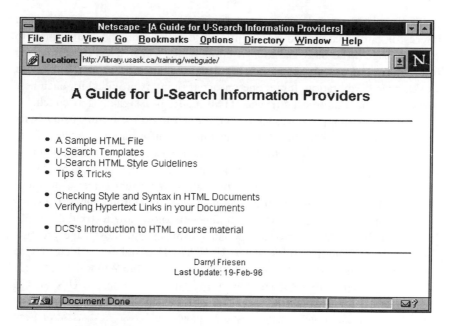

Figure 1.2. A guide for U-SEARCH information providers

Windows 95 as secure as possible by modifying the Start Menu to remove access to the DOS prompt, Windows Explorer, and all but the most critical applications. Shell restrictions were used to hide drives, and the Run command and the Control Panel were removed.

The Windows 95 stations are currently running Netscape 3.0. The Netscape Options Menu has been disabled, but most other Netscape 3.0 features have been retained. Netscape loads the U-SEARCH home page, but thereafter users have open access to the Internet. They may launch their own URLs, and may load their own bookmark files from the A drive. Most of the OPAC stations were converted to the Win95/Netscape platform by December 1996. DougLynx will be phased out in the first quarter of 1997.

PHASE 3: INVOLVEMENT OF SUBJECT SPECIALISTS

In January 1996 the U-SEARCH II Committee conducted a workshop for library subject specialists: Collections and Reference librarians. At this session the U-SEARCH Objectives and Design Principles were reviewed and the Subject and Branch page templates were introduced.

Subject page development is analogous to collections work. The U-SEARCH Committee provides the standards for page development and maintains the "top level" of the Web site. Within the established framework, subject page developers have complete freedom of choice over the content of their pages.

The only criteria to become a U-SEARCH "information provider" are an interest in participating and a commitment to follow the style guidelines, to keep the page up-to-date, and to answer questions received via the comments form. In several cases pages are being developed by two or more librarians working in collaboration. Initial one-on-one training is provided for each new participant, and a more experienced HTML coder is assigned as a "coach."

New information providers have been trained to do their work using Lynx and pico. The committee has discouraged novice information providers from using HTML editors initially for two important reasons. First, we wanted new information providers to gain a firm grasp of the basics of manual HTML coding before attempting to use an editor. In their current stage of development HTML editors can sometimes produce strange and unexpected results. We felt that it was important for the trainees to know how to fix these problems manually if necessary. The second reason is that most page creation involves simple modifications to the U-SEARCH templates, which can be done easily enough with a text editor such as pico, or the Windows Notepad.

The subject specialists have responded to being "set loose" on U-SEARCH with a flood of energy and creativity. Since January numerous Branch and Department pages, subject pages, resource pages, and reading lists have been added to U-SEARCH. Extensive "webliographies" for law, music, and government information have been developed. Nearly one third of the librarians are now contributing to U-SEARCH, and others are preparing to do so.

BACKROOM MAINTENANCE AND TECHNICAL CHALLENGES

Technical and licensing restrictions and some early design decisions have resulted in the development of six different versions of U-SEARCH: DougLynx (OPAC) version, faculty/student dial-in/telnet version, public dial-in/telnet version, campus WWW version, public WWW version, and the library WWW version (Win95/Netscape prototype).

The OPAC version of U-SEARCH, as has been mentioned previously, provides access to all local electronic resources but has no access to the Web.

An important early design decision was that U-SEARCH should be available by remote access, both to university staff and students and the general public. Because U-SEARCH makes available thirty-two databases governed by licenses which restrict access to students and faculty of the University of Saskatchewan, this meant that there would have to be at least two remote access versions of U-SEARCH, one for authorized university users and one for the public, plus a method of distinguishing between these two groups. Dial-in and telnet users are required to enter their name and library barcode number on an authentication screen to gain access to the full version of U-SEARCH. Those who cannot, or choose not to do so are connected to the public version of U-SEARCH which omits the licensed databases. The authentication process matches the user-keyed information against the library patron file on the INNOPAC server.

The dial-in/telnet versions of U-SEARCH connect to the library Web server and run Lynx. Automatic logins to databases running on our VAX system are scripted using the Expect script language. Since Netscape and other Web browsers do not have a scripting capability, users connecting to U-SEARCH with a Web browser must log in to the Vax databases manually. This has resulted in the creation of another two versions of U-SEARCH, the Campus Web version and the Public Web version.

Finally there is the new Windows 95/Netscape version of U-SEARCH which has now largely replaced DougLynx on the OPAC stations. This version provides access to the Internet and integrates all local U-SEARCH resources in a graphical environment.

If you think all this is confusing, you're right! Maintaining all the different versions of U-SEARCH is tedious and time-consuming. At times we think we've created a monster! However, since the generation of the alternate versions of U-SEARCH is largely a mechanical exercise, we are planning to develop a database to automate the process.

The chief problem with all the different versions of U-SEARCH is that it is confusing to patrons. It is difficult for them to understand (and difficult for library staff to explain) why they see a different set of resources depending on whether they are sitting at a library workstation, dialing in from home, or connecting via Netscape from a faculty office. Moving to Web clients for most of our databases and consolidating them on UNIX based servers should enable us to reduce some of the versions of U-SEARCH.

THE LIBRARY WEBSERVER—MOONDOG

We called our Web server Moondog, and its utilization has escalated from 10,000 connections per month when first installed to a peak of over 780,000 connections per month in October 1996.

University of Saskatchewan Libraries Systems Department is the home of acclaimed Internet pioneer Peter Scott, creator of Hytelnet, the comprehensive directory of telnet accessible library OPACs, and WebCATS, the equivalent to Hytelnet for Web-based OPACs. Because Hytelnet attracts thousands of users per day from around the world, this added to the number of connections to Moondog. WebCATS, which was only introduced in April 1996, looks like it will be an international hit of similar magnitude.

Webserver activity is expected to continue to grow at a rapid pace. Conversion of all library OPAC stations from DougLynx to U-SEARCH II, as well as the continued popularity of Hytelnet and WebCATS will put increasing pressure on moondog. To handle the additional load and to ensure some system redundancy the library may have to consider the purchase of a second Web server.

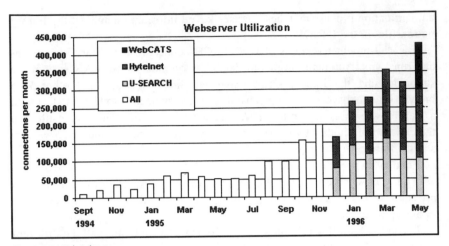

Figure 1.3 Web Utilization

CONCLUSION

We think we have developed a pretty good university library Web site. More importantly, we believe we have put in place a structure to ensure the ongoing updating of the site. Controlled development is the key, and establishing design standards is critical to creating a consistent "look and feel."

If you choose to follow our example, be aware that there are advantages and disadvantages to creating a Web design by committee. Group decision making is slow and time-consuming. Compromises are inevitable. In our case all of the members of the Web design team also had full workloads in their primary areas of responsibility, and meetings were difficult to schedule. Developing U-SEARCH was really no one's top priority. On the other hand, I sincerely believe that U-SEARCH is a better product because of the team approach than it would have been if it had been designed by a single individual.

Design by committee can also help to ensure acceptance of the final product, although this is by no means guaranteed. We have found that you can't please everyone, and that when it comes to Web site design, everyone is an expert! From time to time both the decisions and the membership of the Web team have been questioned by other members of the library staff. Nevertheless, choices must be made and the work must proceed. For this reason the Web team needs to have the confidence and support of the library director. The Web team should encourage and solicit input from staff and user groups but should not be obliged to accept everyone's ideas.

Web maintenance requires continuous effort. Ideally each Web site should have a manager who can devote regular time to its upkeep. Part of the maintenance can be working with focus groups. These groups with students and faculty can help to identify unexpected difficulties users may encounter when using the Web site, particularly in the understanding of library "jargon."

Merging a variety of electronic resources on several unrelated servers and providing access by the Web, telnet, and dial-in, while authenticating users for access to licensed databases, have presented some significant technical challenges. In retrospect I wish we had been more rigorous in thinking though the technical implications of some of our design decisions. If we were starting over I would want to spend more time in the planning stage . . . but then hindsight is 20-20!

In conclusion, a library's Web site plays many roles. Beyond the purely functional level it can be an important public relations tool. The quality of the Website is a reflection of the skills and commitment of the library staff, and the site can serve to attract students to the university. It behooves all university libraries to make a serious investment in developing an excellent Web site.

APPENDIX

U-SEARCH Overview

Webserver

Name: moondog

URL: http://library.usask.ca

Hardware: DEC Alpha 3300X AXP, 96MB memory, 9GB disk storage

O/S: OSF/1 v. 3.0

CURRENT FEATURES:

250 Web pages

1,000 hypertext links to external resources

Access to 57 locally mounted bibliographic databases: 37 licensed, 20 public domain

INNOPAC WebPAChttp://sundog.usask.ca

Multidisciplinary Journal Index (4 HW Wilson indexes merged into one file using the INNOPAC WebPAC interface)

Hytelnet   http://library.usask.ca/hytelnet

WebCATS   http://library.usask.ca/hywebcat

E-journals and Data Files

49 subject guides

online ILL forms

PLANNED FUTURE ENHANCEMENTS:

Continuous expansion and updating of subject content

More online forms. Forms for reference questions and requests for service from off-campus students

A form for searching U-SEARCH using Harvest

Continuous upgrading of the U-SEARCH design to keep up with the evolution of Web browsers and HTML standards.

Java?

University of Saskatchewan Libraries
Networked Bibliographic Databases by Server

Service Name:	The Catalogue; Multidisciplinary Journal Index
Hardware:	DEC Alpha 3800S AXP, 320MB memory, 11GB disk storage
O/S:	OSF/1 v. 3.2c
Software:	INNOPAC release 10.0, WebPAC release 10.0
Databases:	The Catalogue, Multidisciplinary Journal Index (General Science Abstracts, Humanities Abstracts, Index to Legal Periodicals, Readers Guide Abstracts, Social Sciences Abstracts)

Service Name:	Health Sciences Network
Hardware:	SUN SPARCserver 20/71, 192 MB DRAM, 40GB disk storage, 6 CD-ROM drives
O/S:	Solaris 2.4
Software:	SilverPlatter ERL v. 2.05b, WebSPIRS 3.068, UnixSPIRS 1.01
Databases:	Agricola, Biological Abstracts, CAB, Chembank, CINAHL, Current Contents, HealthStar, Medline Express, PolTox, PsycLIT, Social Work Abstracts, BNNA, CBCA, Canadian Education Index, Geo Ref, MLA International Bibliography, PAIS, Sociofile, Sport Discus

Service Name:	Public Services Network
Hardware:	DEC Infoserver 150 with 13 CD-ROM drives, 4GB HD
	DEC Infoserver 1000 with 7 CD-ROM drives
O/S:	DEC Infoserver 2.1, 3.0
Software:	PCSPIRS (SilverPlatter), ProQuest (UMI), CD-Answer (ABC-CLIO), Online Computer Systems Inc.
Databases:	ABI Global, America: History & Life, BNNA, Dissertation Abstracts, E-Stat, GeoRef, Global BIP, Historical Abstracts, MLA Bibliography, PAIS, Romulus, Saskatchewan Theological Union, Sociofile

Service Name:	INFOACCESS
Hardware:	VAX 3100/90, 80MB memory, 11.6GB disk storage
O/S:	Open VMS 6.2
Software:	BUCAT v. 3.2 (TKM Software Ltd.)

Licensed Databases: PsycINFO

Public Domain Databases: Co-op Studies Database, DAVS Film Library, Diefenbaker Library and Archives, E-Journals Bibliography, ERIC (RIE & CIJE), Native Resource Centre, Special Collections databases (manuscripts, pamphlets, Becker, Sorokin), Saskatchewan News Index, Saskatchewan Research Council, Saskatchewan Indian Cultural Centre, Saskatchewan Teachers Federation, Saskatchewan Theological Union, Theses on the Geology of Saskatchewan, University Archives, USGPO

Chapter 2

THE WEB PAGES OF CAPTAIN JOHN SMITH LIBRARY

Amy W. Boykin

Assistant Reference Librarian
Christopher Newport University
awobykin@cnu.edu
(http://www.cnu.edu/library/libhome.html)

Captain John Smith Library is part of Christopher Newport University (CNU), a growing liberal arts institution within Virginia's public university system. In the fall of 1994, the university developed a Web presence and Smith Library joined other university departments on the Web site. Since then, the library's pages have grown and expanded to provide a wealth of information to CNU students, faculty, and anyone browsing the Internet.

HISTORY

Cathy Doyle, Access Services librarian, and Paul Pival, Collection Development librarian, started the Internet work for the library. They were instrumental in getting the library's information on the university Web pages.

CNU's Web development began in the College of Science and Technology in 1994. Most of the development was done by students in the college. In late 1994, the Computer Center took over and set up an official university Web page. Information about Smith Library, taken directly from a two-page brochure about the library, was available on CNU's home page.

At the time, there were two reasons for the librarians to get involved in the process of Web page development. The Computer Center staff and the university's administration were anxious to present a more professional image to the world, and the library staff wanted to present more information (about the library and general reference material) than was available on the library's Web page. In consultation with the Computer Center, the librarians took this opportunity to create a Web presence for the library. After receiving permission from library administration to proceed with the project, the librarians took a short one-hour training session at the Computer Center. During the training session, the systems administrator suggested the "Beginner's Guide to HTML" (http://www. ncsa.uiuc.edu/General/Internet/WWW/HTML Primer. html). The session also covered the basics of HTML and how to store HTML files on the university's server. Now, the librarians were ready to work.

Before creating the actual Web pages, the librarians considered their options. As before, the Web page information could come from printed brochures Smith Library already had available. Another option would be to create the Web page information from scratch, but the librarians chose a third option which was a combination approach. Basically, the printed brochures ended up being rearranged and linked together, with additional information thrown in.

An example of how this approach worked is found with the Interlibrary Loan information on one of the Web pages (http://www.cnu.edu/library/libcirc.html). One of the paragraphs mentions the copyright law, but in the print version, the text of the law was not included; however, through a hypertext link, it is now available. The brochures mentioned earlier are also described in the text of several Web pages. They are also available and can be seen with just a click of the mouse button (http://www.cnu.edu/library/libref.html).

THE IMPLEMENTATION

The main goals for Smith Library's Web pages were to keep them simple, clean, and effective. The librarians tried to use true HTML protocol so that Web page information would be available regardless of the user's browser or server. (Lynx was used to test potential Web pages.) "[We] Don't want to shut people out of information just because they don't have Netscape," commented Paul Pival, one of the librarians involved in the project.

WordPerfect 5.1 was used to create the documents and then they were printed out. A highlighter marker was used to indicate where in the document the hypertext links should be. Most of the Web page text, however, came from existing brochures, and librarian was responsible only for links and HTML conversion.

THE BEGINNING PAGES

Smith Library's first Web pages contained lists of information resources and services available at the library. The Web pages provided access to the online catalog through telnet and provided access to information about the networked databases available in the reference area. They also provided information about hours and library departments, with staff names and phone numbers listed under the appropriate department. All of the pages and links were simple, providing the basics although some of the pages were under construction, such as various forms and a map of the library.

The graphics for the pages were small and appropriate for the content because the emphasis was on the text. Larger graphics were found to slow reception of the Web pages, especially for users with smaller computers and/or modems. For the large ship image, the librarian went to the computer center and asked to have a ship graphic scanned onto the network. The ship plus the words "Captain John Smith Library" were placed on the library's home page, flush right. Simple red dots accented the links and the home page's heading was underscored by a rainbow line.

NEW INFLUENCE ON THE WEB PAGES

I arrived at Smith Library as assistant reference librarian in September 1995. It was about then that the staff learned that one of the Web page creators would be leaving soon. I inherited the job of Web page maintainance after he left—and I had to quickly learn HTML and FTP to work on the library Web pages.

I am happy to say it is not scary or difficult to master the steps in updating and creating Web pages! Two resources helped me get started. The *HTML Sourcebook* by Ian S. Graham (NY: Wiley, 1995) helped me learn the basics of Hypertext Mark-up Language. The Netscape feature "view document source" also showed me how HTML worked, such as what commands did what to the Web text. I quickly learned to copy, change, and create the library Web pages as required.

As a side note, the commands in HTML are easy to master. It reminds me of my college Spanish; if there is punctuation at the end of a word or phrase, it must have a corresponding command at the beginning. The "bold" function is an example of HTML commands and it allows you to create bold-looking text. Type "" (without the quote marks) before the phrase and insert "" after the phrase to be bolded. The text or phrase will appear darker and in bold print on the Web page.

EQUIPMENT

I am not very technically inclined but I will provide you with this much information. The local Web server for the university is a silicon graphics workstation located in the Computer Center. The host for the library pages is Kidd, a computer also located in the Computer Center. The University uses Netscape as the browser, and this is our connection to the Internet. I use a program called FTP Client for Windows to download files from the host to a formatted disk or to my system drive, and to make changes on the Web pages, I use the Microsoft Windows Write program.

At Smith Library, there are about four steps to changing or correcting information on existing Web pages. The necessary file/page is downloaded from the remote university system via FTP to a formatted disk. Using Write, the file is recalled and the changes or updates are made. The file is then saved in .htm format (because the program only accepts three digits after the period in file names), and is then sent back (via FTP) to the remote host. While in the FTP program, the file is renamed .html and everything is set.

I was able to get the hang of that pretty quickly; however, it was more difficult to make the page look as I envisioned. Sometimes, it took several FTPs to get the commands correct and to make the text appear as it should.

PAGE EVOLUTION

The more I learned, from books and Web pages, the more it seemed that there could be a lot done to enhance the library's Web pages. I had great visions of graphics and tables. (That was a little beyond my reach at the time but it did not stop me from dreaming!)

The library director had ideas, too. In November 1995, he suggested that the library pages should include a current-events page. This potential site would provide worldwide, nationwide and/or local events plus links to relevant Internet Web sites. I thought there should to be some fun at the bottom of the page so I took *Chase's Calendar of Events* (Chicago: Contemporary Books, 1996), a "day by day directory to special days, weeks and months," and began to create a monthly current events page.

I would check the Internet news, CNN (http://www.cnn.com) and USAToday (http://www. usatoday.com) for the latest information and stories. Sometimes, these events would be incorporated in the library's current events list. My fun at the bottom of the page was to say that this was the national month of something. For example, April was National Strawberry Month. I searched the Internet for Web pages dealing with strawberries and added links to them on my current events page.

As the current events page developed, I began to notice that there should be some information about what was happening in the library. There were changes in the library administration as well as new databases available for our patrons to use. A natural hierarchy was established: first giving information about library happenings, then the local and national news, and then worldwide news. Of course, the fun stuff was at the bottom. This order seems to work well.

A NEW LOOK

In December, the library director showed me a brochure that included a picture of a California university's home page. The page incorporated a table to display the options available to the user. This sounded like a good way to make our page more accessible and neater in appearance. It would provide links to information that our students and faculty could use.

I searched the Internet for information on how those tables worked and how to create one of my own. After using the "view document source" Netscape function and downloading some valuable tutorials available on the Web, such as the one on Joe Burns' home page (http://www.cs.bgsu.edu/~jburns). I felt confident enough to try a table. The whole process turned out to be a matter of plugging in values and text to make the table work. With the help of a highly competent student assistant, I began to create this table.

The table ended up having several advantages. Instead of a long list of available information, the table kept the information toward the top of the Web page (see Figure 2.1). For the user, a quick look will show what is available on that page with no scrolling to find information. One drawback to the tables, however, is that they may not work well with browsers other than Netscape, and it is still a concern that everyone have access to the information on the library Web pages. In the end, it was determined that other browsers could handle such a simple table as ours and the conversion to tables went ahead. We noted, however, that an alternate text-only page should be added at a later date.

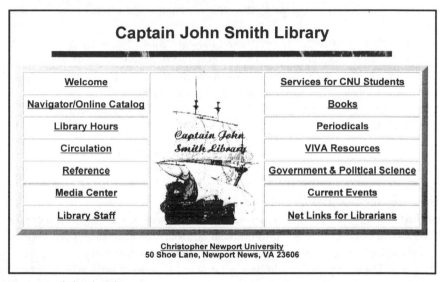

Figure 2.1 A look at the Web page

Other simpler changes were being made around the same time. Some names were changed on the links and we added a "Welcome" page—just to give background information on Smith Library. The background information came mostly from the information found in the university catalog. Please see the Appendix for all the minor changes and developments that Smith Library's Web pages went through during the past year or so.

LOOKING BACK

Creating and maintaining the Web sites for Smith Library is rewarding but time-consuming. In addition to other job duties, this is work that must be continuously updated. It is easy to get behind, to let May slip into June without making changes.

I have gotten good advice by asking colleagues to check the Web pages — the more eyes that see it, the fewer errors will show up on the pages. I am extremely careful about spellchecking, because it is just too easy to end up with unintentional mistakes on the Web pages.

There are several things that work together to make a successful Web page or pages. The best suggestion is to keep it simple! It is easy for the number of Web pages and links to get out of hand. The fewer pages the better and remember that less is more when it comes to Web pages. The reader may get lost or not find information if it is down too far on the page (and may not know about scrolling down for a peek.) Use bullets or outlines to present the information in an eye-pleasing manner; this technique uses the least amount of page space. By keeping the information close to the top of the page, the viewer doesn't need to scroll down.

At a recent workshop, I learned about the "Six Rule." For presentations, it is suggested that no more than six words per bullet be used and no more than six bullets per page. This is a reasonable amount of information for someone to digest and it just happens to fit right on the size page viewed by most browsers.

LOOKING AHEAD

In addition to the general maintenance—hours, staff, current events, etc.— I plan to provide information to our students based on their major and the courses that they are studying. The goal is to provide the library information they need for their classes and assignments.

Just recently, the university has added a new way for students to get credit for classes. CNU Online is a program that allows students to take a class without spending a lot of time on campus, ideal for students who work or have families. The library's pages would be a great place to provide library information for these students. There will soon be a folder of the library available through the CNU Online program.

Last but not least, I am looking into making an image map—something pretty—for the library's main home page. A picture of our library would be appropriate for the center graphic and links to other information placed around the image map would be good. I would also like to get that map of the library done. Since the renovations to the library, there is no good map of where collections are located—or where bathrooms are! Some sort of guide to the library would really help our in-house and online patrons.

I invite you to visit the library's home pages and hope that you will comment on them because any suggestions and recommendations are welcome. Good luck with your own Web pages and keep it simple!

APPENDIX

Partial Chronology of the Web Page

about 11/95   Library director suggested "Current Events" page

about 12/95   Library director suggested a table for the home page

Changed the name "access networked databases" page to "networked databases"

Added a Welcome page

by 1/22/96   Changed heading of home page from "Learn more about the following services at the Captain John Smith Library at CNU:" to "CNU's Captain John Smith Library"

Changed underline of home page title from a rainbow line to a blue line (more in line with school colors)

Added "Services for CNU Students" page

Added "Library Staff" page

Changed contact/Web master names from "Created by Paul R. Pival and maintained by Cathy Doyle" to "Maintained by Amy W. Boykin and Steven Moore (student)"

by 2/26/96   Deleted link to library map because it is not ready yet

Created (at the request of the department) the "Government & Political Science page"

Changed "Networked databases" page to "Viva Resources"

Added a link to the CNU home page (at the bottom, outside the table)

CONTINUOUS CHANGES

These include the library hours, acquired books list, changes in the Navigator/online catalog, staff updates and corrections, the Current Events page as well as the Political Science page.

Chapter 3

THE WORLD WIDE WEB AT UNIVERSITY COLLEGE LONDON LIBRARY

Judith Edwards

Assistant Librarian
UCL Library
j.a.edwards@ucl.ac.uk
http://www.ucl.ac.uk/Library/

University College London (UCL) is the oldest and one of the largest of the many institutions which make up the University of London. It is a multifaculty university, with over 12,000 undergraduate and graduate students, and around 5,000 staff. As well as being a major teaching institution, it is particularly strong in research, ranking only behind Oxford and Cambridge in the United Kingdom. It has grown to occupy many sites, with the main campus in Bloomsbury in central London. Departments at UCL have a tradition of a degree of autonomy in running their affairs, which has influenced the way in which UCL's Web site has developed.

UCL Library contains around a million and a quarter items and has about ninety full-time staff, based in two large and eight smaller libraries. It was one of the first university libraries in the United Kingdom to base its services on a team of subject librarians with close links with academic departments, a tradition which remains strong today. The computer applications team is in charge of the library management system, online and CD-ROM databases, and IT applications in the library generally. As well as being a member of this team (which is where my responsibility for the library's Web pages[1] comes in), I'm also subject librarian for physics and astronomy. These two jobs help me to see both the central and subject-related aspects of UCL's Web services.

The two departments at UCL which have been most involved with developing the WWW site are External Affairs and the Information Systems Division (ISD). External Affairs is responsible for UCL's internal communications, publicity, and publications (the WWW being, after all, just another medium to present these), and ISD runs computer systems for the college as a whole, including the main Web server.

THE HISTORY OF THE WEB PAGES

In early 1994, External Affairs and ISD set up a working group to implement a Campus-Wide Information System (CWIS). The group's brief from the provost (the head of UCL) was to improve information and communication within college by electronic means. It has representatives from External Affairs, ISD, and the library, and continues in this form today, expanded to include a representative from an academic department. As I was then the newest member of the library's computer applications team, I was nominated to the CWIS working group.

The CWISs of individual colleges then were mainly based on gopher servers, so this was how we decided to implement UCL's CWIS, soon christened UCL-Info. Some early objectives were to

- produce a guide to the many events at UCL, for members of the college and the public
- to provide information about central services (such as the library and ISD)
- to provide links to information "out there" on the Internet—although this was seen as less of a priority

I devised a structure for the whole UCL gopher, which was adopted more or less unchanged, although most of it was never implemented because the WWW, which needed a less rigidly defined structure, came along. June 1994 saw the first discussion by the working group of putting the CWIS onto the WWW, and in September of that year, ISD got funding for a half-time student to write WWW pages for the CWIS, starting with the UCL home page.[2]

Further milestones were the Events Diary and "going public" with the library pages at the end of 1994, the Internet Resources Guide in June 1995, and the Undergraduate Prospectus in August 1995. Expansion and development of UCL-Info continues, still with the major technical input being from ISD. The focus has expanded too, as it was realized that the Web had the potential to attract prospective students and to disseminate information about what UCL has to offer. However, the debate still rages about the appearance of the home page.

DEVELOPMENT OF THE LIBRARY'S WEB PAGES

I'd been using various Internet resources enthusiastically for a year or two, and I was keen to contribute information as well as receiving it. I was the sole library contributor to the UCL CWIS, but as this was only part of my job, I had no time to learn how to set up and manage a gopher or WWW server myself. This was an ideal situation for ISD to work out how to manage another department's information on the central server, rather than that department running its own server as several were already doing. (The pros and cons of this approach will be discussed later.) I was given an account on the central server which linked to a directory in the gopher server (and later, the Web server).

Another problem was that I had neither the time to write a lot of new material for the gopher/WWW myself, nor the knowledge in every area. To start with, I collected all the library's existing printed leaflets, turned them into gopher pages, and put them into a logical structure. In most cases, I simply asked the producers of the leaflet for their word-processed file and reformatted it, but a few leaflets had to be rekeyed. I continued this approach when the gopher gave way to the WWW, although tagging the files with HTML and restructuring them to suit the new medium obviously took a little longer.

My approach has always been to get the information online quickly. I believe that some information is better than none, even if it is not perfectly structured. Many of my Web pages are still too long and boring but revamping them is not at the top of my list, although I often tidy up and restructure pages as I'm updating them. My priority has always been the information itself rather than its presentation, although I hope the latter is improving a little.

PLANNING THE LIBRARY WEB PAGES

This was easy because there wasn't much planning involved! From an outsider's perspective, I put up what pages I liked, when I liked. The downside is that I have no committee within the library to guide, advise, or encourage me; the upside is that I have no committee to report back to, revise my pages, or generally hinder me. Of course, that's not to say that I didn't plan the structure of the site, and the structure and content of the pages in it. Of course I did, and do. Having just one person doing this has two big advantages over the "committee" approach. First, the whole process is a lot faster. Consultation would inevitably take time, even more so if it was within a formal committee structure. Second, the pages have a consistent "look and feel" without any corporate effort.

I also try to consult other people. All new Web pages go into a test directory, and I ask the appropriate people for their comments before the pages are made public.

The structure of the library Web pages (see Figure 3.1) originally followed that of the gopher. After about a year, I had a major shake-up of the home page, and I collected information about the library itself (most of the original gopher information, in fact) into a separate section. Since then, the structure has remained stable; I've felt no need to change it, nor had any requests to do so, so I think I must have got it about right. One underlying feature that has been criticized is that I have very few subdirectories. This has the disadvantage of making some housekeeping and file naming more difficult, and it means that I need a clear picture of the virtual structure, as it is not reflected in the directory structure. The structure must be written down (it needs updating), just in case something happens to me. On the other hand, moving the structure around is easier as URLs will stay the same, and links to relative path names are a lot easier to construct.

There are two major parts of the library Web pages that I did not write myself, those about the library's own "ELIB" project, and the RNID pages. The library's ELIB project[3] is concerned with campus-wide networking of CD-ROM and online databases. The programmer responsible for the technical work has written a set of pages with full details of all the databases and how to access them. As I'm happy with his work, he has access to the library Web account so that I don't need to be involved. As far as the RNID pages the Library of the Royal National Institute for Deaf People (RNID)[4] is closely associated with UCL Library. Its librarian was keen to provide further information services for deaf people and those working with them, and was fortunate to have an enthusiastic and computer-literate assistant. She wrote Web pages on RNID library services (see Figure 3.2), including a set of reading lists, and collections of links to resources elsewhere. I advised her on the header and footer information on each page (to ensure consistency with other pages), discussed the structure, and checked the pages. The RNID librarian checked the information content, and then all I had to do was to copy the Web pages into their own directory and add a link to them.

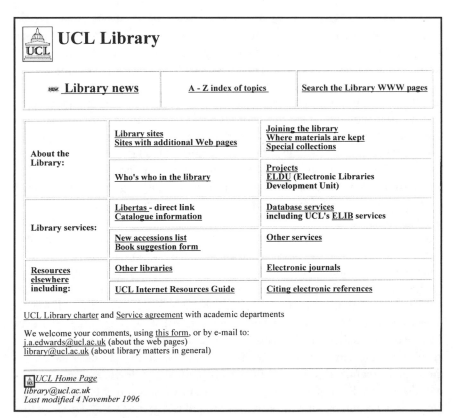

Figure 3.1 The Web page of the UCL Library

RNID Library

The RNID library is a co-operative venture between the Royal National Institute for Deaf People and University College London Library.

The library covers all aspects of hearing, speech and language and specializes in literature on deafness - from academic journals, research reports and student textbooks to children's books and novels with deaf characters. Its collection of historical material has earned it a reputation as the archives of the deaf community.

Anyone can visit or contact the library for advice on literature and help in obtaining it. You do not have to be a member of the library in order to use its services.

We can be found at:

The Royal National Throat, Nose and Ear Hospital
330- 332 Gray's Inn Road
London. WC1X 8EE
0171-915-1553 (Voice/Minicom)
0171- 915-1443 (Fax)
email m.plackett@ucl.ac.uk

RNID library services
        What the RNID Library can do for you!
Internet resource lists
        Selected Internet resources in the fields of audiology and deaf studies
RNID library reading lists
        Selected literature resources in the field of deaf studies

---

UCL Library

ucylmpl@ucl.ac.uk
Last modified 2 October 1995

Figure 3.2 The RNID Web page

THE INTERNET RESOURCES GUIDE

Also part of our offerings is the Internet Resources Guide.[5] This involves management of links to subject and other resources on the Internet and it varies by university Web site. Some, such as Cambridge,[6] have a link from the university's home page, and others, Exeter University[7] for example, have subject guides managed by library staff. Some of the CWIS working group (including myself) were keen to develop a "subject tree" of resources relevant to work at UCL, but I knew that few subject librarians had the time (or the inclination) to do the work themselves. We therefore decided on a flexible approach. The basic structure was set up by ISD staff, who give me access to its Web account. Contributions come from a variety of sources in a variety of ways:

- Subject librarians compile a list of resources in their area and write their own Web pages, held in the Internet Resources Guide (IRG) Web account (e.g., my own pages for physics and astronomy).
- Subject librarians or academic staff compile a list of resources and my assistant or I write the Web page for them. Examples are in law, where the subject librarian found the resources, and Greek and Latin, where a professor liaised with me directly.
- Departmental Web server managers compile a list and hold it on their server; the IRG then links to it (e.g., anatomy and developmental biology[8]).

We encourage feedback, and a few readers of the Internet Resources Guide have sent us useful URLs, but there is still some way to go in developing this cooperative approach. Debate also continues on whether we really need to maintain our own guides to subject resources, as so much is already available, such as the following:

- Large collections, e.g. the WWW Virtual Library and Yahoo, are well-known but list a very large number of resources with little evaluation of their quality.
- Collections developed in other universities are often well evaluated, but may not be very comprehensive or relevant to UCL's particular strengths.
- Information gateways being developed as eLib (the Electronic Libraries Programme) projects[9] seem likely to be the most useful resources, particularly relevant to the needs of United Kingdom universities. (The eLib projects are being funded by the Higher Education Funding Bodies in the United Kingdom to "transform the use and storage of knowledge in higher education institutions"). Current developments include SOSIG[10] in social sciences, EEVL[11] in engineering, OMNI[12] in medicine and ADAM[13] in the visual arts. Resources in these collections are well evaluated and of high quality.

NEEDED RESOURCES

Because the library does not run its own Web server, we need no extra hardware or software resources. I, and those who contribute, use our normal networked PCs, with the software provided by ISD. I was already comfortable with word processors and Internet use and taught myself HTML from material I found on the Web itself. I already knew a little UNIX, but found I needed more, particularly when managing the gopher pages. I learned some on a half-day introductory course run by ISD, picked up even more from ISD staff, and also found support in books such as John R. Levine's *UNIX for Dummies* (2nd ed. Foster City, California: IDG Books, 1995).

Time to do the work has been the biggest problem, and I've had to fit in the (single-handed) development of Web pages around my other jobs. Perhaps the hardest thing has been to discipline myself *not* to spend a disproportionate amount of time on Web work—it's such fun! Since October 1995, I have had an assistant for a few hours a week, which is a big help. She taught herself HTML and now produces Web pages "on demand" when given the appropriate information.

I write all my HTML "raw" with an ordinary text editor or word processor. I have a puritanical mistrust of HTML editors, although no objection to others using them as long as the final result is up to scratch (my assistant uses Internet Assistant). I do use an HTML validator[14] to check the final result, which I try to examine on a variety of browsers as well.

WHY NOT RUN MY OWN WEB SERVER

While I feel confident that I *could* manage a Web server myself, I have neither the time (although doubtless I could find it if necessary) nor the inclination. I'm still very much a librarian and have little desire to become involved with the intricacies of the likes of CGI (Common Gateway Interface) scripts (used, for example, to process forms). I suspect that I'd need so much advice and help from ISD, at least in the early stages, that they'd rather do it for me!

There are, of course, problems with not running my own Web server. I can't write or use my own CGI scripts and have to ask ISD to implement forms for me. I find it difficult to get statistics on access to library Web pages, and can't experiment with new tools, such as search engines. I have to know the right people in ISD to ask for help and get on with them—but as I said above, I'd have to do that anyway.

The advantages of not running my own Web server are that there's no equipment or software to obtain or maintain, and it is easier to keep all the pages consistent in style. I feel I can more easily ask for help from ISD, as they know the library Web pages depend on their service. It also ensures that the pages are kept simple, and I'm not tempted to put the latest (unnecessary!) toys on them.

USE OF THE LIBRARY AND INTERNET RESOURCES GUIDE WEB PAGES

As I said, one of the problems in not running my own Web server is the lack of statistics on access to the library pages. Although ISD will provide some figures on request, they only collect statistics routinely for some of their own pages, which means that I really have little quantitative information on what people are looking at. The information I've provided is based large-ly on my opinion on what users might find helpful. I've adapted existing library leaflets for the Web, and I get feedback from some of the user educa-tion courses the library runs. As I work regularly on both the main and sci-ence library enquiry desks, I know the sort of questions that users ask, and I'm increasingly using the Web to answer them.

As UCL has one of the largest United Kingdom university libraries and is in central London, people from other universities worldwide use it heavily. While information for UCL staff and students must always be the priority, the Web pages are an efficient way of telling others about our collections and services.

My e-mail address is on the home page, and there is a link to a form for comments. I do get some useful comments by e-mail—usually only one or two a week, and often telling me about broken links. I'm not sure if this poor response means that no one is looking at my pages, that they can't cope, or can't be bothered, with e-mail, or that users are satisfied. I hope the last holds true!

NEW DEVELOPMENTS

Having a well-established Web structure makes many new "electronic library" developments much easier, as I can fit them into the existing Web page framework. For example, we haven't had a printed Accessions List in recent years, and there was demand for one. We can extract the information from our Library Management System (Libertas[15] from SLS Ltd.), but piles of printout seemed too unwieldy to be very useful, especially with ten library sites, and no staff time is available for a proper editing job. Instead, I FTP the "New Accessions" file to the Web account each month, treating it as <pre>formatted text with a minimal amount of tidying up, while adding a header and footer from a template. The whole job takes only an hour or two a month; the page is functional (searchable using Netscape) if not exciting, and has proved extremely popular with library users.

I've had an "Electronic Journals" page since the early days, with links to directories and general titles. With our multiple sites, online access to electronic journals could be particularly useful at UCL, and we have taken out a few subscriptions to see how they go. More excitingly, recent HEFC (Higher Education Funding Council) initiatives have given United Kingdom universities free access to the electronic versions of hundreds of printed academic journals. Given an existing library Web page structure, it has been relatively easy to provide links to these journals and instructions for using them and easy to limit their use to members of UCL.

We are working on making our exam papers available online and again, access to them will be linked via the library's Web pages, where information on printed exam papers is already available. This may well be our first venture into using *Adobe Acrobat* software for publishing, rather than just for viewing, and we hope to use the experience gained to digitize our course study packs.

We can use the Web pages to link to information about other new projects the library's involved in, such as the LAMDA project.[16] LAMDA—London And Manchester Document Access—is an eLib-funded project investigating document delivery systems using *Ariel* software that coordinate several United Kingdom university libraries. We'll also be adding images of some of our manuscripts and archives.

The main problem in developing both the UCL and the library Web pages is, and will continue to be, a lack of staff resources to do the work. We need the time to improve and add to existing pages, to investigate new resources, and to keep up with technological developments, but everyone involved is a part-time Web person and has other work demanding their attention. Because of cuts in the funding of United Kingdom higher education, we are very unlikely to be allocated more staff time; therefore, I see that the way to progress is to encourage other people (particularly subject librarians) to contribute to our Web pages.

NOTES

1. UCL Library: http://www.ucl.ac.uk/Library
2. UCL Home Page: http://www.ucl.ac.uk/
3. UCL Library "ELIB" project: http://www.ucl.ac.uk/Library/ELIB/
4. RNID (Royal National Institute for Deaf People): http://www.ucl.ac.uk/Library/RNID/
5. UCL Internet Resources Guide: http://www.ucl.ac.uk/Resources/
6. University of Cambridge: http://www.cam.ac.uk/
7. Exeter University Library: http://www.ex.ac.uk/~ijtilsed/lib/libintro.html
8. UCL Department of Anatomy and Developmental Biology: http://www.anat.ucl.ac.uk/
9. Elib (Electronic Library) Projects: http://www.ukoln.bath.ac.uk/elib/
10. SOSIG (Social Sciences Information Gateway): http://sosig.ac.uk/
11. EEVL (Edinburgh Engineering Virtual Library): http://eevl.ac.uk/
12. OMNI (Organising Medical Networked Information): http://omni.ac.uk/
13. ADAM (Art, Design, Architecture and Media information gateway): http://adam.ac.uk/
14. HENSA HTML validation service: http://www.hensa.ac.uk/html-val-svc/
15. SLS Ltd. (Suppliers of the Libertas Management System): http://www.sls.se
16. LAMDA (London and Manchester Document Access): http://www.ucl.ac.uk/Library/lamda.htm

Chapter 4

A WEB PAGE FROM SCRATCH: ONE LIBRARIAN'S EXPERIENCE

David King

Electronic Services Librarian
University of Southern Mississippi
dlking@ocean.st.usm.edu
http://www.lib.usm.edu/

The World Wide Web, the newest form of information on the Internet, is growing daily. In fact, some of the search engines out there report millions of sites that can be searched, and these sites frequently add new links. As information providers, libraries need to jump into this information revolution. One way to do this is for libraries to create their own World Wide Web home pages. In this chapter, I hope to explain the processes involved in creating a home page for the World Wide Web and to show how I did it (as anyone can) from scratch.

WHY CREATE A WEB PAGE?

The first question that needs to be asked when creating a World Wide Web home page is "why?" Why does our library need a home page? Who is the intended audience of the home page? How should information in the home page be presented?

The University Libraries at the University of Southern Mississippi became "hardwired" to the university computing network soon after I began my job as Electronic Services Librarian. One goal our library had after being networked was to create a library World Wide Web home page. There were four primary reasons for this goal:

- On-campus public relations for the library
- Off-campus public relations for the library and university
- Staff interest in the Internet
- Availability of necessary equipment

On-Campus Public Relations for the Library

One goal of the USM Libraries has always been to be technologically up-to-date. Some examples of how we're currently meeting this goal are the library's large CD-ROM collection (some of which are networked), a gopher page (which was recently phased out in favor of using only the World Wide Web), and the library's use of ARIEL, a system designed to digitally deliver interlibrary loan items to the ILL department.

We decided that creating a library Web page would help us continue to stay in the technological forefront of the campus community. In addition, since many students/faculty on our campus have begun asking questions about searching the World Wide Web, this home page would allow us to give them a front end—a place to begin their search.

Off-Campus Public Relations for the Library and University

Having a library Web page is also good for our library and our university off-campus. Other libraries in our state library association might see our Web site and be interested in how we created it. In turn, this interest could spark other Web projects within the state, and it has the potential to make our library a leader among other state libraries in regards to the World Wide Web, as well as put us in touch with other libraries that may be using some of the same Web techniques.

Also, a library Web page makes the university look good. Prospective students could be directed to our home page (and other campus home pages) in recruitment literature. Prospective students might "surf" the Web and become interested in what our campus has to offer. Seeing our home page will let them know that our library is up-to-date technologically, and it could help them become more familiar with our library, even before they arrive on campus. This is also true for scholars applying for faculty positions.

Staff Interest in the Internet

Other librarians in our public services department had been wanting our library to begin work on a home page. However, this project had been stalled for two reasons: first, the library building wasn't yet networked, and second, no one was willing to tackle the project. So, once our library building was hardwired and I mentioned that I had the desire to work on this project, I had full support.

Availability of Necessary Equipment

The library I work in recently moved to a new building, which included an upgrade of computing equipment. The computer I used for this project was a Gateway2000 P5-100 personal computer, and the software used for this project consisted of WS-FTP, HTML Writer, Netscape Navigator, LView Pro, and EWAN (a Windows-based telnet emulator). All these programs are either shareware or freeware, and I downloaded them from the World Wide Web, used the *Stroud's Consummate Winsock Applications: The Resource Center for the Internet* home page (http://www.cwsapps.com/) for most of the programs, and went to the Netscape home page (http://home.netscape.com/) to download its Web browser. I also used HTML code and UNIX.

IN THE BEGINNING

When I began this project, I had no prior experience writing HTML code or designing home pages. I had merely learned to "surf" the Internet and had a desire to learn what I needed in order to complete this project. I knew that I had a great deal to learn.

Before I began to gather information or design the site, I decided to examine other libraries' Web pages to see what they did, both in terms of content and design. When I examined other university library Web pages, I concentrated on two things: design and content. I looked at how the home page was designed visually, which included what colors or images were used for the background (if any), what other images or pictures were used, what size and color of fonts were used, what type of information was placed on the home page, and how it was arranged. For example, did this site use an outline form or a paragraph form? How much descriptive text was included? What types of links were included on the home page?

The next step in the process involved learning Hypertext Markup Language (HTML). I did this in two ways. First, to learn the basics of HTML, I looked at a few beginner's HTML guides that I found while browsing the World Wide Web. One that I particularly liked (mainly because of its basic outline format) was *A Beginner's Guide to HTML* (http://www.ncsa.uiuc.edu /demoWeb/html-primer.html). From these sources, I gained a basic knowledge of HTML code.

Another way I learned HTML code was through the library home pages I examined. If I saw something I really liked, I'd examine the HTML code to see how the part I liked was constructed. Since I use Netscape, when I wanted to examine HTML code for a particular Web site, I clicked on VIEW, a pull-down menu, and then clicked on Document Source. This pulls up the HTML code for the home page, and allows me to see exactly how the HTML code was used.

The last part of the learning process involved "playing around" with HTML code. To do this, I used HTML Writer, a Windows-based HTML editor. This editor is one of many that allows a user to design a home page and test it out using Netscape browser software before actually placing the page out for the public to see. This allowed me to experiment with HTML code and eventually to create a final product before setting it up in a public environment.

THE PLANNING PROCESS

My initial planning was described above. Basically, I looked at ten to twenty university library Web pages and assessed the good and bad on each site (both in terms of content and design). From there, I made a list of the "good stuff" that I had found. Then I made a list of what I wanted our library's home page to include, and shared this list with the reference department, in order to get comments and feedback. Once I had received staff input, I had a working list of what the content of the home page should include.

From this working list, the main home page included seven different headings:

1. *About the University Libraries*—This heading was created to give people general information about our library. It included brief descriptions of our individual libraries and special collections, a library departmental telephone directory and each library's hours of operation.
2. *OSCAR*—*OSCAR*, or the Online System for Computer Assisted Retrieval, is our library's online public access catalog. It was included so people using the World Wide Web would be able to access our catalog, either on or off campus.
3. *Library Publications*—Our library's user guides and our library newsletter, *Library Focus,* were placed here. The user guides were included so that people with World Wide Web access did not have to come to the library to get a user's guide. Also, this way our reference department always has an online copy of each user guide that can be easily printed out for a patron, even if we run out of paper copies. The newsletter was included for primarily the same reasons, with a twist. Since we place each issue of *Library Focus* online, we now have an online archive of our newsletter.
4. *Orientation Tour*—This section has yet to be developed but was listed as an unlinked heading primarily as a teaser. The plan for this section is to create a floor by floor image map of our library that visually shows the location of each department/collection and gives a brief text description of each area.
5. *Electronic Reference*—This section listed twenty-four Web sites that might be useful to people browsing our home page. Some of the sites included were the White House home page, the *AT&T Internet Toll-Free 800 Directory*, and *Bartlett's Quotations*. The plan for this section is to continue developing it as the reference department finds other helpful sites.
6. *USM Libraries Gopher*—This was included as a link so people who needed access to our gopher server could get to it through the World Wide Web.
7. *Other places*—This last section included a link to our university's main home page. This way, people browsing our library's home page can easily access more information about the university and the surrounding area of Hattiesburg, Mississippi.

DESIGNING THE PAGE

Once the content for the home page was decided, the next step was to plan the visual design of the Web page—what people would actually see when they found our Web site. This involved two steps: first, choosing the Web browsers with which to make the site compatible and using that "style" of information; and second, deciding how the Web page should look.

Different Browsers, Different Designs

In choosing a browser, I learned that different browsers present the user with different designs. For example, Lynx is a Web browser, but it only browses the text found at a Web site; it ignores all images, other than displaying the word "IMAGE" on your screen while accessing the Web site. On the other hand, many browsers will also allow the user to view images as well as text. Netscape, a popular browser, has additional capabilities, like displaying background images or centering text.

I decided to design for Netscape users, since approximately 80 percent of World Wide Web users are using Netscape as their browser,[1] and other browsers are beginning to use features previously found only in Netscape.[2] Additionally, Netscape is our university's "official" browser on campus, so our students/faculty will be most familiar with this browser. Finally, Netscape allowed me the widest range of design, in regards to both placement of content and visual design.

Visual Design

Once the Web browser was chosen, I began to think about visual design. Visual design decisions included the following:

1. Background color/designs: Should they be used?
2. Color and size of text and text links
3. Placement of text
4. Graphics: Should they be used, and, if so, where should they be located?
5. Headers and footers: How should they look?

Since our library recently moved into a new building, I decided that our home page should look "new" and so I used a background design. I found some background image Web sites and chose a few (using Yahoo, a popular Internet search directory, I found fifty-two Web sites devoted to background images). Then, I tested each of them, using HTML Writer. I decided on a background design that was visually appealing and didn't get in the way of the text.

Text Placement, Color, and Size

Most Web sites use the default size for fonts in both text and text links. I think the default sizes are the easiest to read, so I stayed with them. Also, it seems that most Web sites use the default colors for text and text links (black and blue, respectively), and I opted for these, too. I chose black for the text because that is the traditional color for text in books, and it is easy to read. I tried different link text colors, but I decided that blue worked best with the tan background design I used on our library's Web page.

After reviewing several formats used to present the information on library Web pages, I decided to use an outline format. This format allowed me to have five to eight main headings on the home page that were linked to other pages containing either text or groupings of links. I decided this arrangement would be simple and clean, especially compared to a jumble of fifty-eight links in no particular order. Originally, I decided to place the links on the left side of the home page, which is the default in HTML code.

Graphics: Use and Location

Since we had a new building to show off, I decided to place a picture of the building on our home page. Also, I decided to use Horizontal Rule (hr) lines to visually separate sections—the header, the body, and the footer—of the home page. Also, on the subpages, I used an arrow icon with a link to enable the user to go back to the previous page.

Headers and Footers

I decided to use a simple typed header that referenced our library and university, separated with an hr line. This way, visitors to our home page would know where they were. The footer also used a simple typed design. It originally gave my name with an e-mail link for comments about the home page. Also, the name of the university and the library was given, and all this was separated by another hr line.

THE ACTUAL PRODUCTION

Once the planning was completed, I made a simple sketch of how I wanted the end product to appear. Now began the actual production of the Web site. There were many steps involved in production. First, I created the main home page, then I produced subpages using HTML Writer for all pages. To create the primary pages, I arranged all images, links, text, and colors and then tested the page using Netscape (through HTML Writer) to see if everything was placed correctly. I then made changes accordingly.

The one thing that was done outside the reference department was transferring the final graphic image of the library from a slide to a JPEG image. Our library's graphics department did this. They also used some graphic design magic and removed an unsightly smokestack and a large crane from the picture, thus producing a less cluttered image of the new library building.

I had to edit the size of the library building image using LView. LView is a viewer/editor for computer-generated images and allows me to edit many different image formats, like JPEG, GIF, and BMP images. The image I received from our graphics department was very large. When I created the HTML link on the test home page, I found that the image was a memory hog and a screen hog, as well. It was about three screens too big! I wanted it to appear as a four inch snapshot, so I resized the image using LView.

No, I didn't know what I was doing. However, I've used several graphics and paint programs, so I had an idea of what to look for. I simply played around with the image in LView, then viewed it in Netscape, until I found the size I wanted (51,008 bytes). This size looked much better on the home page, and it doesn't take thirty seconds to load.

Once I was pleased with the main home page, I began creating the sub-pages, which are connected by links to the main home page. I found that an easy way to create subpages is to create one page, then use that page as a model for the other subpages within the library's Web site structure. This system allowed me to make all the subpages visually match the main home page. This was accomplished by using the same background color on most of the pages, and by using similar headers and footers within each subpage. Also, all text-based links use the same size font, all the text is the same font size, and all the subheaders are the same font size. I feel that this similarity in design helps establish the library's Web site as an entity, rather than just a page of links to other pages. Once I had the main home page and over twenty subpages created, I tested every page to make sure each link worked properly. I also double-checked for spelling errors.

Next, I demonstrated the Web page for the director of public services, the head of reference, and the library director, and received permission to place the home page on the library's network. This process involved another learning curve for me, because although I knew how to read my e-mail and FTP in the UNIX environment, I didn't know how to do much else.

I found out that there wasn't really much more that I needed to know, however. First, I FTPed each home page file from my computer to the library's UNIX network, with an .htm extension. As a second step, I also FTPed the image of the library and the background color, making sure to transfer them as binary files—otherwise, they appear in UNIX as gibberish. In the final step, once all the files were in the proper UNIX account, I was able to change the links to match the computer network format. When creating the home page in HTML Writer, all links created were set specifically for my computer, and read something like this: localsite://c:util/htmlwtr/about.htm which needed to be changed to about.html in order for the link to properly connect. So, I bounced back and forth between UNIX and Netscape for a few hours, changing links where necessary, until everything worked properly. This was very easy to do using EWAN, a Windows-based telnet emulation program. Using Windows, I was able to employ its multitasking feature, in order to keep both EWAN and Netscape open at the same time. Therefore, I could quickly switch back and forth between the two in order to view changes, rather than having to exit out of UNIX, reload Windows, open Netscape, and then repeat that process many times.

Once all the main pages for the Web site were created, I was able to focus on two special sub-groupings: library user's guides and the library newsletter. Unlike other parts of the library Web site, these two subpages originally existed in paper form. My goal was to format the electronic versions to look similar to the paper versions, while using Web technology.

To produce the newsletter, each page was scanned and saved as a JPEG file. Then, using LView, I cut out the parts of the graphic that I wanted to use (for the next issue, I'll be given the graphics; for this issue, I had to "scan" them). Then I resized each image to visually match the size of the paper version. Next, I had to rearrange the design of each page to work within the boundaries of HTML code. For example, you can't use columns of text in HTML code like you can in a newsletter, so all text for each article had to have one continuous flow. Graphics that were used for each article needed to be downloaded to UNIX, and links to the graphic files were placed within the text of the article in a logical place. Headings that were used in the paper version of the newsletter needed to be used for the electronic version, too. In addition, I designed a table of contents for the electronic newsletter, since the paper version didn't use a formal table of contents, but a "What's Inside . . ." graphic that gave article titles. A formal table of contents with the titles of the articles as links works better for the electronic version of the newsletter (see Figure 4.1).

The text for each article needed to be marked up in HTML code. Since no one had saved the articles on disk, I retyped each article that had appeared in the first newsletter. Next, I saved the articles as text files and imported them into HTML Writer, where I then marked up the text in HTML code. Primarily, I added things like **boldface** and *italic* font commands, placed graphic links within the text, and provided headers and footers for each article.

I went through a similar process with the user's guides. A black font/white background color combination was used, to resemble paper on print—easy to read and print. I created a header/footer design that looked similar to the paper versions of our user's guides, and then I marked up the text of each user's guide using HTML code.

INITIAL RECEPTION

Once the home page was up and running, our library director decided that I should "show it off" during an all-staff meeting. Since the meeting was taking place in an auditorium with a network connection and a large projector screen, this was relatively easy to arrange (other than wheeling a computer, a projector and an LCD panel down a hill on a cart to get it to the auditorium).

I gave a simple five-minute presentation, which explained why our library needed a home page and what type of information was included on it. Also, I

USM
UNIVERSITY LIBRARIES

Volume 1 • Issue 1 • University Libraries • Fall 1995

LIBRARY FOCUS

This is the electronic version of *Library Focus*.

Contents:

Phase I of Renovation Complete
OSCAR Delivers Information Online
Coast Connections
Collection Profile: Feature Films at the TLRC
de Grummond Collection Goes International

Return to the Library Focus Index

EDITORIAL STAFF

Sarah Armstrong
Pollyanne Frantz
Dee Jones
Sherry Laughlin
Sheri L. Rawls
Stella Wheat

LIBRARY FOCUS is published once a semester by University Libraries, The University of Southern Mississippi, Box 5053, Hattiesburg, MS 39406

Copyright: 1995 University Libraries, University of Southern Mississippi
Revised: March 18, 1996
URL: http://www.lib.usm.edu/libraryfocus/focusfall95.html

Figure 4.1 Contents of *Focus* newsletter

asked for suggestions for improvements from the staff. This presentation (and the home page) was well-received. All responses about design and function were positive and enthusiastic. Suggestions for change concerned errors like "these hours are wrong" or "your spacing's off here." I think that careful pre-planning really helped make that initial reception a positive one.

CHANGES SINCE CREATION

I have made many changes since this site was first created and made public. One change concerns the arrangement of information. For example, the Web site had individual libraries listed under "About Libraries," but once individual libraries/collections, like the deGrummond Collection, began creating their own home pages, I decided to get rid of the "About Libraries" link, and instead list that information alphabetically on the main home page (see Figure 4.2). This, in turn, forced me to redesign other parts of the home page. Removing the "About Libraries" link meant that the "Hours" and the "Library Directory" pages needed to be placed somewhere else, too. I ended up using three main headings: "Individual Libraries/Collections" lists each library and collection, with links to information about that library/collection, or links to a home page, if available;" Other Library-related Information" includes the library catalog, hours, library directory, and an electronic reference section; and "Other Sites of Interest" links to the main university home page. It also links to other helpful Web sites, like other Mississippi library home pages (still to be added).

I also changed the home page's header. Initially, the header said "USM University Libraries." After a suggestion by someone and an examination of other libraries' home pages, I changed the header to more fully reflect the library's mother institution. It now says, "University Libraries at the University of Southern Mississippi." This new header clearly indicates the page's origin.

I changed the footers as well. Originally, the footer included only a link to my e-mail address for questions and comments. After some searching of other library sites and the *Web Style Manual,*[3] I decided more information would be helpful to visitors of the Web site. Now, I have an e-mail link to myself as Webmaster (for comments and suggestions), a revision date, and the URL for the home page. This way, people citing information found within our Web site will have all the information they need for a complete citation.

I also made an addition to the "Hours" subpage. Originally, I had created an attractive table that gave day-by-day hours for each of our libraries. However, someone not using Netscape went to that page and the table was displayed through his or her Web viewer as a jumbled mess. When I found this out, I added a simple text-based hours listing for each library under the table.

I have also changed the "Electronic Reference" subpage. Originally, this was an alphabetical list of helpful Web tools and links. However, the list was becoming rather large, so I changed it into a subject listing, under headings

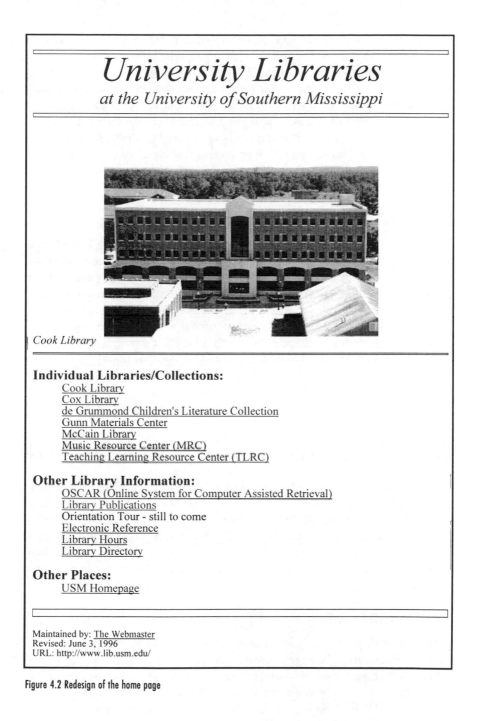

University Libraries
at the University of Southern Mississippi

Cook Library

Individual Libraries/Collections:
Cook Library
Cox Library
de Grummond Children's Literature Collection
Gunn Materials Center
McCain Library
Music Resource Center (MRC)
Teaching Learning Resource Center (TLRC)

Other Library Information:
OSCAR (Online System for Computer Assisted Retrieval)
Library Publications
Orientation Tour - still to come
Electronic Reference
Library Hours
Library Directory

Other Places:
USM Homepage

Maintained by: The Webmaster
Revised: June 3, 1996
URL: http://www.lib.usm.edu/

Figure 4.2 Redesign of the home page

like telephone directories, databases, government information, and search engines. This way, users can quickly find appropriate information.

One last thing that changed during this project was my job description. When I was hired, the creation of a Web page was an idea that needed to wait until the library was "hardwired" to the campus computing community. Once this was accomplished, I was able to jump in and begin the creation process. In the midst of this project, it was quickly discovered that part of my job was going to involve working on our Web pages, making changes and updates, keeping all links working, etc. So, my supervisor thought that it would be a good idea to formally add "Webmaster" to my job description.

MARKETING STRATEGY

The marketing strategy for this home page has been low-key. We haven't sent fliers out to the campus community, or anything like that, but here is what we have done. First, I demonstrated the Web site for the entire library staff, which was discussed earlier. The demonstration was an important educational strategy that ensured everyone on staff would know we have a home page and how to use it. We hope staff will tell others on and off campus about our Web page.

Second, the library participated in a technology fair day for campus faculty. Our home page was used to gain access to OSCAR (our library catalog and networked citation databases can be accessed through OSCAR) in a presentation our systems director gave. The presentation was not about the home page, but as it was used as an access point, faculty became aware of its existence.

Third, we have also mentioned the URL of our home page in our library newsletter, *Library Focus*, which is distributed campus-wide and is also available in the library. This also helps to inform the campus community about our home page.

Fourth, we have plans to begin teaching how to find information through the World Wide Web within two semesters. Probably the library's home page will be used prominently at that time, as well.

Finally, I have sent the address of the main library home page to several address registration sites (for example, one called *Submit It!*[4]), which then sends the address to a number of Web search engines. Now, people performing a search using the World Wide Web will be able to find our library.

MAINTENANCE OF THE SITE

Once a home page is up and running, the work is not over. In fact, most of the work comes after the page is created. After creation it needs to be "maintained." A Webmaster needs to make sure all the links to different sites function properly and, if they don't, has to search for the new address, if available, and edit the HTML file to make that change. If the site no longer exists, the Webmaster needs to delete the link from the home page.

The Webmaster also needs to fix things once in awhile. For example, if someone notices that a link no longer works, something is spelled wrong, or the information about an individual library collection is out-of-date, the Webmaster should try to correct the problem. Another example is when someone sends a message saying "my browser isn't reading your page correctly"; in this instance, I need to figure out what the problem is and reply to the person, letting them know that I'm working on the problem.

It helps to keep current with the Internet and Web technology. If, for example, something new and useful hits the market, that product should be assessed and added if it will enhance the Web page in any way. Two current examples of this are Java applets and CGI counter programs.

CONCLUSION

If I had it to do over, I'd create our library home page in much the same way again. I enjoyed the entire process (but that's because I enjoy working with my computer for hours on end). If you don't enjoy this type of work, then I'd suggest forming a committee in order to share the workload and focusing on committee members' strengths. For example, if one person is a computer whiz, another loves to dabble in graphic design, and a third is a good writer/editor, then the work can be divided up accordingly and the end result will probably be a nice looking product in both design and content. Another way is to do it my way—surf, experiment, play around, and . . . create.

NOTES

1. Browser Statistics: BenLo Park Research, [Online]. (July 1995). Available: http://emporium. turnpike.net/J/jc/public_html/stats.html [1996, May 5]. An analysis of 2.1 million visits to 1,727 different sites tracked from June 24, 1995 to August 13, 1995.

2. ThreeToad WWW Browser Comparison Page, [Online]. (April 15, 1996). Available: http://www.threetoad.com/main/Browser.html [1996, May 5]. A comparison of Netscape 2.0 and 1.1, the MS Internet Explorer, Spyglass Mosaic, NetShark, the AOL Browser, NCSA Mosaic, Tiber (Video On Line), WebSurfer, the Oracle Power Browser, and MacWeb in both Macintosh and Win95 formats.

3. Lynch, Patrick J. (1996, January 24). Web Style Manual, [Online]. Available: http://info. med.yale.edu/caim/StyleManual_Top.HTML [1996, May 10]. This is a style manual for Web developers. It helps lay out pages logically.

4. Banister, Scott. (1996). Submit It!, [Online]. Available: http://www.submit-it.com/ [1996, May 10]. This is a free service that submits URLs to over 15 different Web search sites, like Lycos or Alta Vista.

Chapter 5

CREATING A WORLD WIDE WEB SITE FOR LANE MEDICAL LIBRARY, STANFORD UNIVERSITY

Jane Goh and Marilyn Tinsley

Lane Medical Library
Stanford University Medical Center
jg@krypton.stanford.edu
mt@krypton.stanford.edu
http://www-med.stanford.edu/lane/

WHY CREATE THE WEB SITE?

Lane Medical Library's home page is the latest in a long line of attempts to provide our users with easily accessible information about the library and its services. Previous efforts include improving our signs; creating a library fact sheet listing hours, phone numbers, and services, with a floor plan on the verso; devising a "finger" site that provided electronic access to phone numbers and hours; and then creating a gopher. In 1993, when the World Wide Web became a viable means of communication, the gopher project was set aside in favor of creating a Web site for the Stanford University Medical Center (SUMC). Lane's home page was begun in January 1994, as part of this effort. The SUMC Web site was initially developed by the Information Services Group (ISG), which supports networking activity throughout the medical school. Lane Library was a natural partner in this effort, since the library was already a leader in networking the medical center and had pioneered in bringing literature searching capability to end users and to sites outside the library.

PLANNING AND PERSONNEL

Lane's library director had been meeting with the ISG team and others about developing a gopher and other innovations for the medical school information system, and this group originally formed the idea of a Mosaic site in late 1993. Lane was to provide one component of the medical center site and then to develop a more complex site for the library itself. As Lane's user education librarian, one of us, Marilyn Tinsley, was asked to participate by selecting and organizing library handouts, which would then theoretically be transformed into Web documents.

The original vision was to keep the Web site simple, using the fewest possible number of links and providing only basic information about the medical center and about the library and its services. The Web seemed to be an attractive way to provide this type of information because of its apparent ease of use and flexibility, for both users and providers of information. Our first step was to provide bare-bones information about the library on our home page, much as the finger site had done (hours, phone numbers, list of services, etc.). Then we tried to add existing handouts on searching databases, downloading, and other commonly used techniques. The necessary reformatting (and, in 1994, retyping) of highly formatted print documents into HTML format proved to be more difficult and time-consuming than expected. We had tried scanning, but it did not work quickly and reliably.

Our first major reassessment of our goals for this Web site followed the discovery of how difficult it is to transform static paper documents into useful Web documents. There were several things to be considered. What kind of information is attractive and easy to use on a Web page? How do the links and HTML formatting affect the presentation of information? How can we take advantage of the linking ability? What questions are people going to bring to the Web site? What information do our users need, versus what information would be helpful to "visitors" to Lane's site? How much time is worth investing in the presentation of a single document, i.e., how much time can or should be spent on reformatting? How will users retrieve and use our information, on screen or by printing?

To give focus to the project, we decided to concentrate on the information needs of our library clientele. We envisioned Lane's Web site as our local "on ramp" to the whole Web, as well as a source of information about the library, its services, and its classes. Via Lane's Web site, users can explore the Web, communicate with the library, read about library services and how to search databases, link to a telnet session for database searching, or submit online request forms for interlibrary loans and class registration. In addition, we created links to Stanford, community, and biomedical resources that would be of interest to our user community.

We set up a basic outline to help organize our efforts and to make it easier to find items on the Web site. The basic headings are Lane Library Resources and Information with subheadings of databases, telnet searching sessions, search guides, request forms for ILL, and schedule of classes, with online registration form; What's New at Lane; Other Biomedical Resources (constantly being revised); Campus Resources; and Community Resources.

We developed a policy for our Web site, delineating our goals or mission, whom we would primarily serve, and selection criteria for sites to which we would link. In accordance with Lane's overall mission statement, our primary clientele are the medical school at Stanford University and Stanford Health Services faculty, staff, and students. We also decided not to duplicate sites already in existence, and to link only to sites which fit the needs of our clientele and seem to be robust and reliable.

When one of the writers, Jane Goh, joined Lane's Information Services Department, one of her assignments was to take over as much of the technical part of the Web project as possible. As a team, we explored the Web for ideas and inspiration and then experimented with various ways of outlining and mapping the information we wished to include in our site. The structure and content of our plan were reviewed by the head of public services and the director of the library, and additional ideas for links and documents came from other librarians throughout the library. Final approval of our basic outline of five major topics came in December 1993 (see Figure 5.1).

For efficiency, we have now divided the tasks, with Marilyn doing most of the writing and checking new sites for inclusion, while Jane handled the technical aspects and Webmaster duties. All design work has been done by Lane staff, drawing on our own abilities and taste, and using sources on the Web for design ideas and clip art.

In late 1994, we supplemented Jane's technical skills by hiring our own student programmer, Ed Jajko, who worked full time for us for several months. His technical abilities, creativity, and knowledge of how the Web worked allowed us to add the more sophisticated touches, such as a clickable floor plan and the forms on which a user can request an ILL or sign up for a class. Jane worked with the programmer intensively for one to two hours a day during the whole month of December, both to keep his efforts on track and to be able to maintain the site after the student programmer's departure.

DEVELOPMENT AND PROBLEMS ENCOUNTERED

On March 11, 1994, Lane's first attempt at a home page (basic library information only) was mounted on ISG's server. We were on our way, and constant revision and addition of materials would be our lives for the next several months.

For the first several months of our project, all the actual creation of links and documents had been done by a computer science student who worked 25-percent time for ISG, or by the head of ISG. Progress was understandably slow, due to the many competing priorities of developing the multifaceted SUMC Web site. We often had to wait for editing and additions to our pages. This difficulty was overcome by obtaining direct access to the server. Technical skills were needed in order to have direct access to the server and to be able to directly create and edit our own documents, so Jane focused on learning UNIX and HTML (Hypertext Markup Language, the language used for creating Web pages). This allowed us to move ahead much faster and to edit individual pages several times.

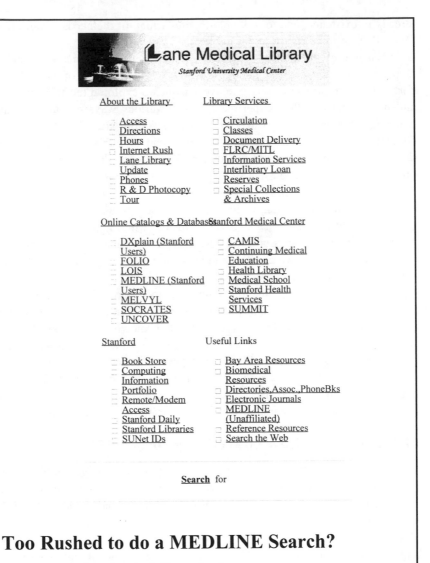

Too Rushed to do a MEDLINE Search?

Free Search Service and Consultations

Figure 5.1 A Web page from Lane Medical Library

Another difficulty was that the conversion of highly formatted MSWord documents to HTML—a tedious process. We found the manual tagging of HTML code to be very labor- and time-intensive. We struggled with the options of mounting the documents as plain ASCII text or scanning them in as graphic files. Although it was fast, scanning was not a practical solution due to resolution problems. We also encountered problems in converting many of the "screen-captured" images embedded in our Word documents into "GIF" format, a standard graphic format. We experimented with the rtftoHTML converter, one of the few HTML editors that was available at the time. We found this utility to be useful in converting existing Word documents that were not highly formatted (i.e., without a lot of tables) into HTML files, although we had to edit and remove the errors in HTML code generated by the program. Our student programmer wrote a document server in PERL to allow users to request our handouts in several alternative formats: HTML, ASCII, or MSWord. PDF (portable document format) software converters such as Adobe Acrobat and Common Ground were also considered as alternatives for serving our documents. Our student programmer also wrote an HTML checker to enable global checking of the Web pages created against standard HTML code.

Due to the limitations of HTML and to the fact that we had decided to stay with mainly standardized HTML (version 2.0), a lot of the formatting of the Word documents was lost. We found that what is pleasing on a page of paper was not necessarily pleasing on screen, so we were faced with redesigning and reorganizing the information to better fit the medium. We also changed our original goals of merely putting static handouts on our Web pages, in order to take advantage of the hypertext medium. Our Web pages generally are shorter than their print counterparts, and hypertext links guide the reader to sections of documents and to related information.

One of the unique services we offer on our Web site are the interactive forms for ILL requests and class registration (see Figure 5.2). In an effort to prevent non-Stanford people from sending ineligible requests, we wanted to restrict access to these services. To accomplish this, we put the interactive forms into a directory that was restricted to Stanford IP addresses only. Another unique feature of our Web site is our customized search engine, written by our student programmer to search the full text of files on Lane's Web site only. For searching the Stanford University Medical Center and Stanford Web sites, we provided links to the respective search engines at these sites.

Both information services librarians worked on compiling the lists for biomedical resources outside of Lane and ended up with a large selection. We decided to restrict our topics to specialty areas that we felt were of special interest at Stanford, such as AIDS and cancer. We checked each resource on the Internet and reviewed its content, stability, and authoritativeness before a link was made to that site. To provide comprehensive coverage, links were made to "lists of lists" at sites such as Harvard's WWW Virtual Library. We also tried not to duplicate local resources already available at other Stanford Web sites, preferring to link to them. Examples included clickable Stanford campus maps, campus directories, online reference tools, and information sheets about other libraries on campus.

In the design of our home page, we felt that speed of download was just as important as aesthetics, so we minimized the number and size of our graphics.

Unsure of which database(s) may have the key paper you need? Lane librarians are available to do searches for you on a variety of databases.

To submit a search request or set up an appointment, come to the Information Center, send email to laneinfo@krypton.stanford.edu, or call 723-6832.

Note: Free searching is available to Stanford faculty, staff and students only.

Take a Class at Lane Medical Library

Entrez: Molecular Sequences & References
Wed, Jan 8, 1997
1:00 - 3:00 pm

MELVYL MEDLINE Command Class
Fri, Jan 10, 1997
1:00 - 3:00 pm
Fri, Jan 24, 1997
9:00 - 11:00 am

Library Skills
Mon, Jan 13, 1997
1:00 - 3:00 pm

Knowledge Server MEDLINE
Fri, Jan 31, 1997
1:00 - 3:00 pm

Internet Introduction
Wed, Jan 15, 1997
9:00 - Noon

Walking the Web
Wed, Jan 22, 1997
9:00 - Noon

Creating Your Own Web Pages
Wed, Jan 29, 1997
9:00 - Noon

Class Location:
MITL, M202, Medical Center

Note: Registration is limited to Stanford faculty, staff and students only. Exception: Non-Stanford people can register for the **Entrez & HIV AIDS** classes. The **Library Skills** class is open to the public and is free.

Lane Library Webmaster (LaneWeb@Krypton.Stanford.EDU)
Stanford University Medical Center (webmaster@www-med.Stanford.EDU)

Figure 5.2 A special Web page topic: types of classes

We kept individual pages short and provided navigational pointers on all pages.

IMPLEMENTATION

HTML programming language is required in order to create Web pages. Most of the information about HTML was acquired using HTML tutorials that were available at the NCSA and CERN WWW sites and from "lurking" on Web-related listservs such as Web 4lib, netscape-l, www-announce, etc. Since the Web server was located on a SunOS UNIX machine, basic UNIX commands, and shell programming were required to maintain Lane's directory on the ISG server. We decided to have our directory on a server maintained by ISG so that we would not have to worry about server security and administration. Learning to use the UNIX text editor proved useful for editing the pages directly on the server. The Web pages were created entirely on a Power Mac using Simpletext (text editor) and HTML converters. Adobe Photoshop was used to create the graphics and prepare photographs for mounting on the Web site. Our in-house student programmer wrote all the CGI and PERL scripts, which provided the interactive forms and other Web interactivity.

Most of the design work was done by Lane staff, influenced by the decisions and style developed for the SUMC Web site. We also attended local Web design workshops, such as "Putting Your Department on the Web," given by Engineering Computer and Network Services at Stanford.

Since ISG and the Consortium for Applied Medical Informatics at Stanford (CAMIS) were also in the process of creating their Web sites, we found the exchange of ideas in the initial stages of the project to be extremely helpful. We were able to share some of the scripts we created with the other groups on campus. The Web project resulted in more interaction with various technological groups on campus. One of the us, Jane, currently attends the Stanford University Libraries' Web advisory committee meetings.

MARKETING THE WEB SITE

To bring our Web site to the attention of the library and information community, we presented papers recounting the process of developing our Web site at regional and national professional meetings in 1995. We also registered our site with various Web indexers, such as Yahoo!, and announced our site on various listservs, such as MEDLIB-L and www-announce.

To make sure our users know about and use Lane's Web site, we present the site in several ways. We provide Web updates as well as Lane's Web address in our monthly newsletter, *Lane Library Update*. We introduce people to our site in our Internet-related classes and give demos of it at the annual Medical Center and Biomedical Informatics Infofairs. On all our library workstations, we have set the home page to default to Lane's site whenever the Web browser is launched. We have also created and distributed bookmarks and business cards with Lane's home page address.

USER FEEDBACK AND TRACKING

We currently provide a feedback mechanism on our site by which comments and suggestions for upgrading the content of the Web pages could be sent to the Web team. However, we have not found a foolproof way (apart from a disclaimer) to prevent users from using our suggestion forms as a means to make reference requests. User comments are sent to the e-mail boxes of the Web team who may reply directly to the user or forward the comments or questions to the appropriate library department. In response to user feedback, we have reorganized our pages so that frequently used items (such as access to our online catalogs, Medline, and other databases) are easily accessible and visible. We are currently in the process of rethinking the design and organization of our Web site in order to enhance it aesthetically, to incorporate new Web technology, as well as to provide more access points to information on our site.

To assess usage, we wrote a PERL program which displays access statistics such as the number of times each Web page is accessed, the number of hits for each Web page as a percentage of the total, and the date and time each Web page was last accessed. However, so far we have not had the time to formally study usage statistics.

WEB SITE MAINTENANCE

All of our Web pages and our logo were created using a Power Macintosh with a word processor and graphics programs. We have an in-house scanner, but have found it more effective to convert photographs to digital format on a CD. An IS librarian, Jane currently maintains the site in addition to her other responsibilities. Time spent maintaining the site varies from a couple of hours a week to several hours a day, depending on the project required. Since we are in the process of doing a major overhaul of our design and organization, we plan to devote more time to the project.

SUMMING UP

Today, with so much interest generated by the press regarding the Internet and World Wide Web, it is much easier to get training for creating Web pages. When we started, it was still a new and relatively unknown technology outside of academia, so we had to rely on picking up the required skills in piecemeal fashion.

We found that having an in-house programmer dedicated to the Web project in its early stages was invaluable in Web script creation as well as in setting up the directory and in providing technical support to the Web team members. For customized banners, logos, and Web graphics creation, access to a graphic designer would have been helpful, especially in-house or within the campus. Since we did all of our work in-house, we did not experience using contractors or consultants who would be helpful in the initial stages of the effort. However, the issue of maintaining and updating the site would have to be worked out if contractors were used.

Before mounting most of our documents, we spent a lot of time off-line thinking about the overall organization of our Web site. We discussed and outlined our policies, audience, and content. This preplanning proved essential in keeping us from being sidetracked and having to redo a lot of our work as we moved our files online and created our hypertext links. We also found it helpful in guiding the programmer in his creative process of coming up with innovative scripts and programs.

In view of the time and effort needed to keep a complex Web site viable and to keep up with all the advances in Web technology and resources available on the Web, ideally there should be at least one person, traditionally referred to as the Webmaster, dedicated full time to Web site construction and maintenance. Unfortunately, due to staffing restrictions, this option is not always possible. A joint effort by two or more people is another option for keeping up-to-date. At Lane, Jane is primarily responsible for the technical or "housekeeping" tasks of maintaining the site, Web page creation and updating, as well as ensuring uniformity of design across the site. Marilyn serves as editor-in-chief for the content and organization of the site, and in reviewing new Web sites for potential hypertext links. In addition to these Web master duties, which require approximately about 25 percent of our time, other staff members contribute to maintaining the Web site. The project has evolved over time to become a library-wide team effort, with each information services librarian taking responsibility for reviewing and suggesting content in particular subject areas. Lane staff from all departments contribute by updating information, designing graphics, and providing suggestions and comments for improving the site. The Fleischmann Learning Resource Center (FLRC) and Special Collection and Archives departments are currently developing their own individual Web pages.

LOOKING AHEAD

Over the last two years, as the World Wide Web has become more widely used, maintaining a presence on the Web has become a high priority for both Lane Library and the medical center. To support more SUMC departments in developing Web sites, ISG is planning to hire staff dedicated to the Web project. We hope to cooperate in this endeavor and also to benefit from the new expertise being added to ISG's Web support staff.

ACKNOWLEDGMENTS

We wish to thank the following people for their support in developing Lane Library's Web site.

John Reuling, Director, Stanford Medical Center Networking
Bill Merz, News/On-Line Information Editor, Stanford Information Services GroupSG
Torsten Heycke, Symbolic Systems Resources Group, Stanford
Peter Stangl, Library Director, Lane Medical Library
Valerie Su, Deputy Director, Lane Medical Library
Staff of Lane Medical Library
Ed Jajko, assistant student programmer

REFERENCES

Goh, Jane, and Tinsley, Marilyn. "Setting Up a World Wide Web Home Page for a Medical Library." 1995 NCNMLG/MLGSCA Joint Meeting, Napa, California.

Goh, Jane, and Tinsley, Marilyn. "Setting Up a World Wide Web Home Page for a Medical Library." 1995 Medical Library Association Annual Meeting, Washington, D.C.

Quinn, Christine. "Putting Your Department on the Web" Stanford University, Dec 1994. URL: http://cast.stanford.edu/cast/www/class/

Chapter 6

THE WESTERN ILLINOIS UNIVERSITY LIBRARY WORLD WIDE WEB HOME PAGE

Tina Evans Greenwood

Library Instruction Coordinator
Fort Lewis College
GREENWOOD_T@FORTLEWIS.EDU
(formerly Reference Librarian and Library Web Coordinator
Western Illinois University)

Western Illinois University Library's World Wide Web (WWW) site (http://www.wiu.edu/users/milibo/wiu.index.htm) was developed in the spring of 1995. I voluntarily assumed the role of library Web coordinator, and with the help of others, including many library faculty and staff, I developed and presented the major portions of it from January to May of that year. The Web site is very large (several hundred files), offering users a great deal of information about the library itself and helpful links to library and Internet services. After a discussion of why and how the WIU Library Web was developed, there will be an examination of the issues facing us today and the questions that will need to be answered for future development.

WHY THE WIU LIBRARY DEVELOPED A WEB

The real push for WIU Web development was initiated outside the library in Academic Computing. Jim Calhoun, long-time director of the Department of Academic Computing, taught a one-credit class on Web pages that was offered through the computer science department in spring of 1995. Hearing about the class through a friend, and since I was fascinated with learning as much as I could about the Internet, I decided to take it.

The requirement of the class was that each student was to develop a Web presence for a university department, office, or other campus entity. The class was designed to teach students a basic set of skills needed to become Web page designers, but it had another objective as well: to bring a sizable amount of information about WIU onto the WWW.

Forewarned by reference colleague Felix Chu that if I was the only one from the library who took the class, I'd probably end up in charge of a library

Web project, I found he was right. Since I was relatively new in my job in reference—I'd been at WIU less than a year—I was still searching for a real niche for myself, so the thought of taking on this project pleased me.

Although many of us at the library could now give very good reasons why we have and maintain a library Web, there was no clear vision as to why we were doing it at first. There hadn't been a push for Web development from within the library, but I had a sense that a well-organized Internet presence would become increasingly important as the Web developed and as we learned to take advantage of how an established Web presence could offer and organize access to many new resources. However, the vision of the Web's potential as a library service grew over time as our awareness and knowledge developed. Now, of course, we have the understanding to envision how we might apply technology in creative ways to expand access to library services or to offer entirely new services, but then I needed to go through a steep learning curve (bringing others along with me, at least in some areas) to become technically proficient and aware of the kinds of choices to be made and potential to be tapped in the future. It's hard to have vision about that which you don't yet understand.

PLANNING STRATEGIES AND PRODUCTION OF THE INITIAL WEB PAGE

The overall guiding principle in planning for the new Web page was to get people involved. Gretchen Whitney, one of my library school professors, stressed the importance of involving people in a new project involving technology and of having people accept the new product; it is difficult to gain this acceptance after implementation if it has not been cultivated along the way. The shape that involvement took and its extent varied with the library unit and with the individual. The best way to gain people's interest in a new project and to guarantee that they will make use of the finished product is to ask them to take part in producing it. If people feel a sense of ownership in something they help to make, they have a personal stake in ensuring its quality and utility.

Early on, I called several planning meetings open to all library faculty and staff. The turnout was good—about ten to fifteen faculty and staff from various library units attending each meeting. Presenting a variety of information—what was going on campus-wide, possible models for organizing the Web page and possible ways to go about constructing it—I asked for ideas and suggestions from all who attended. The response was a mixture of skepticism and enthusiasm from those attending; however, as the project progressed, the skepticism subsided somewhat.

At these early meetings, we determined, as a group, the basic design of the library's main Web page as well as the organization of much of the information that would be linked "below" it. Unit coordinators, some faculty and some staff, would be responsible for putting together the information about their units to be posted on the Web. The unit information, at a bare minimum, was to include a basic description of the function of the unit together with a contact point for requesting further information. I was to code the material in HTML and perform editorial work necessary to give the Web a consistent look and feel. After posting material about a unit on the Web, I asked the individual unit coordinator to review it carefully and to decide if changes were necessary or desirable. Unit coordinators had ultimate control over the final quality and character of what was presented (see Figure 6.1).

Web development gave the units an opportunity to consider what was most important to communicate to the public about themselves, what their real purpose

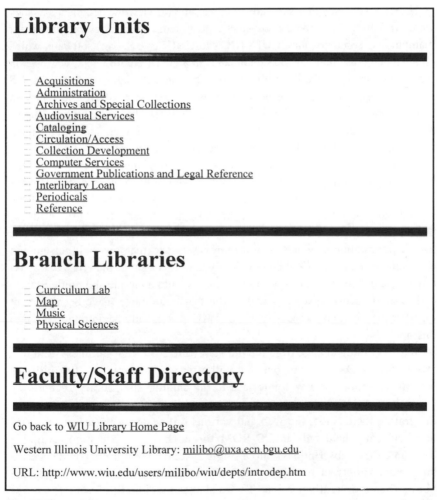

Library Units

- Acquisitions
- Administration
- Archives and Special Collections
- Audiovisual Services
- Cataloging
- Circulation/Access
- Collection Development
- Computer Services
- Government Publications and Legal Reference
- Interlibrary Loan
- Periodicals
- Reference

Branch Libraries

- Curriculum Lab
- Map
- Music
- Physical Sciences

Faculty/Staff Directory

Go back to WIU Library Home Page

Western Illinois University Library: milibo@uxa.ecn.bgu.edu.

URL: http://www.wiu.edu/users/milibo/wiu/depts/introdep.htm

Figure 6.1 Library unit list

was and how they might make use of this new technology in innovative ways. Some units even developed new services as a result of this process; for example, reference offered its services via e-mail, and interlibrary loan (ILL) offered submittal of book and periodical request forms via the Web.

Some units or branch libraries managed at least some of the coding of their documents within their own units by having students or staff learn HTML. For those libraries and units that submitted coded material, I performed editorial functions, making sure that all the coding worked properly and was consistent in heading sizes and other minor design matters. I would also add some graphical enhancements (such as colored bars to set off certain parts of the text) that made the overall presentation cohesive.

HTML Assistant editor software and Netscape (to view the documents as they were written) were used to produce the document while LView was used for manipulating some graphics. DUFS (DOS to UNIX File Server) software, which allowed me to use familiar DOS commands in a UNIX environment, was used in the initial transfer of the large library Web structure, though I currently use WS FTP to transfer updates. The entire Web is housed on a UNIX file server in Chicago, part of the Educational Computing Network shared by several Illinois universities, because the library does not have its own server. This arrangement saves some headaches, but it presents some challenges as well.

Distributing the writing was a great success, though not perfect. The material supplied by library units was generally uneven in its depth and its relevance to the Web user and needed refining. Much of the material was also written from a print-based mindset, some of it even converted directly from printed documents, which does not yet demonstrate the true potential of Web publishing. The library information now presented is more a set of textual material translated to electronic format and linked hierarchically than it is a set of materials that maximizes the potential of the Web to integrate text into a unique and unified fabric and to offer access to services and media that could never have been brought together in a single package before. The WIU Web is only beginning to tap into this potential.

With a coming change from the old statewide ILLINET Online system to a new statewide DRA system, one that will offer a great deal more flexibility as well as an option for a Web interface to the catalog, the Library Technology Committee and the library as a whole are just beginning to see possibilities for integrating the catalog, the Web and various online services (many subscriptions currently held only in CD-ROM format but now becoming available through online subscriptions) into a single system so that users could access a far greater variety of resources from any one terminal inside or outside the library than is currently possible. The road ahead will be filled with new questions but with new potential as well.

STANDARDS FOR LIBRARY WEB DEVELOPMENT

Web Organization

The organization of the WIU Library Web is, for the most part, hierarchical. Although one of the real innovations represented by the Web is that it can present information linked in many configurations (hierarchical being only one of the choices), I felt—and my colleagues agreed—that a basic hierarchy would make the most sense to users. Hierarchy, however, is not the hard and fast rule here. For example, a link is provided within the subject organization of Internet sites (http://www.wiu.edu/users/milibo/wiu/resource/subjects.sht) to "Reference" information (see Figure 6.2). A link to this same file of external links is provided within the Reference Unit section of the library Web (http://www.wiu.edu/users/milibo/wiu/depts/ref/ref.sht). Here, it makes sense to reference the one file from multiple locations. Convenient links to often used library services such as the library catalog (ILLINET Online), UnCover, and Interlibrary Loan are provided from the initial library Web page (see Figure 6.3). In the future, the library Web may vary increasingly from its original hierarchy as more library material is written specifically for the WWW.

Navigational Tools and Graphics

Each document contained in WIU Library's Web provides a link or links "back" to a page or to pages the user probably visited in the process of accessing the current document. For the most part, these links can return the user to the page used to link to the current document. If a page is accessed from several points within the Web, the user is offered a return path to each of these individual pages. Occasionally, "back" links take the user back several steps, back to what would seem a more desirable point for further searching once the current information

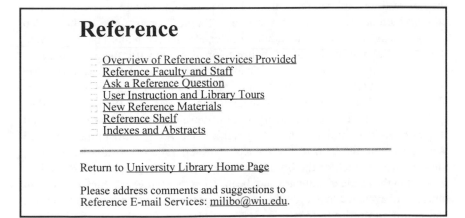

Reference

- Overview of Reference Services Provided
- Reference Faculty and Staff
- Ask a Reference Question
- User Instruction and Library Tours
- New Reference Materials
- Reference Shelf
- Indexes and Abstracts

Return to University Library Home Page

Please address comments and suggestions to
Reference E-mail Services: milibo@wiu.edu.

Figure 6.2 Reference list

Welcome to the

University Library, Western Illinois University

in Macomb, Illinois.

- Library Catalog
- Library Overview
- Hours of Operation
- Computerized Interlibrary Loan Forms
- Library Units, Branch Libraries, Personnel
- Collections
- CARL Home Page (including UnCover)
- Internet Resources by Subject
- Full Text Resources

Free Speech Online
Blue Ribbon Campaign

Return to the WIU Home Page.

Please address comments and suggestions to
The Western Illinois University Library: milibo@uxa.ecn.bgu.edu.

URL: http://www.wiu.edu/users/milibo/wiu/index.htm

Figure 6.3 Introductory page

trail is complete or deemed irrelevant for the user's needs. These "back" links provide effective navigation through a large Web of information.

Many Web sites use navigation "buttons" at the bottoms of pages for the same purpose; I chose to use hyperlinked text since it allowed users the flexibility to designate "back to where?" Buttons can look great, and I'm now becoming interested in developing them, but when they are not well designed, they offer little explanation of the links they provide. When a user is presented with buttons for "back," "forward," and "home," for example, at the bottom of each page, it becomes difficult to offer alternative paths "back" without developing new graphic "back" buttons for many specific pages. "Home" is unclear—a specific page name is better—and "forward" offers very little information at all. For "forward," contextualized links within pages are preferable; they lead users onward, thereby avoiding the need for such a button altogether. Another advantage of using text for these navigational purposes is that it generally loads quicker than do graphics. However, with more and more users accessing the Web with graphical browsers rather than text-based ones, the time has arrived for the library to reconsider use of graphics in its Web.

Although no clear standard has been set concerning graphics other than buttons, I have tried to avoid gratuitous use of them and to minimize their size and number in order to maximize speed of transfer. Graphics have also been placed in somewhat uniform ways in each page—this is particularly evident in the subject-oriented pages—in an effort to give the Web a cohesive feel. As technology improves, heavier use of graphics in Web documents may not necessarily mean sacrificing speed of transfer. Many of the design principles used in the Web pages were gleaned from Laura Lemay's *Teach Yourself Web Publishing with HTML in a Week*. (Indianapolis, IN: Sams Publishing, 1995). A new edition on using HTML 3.0 was published in 1996.

URLs Included in Text

Other important standards were developed for the WIU library pages. The URL for each specific page is included in text in a standardized position at the bottom of each page. At the time these pages were developed, the Netscape version available did not include the URL of a document on printouts from the WWW; thus, for library pages, URLs were included on each so that users would know exactly from where library printouts came and would know how to return there if necessary. These URLs are still useful to many users whose browsers do not automatically include such information on printouts.

Dates of Last Revision

Since the last date of modification or revision of a WWW page is important to users needing to verify the currency of information presented, these dates are included in a standard position at the bottom of each document. Dates of first implementation for each page were not maintained, though they may have been quite useful and perhaps should appear on pages. A Web user can generally expect a higher level of refinement from an older page if that page has been consistently maintained. Knowing that a page is very new alerts the user that it may not be fully developed and may have some rough spots.

Points of Contact

For most library unit divisions included in the Web, contact information is provided should the user need to seek out further information from that unit. This contact information often includes a link to an e-mail form as well as a phone number. My own e-mail address is clickable from the main library page as a general contact for the library. Contact information needs to be further standardized.

SUBJECT-ORIENTED INTERNET RESOURCE LIST

A resource list (http://www.wiu.edu/users/milibo/wiu/resource/subjects.sht) is a subject-oriented set of links to Internet resources, containing over 3,000 unique sites classified under one or more of approximately 150 subject headings. It is accessible directly from the main library page and is organized into an alphabetical list with appropriate "see" and "see also" references provided. An alphabetical "jump list" at the top of the subject page offers an easy means of moving to specific locations within the subject listings, and "return to the top" links at the end of each alphabetical division in the subject page itself further improve the ease and speed with which a user can search for a specific topic. The list of subjects allows users to access separate pages for each subject, each page consisting of a set of links to various pertinent Internet resources. Some of these links are supplemented with annotations to give the user an idea of what is available at a site before linking to it.

Many of the sites included in the list were gathered and organized into a database used to generate a subject-oriented list of Internet sites for an Internet provider. These sites were to provide links of general interest on a variety of subjects to give new Internet users the opportunity to explore the WWW with ease. The database originally worked in conjunction with a software program written specifically for the provider, but this program was incapable of handling annotations, so none were included in the original database. When the library produced its Web, I thought it would be a good idea to make use of information from this large database to aid in generating subject-oriented Web pages for the library. Since the information contained in the database was strictly factual, directory information, it did not seem that there would be a copyright problem with using it. However, the consent of the provider was obtained before proceeding to use portions of the database contents in the library's Web.

The list of subject headings were formulated by drawing upon the subject listings in two major periodicals directories, *Magazines for Libraries* and *Ulrich's International Periodicals Directory,* and several other books, including *The Whole Internet: User's Guide and Catalog* by Ed Krol (1992) and *The Internet Yellow Pages* by Harley Hahn and Rick Stout (1994). These subjects were used to produce an authority list in ProCite for DOS. Information regarding various Internet sites was keyed into the database (as is necessary with a DOS program), each site having its own record. Each record was classified under one or more subject headings so that it could be output as listed under multiple applicable headings. A ProCite punctuation file was written to output the database into an unordered list of hypertext links classified by subject. However, since the right angle bracket (>) has a special meaning in the ProCite puncuation file, it could not be used like an ordinary character. I worked around this by substituting an accented "a" to hold the place of all the right angle brackets, then used WordPerfect to search and replace these accented letters with right angle brackets. Each time the subject pages are updated, spell checking is also done in WordPerfect 5.1 or Microsoft Word, and corrections are made to the database. A search for duplicates is run in ProCite as well and true duplicates removed from the database. Sorting the database by the titles of the sites results in an alphabetical arrangement of sites under each subject when the subject "bibliography" is printed from ProCite to produce the Web pages. Once the final version of these subject listings is printed into one large file, that file must be divided to produce individual subject pages— work that is extremely time-consuming!

There are probably better ways to produce such lists now. I used what I knew at the time, inventing my own way to do it with software not even designed for that purpose. Database programs capable of creating subject pages on the fly in response to user requests can be much more efficient. Several such products have been mentioned on the Web4Lib listserv, and I will be checking into new software for future Internet database construction and use. When searching for new software, it would also be a good idea to address maintenance needs by searching for software capable of automatically checking links included in the database and capable of generating periodic reports of bad links found during such checks.

I am the sole selector of sites for the subject list, although other librarians and teaching faculty often send material they think is worth including. There has never been a time when a request was not honored. Since I originally drew heavily on my previous work for the Internet provider in producing a new subject-oriented list, the criteria for inclusion was less restrictive than it would have been had I had an academic library audience in mind from the start. There has been some help in weeding out and annotating resources. Annotations to resources were included beginning in summer of 1995, with students who have worked on the library database assisting with annotations (all checked by me), and Susan Avery weeded and annotated all of the reference resources during the fall of 1995.

The library subject database needs to be weeded and its focus more clearly defined if it is to serve a truly unique purpose. With proper annotations, it has the potential to serve a helpful "reader's advisor" role to a primarily academic audience. There is no need for WIU to keep building its own "little Yahoo," but the existing subject list offers an excellent starting point from which to create an even better product for our library users.

Teaching faculty should be drawn into this process of site selection, just as they are involved in selecting other materials for the library. They could also become an excellent resource for producing annotations that would be meaningful to their colleagues and students. Until such efforts are rewarded when it comes to teaching faculty evaluation, few will probably demonstrate an interest. Perhaps librarians would be better off utilizing subject specialists within the library for such purposes, if they are present.

Up to this point, no links to Usenet news resources have been included in the library subject listings. Newsgroups are certainly a valuable source of information, but they are not easily documented, and their nature changes constantly; they are even less rigid than Web pages in this respect. As ideas about what shapes research information can take change and evolve, this decision may need to be reconsidered.

These subject-oriented pages, of course, present some real maintenance problems, though they are not by any means insurmountable. I recently installed MOMspider, a PERL program developed by Roy Fielding of the

University of California, Irvine, which automatically checks links on a UNIX system. I ran a check which included all the subject sites at the end of November 1995 and corrected the library's database of Internet sites (a long process which I will not describe here). As of this writing, I am currently in the process of running another check, and new subject pages are due out in the summer of 1996.

Although a maintenance scheme is being developed and implemented at present, the subject listings almost certainly still contain out-of-date links. Such links can be frustrating to users. Maintenance of the growing number of abstracts associated with information resources contained in the subject listings has not yet been addressed and will certainly need to be. I cannot think of a program yet capable of assessing content! A PERL search engine, which would add speed and flexibility to subject retrieval, would also be a nice addition to the subject listings in their current implementation.

USER RESPONSE AND MARKETING

Initially, the WIU Web pages were not marketed effectively. As the leader of the project, I am the one most responsible for this lapse, but at the time initial implementation was completed, I was exhausted! On a ten-month contract, I was soon temporarily off contract as well. Some of the marketing took care of itself in time, at least where marketing outside the WIU community is concerned, and many of the automated indexing services providing Web search engines have found the Web pages. The WIU library has been included in several online lists of libraries on the Web, and there are regular e-mail requests, from an international audience, requesting that more sites be added to the subject listings.

Another question regarding marketing has yet to be resolved: just how much marketing outside the institution should be done. The focus of the Web pages, as it is in many other libraries and universities, is somewhat schizophrenic; some of the material was designed for an internal audience and some for either an internal or an external audience. It seems, however, the most pressing concerns are in serving the university community; therefore, there has not been a great deal of effort to market outside WIU.

Because the Web pages were not being noticed on campus, I began to advertise its services via an electronic bulletin board accessible to faculty and staff. These same announcements were also published in the *Campus Connection*, a weekly printed newsletter distributed to WIU faculty and staff. According to access counters placed on some library pages as of March 1996, it seems that use has increased following these announcements. To market effectively to students, as well, there may be a need to step up efforts to offer Web instruction directly to students.

The page access counts that are documenting use by the WIU community may be incorrect, especially where pages such as the "Internet Resources by Subject" page are concerned. Use of this page may well be growing outside the institution as quickly or more quickly than it is inside. After all, this list is useful to a broad community; one need not be a student, faculty, or staff member at WIU to find it a valuable resource.

To effectively target areas of the Web for further development, a tracking strategy should be implemented that more accurately defines who uses the Web pages and what portions are most useful. It may also be helpful to implement some sort of survey on campus or on the Web itself. With any tracking strategy, it will be important to maintain security and anonymity for our users. Just as librarians do not want patron borrowing habits made public, data about the library's Web users must not fall into the wrong hands. There must be concerns about what kinds of data should be collected and how it should be used and stored.

MAINTENANCE AND FUTURE DEVELOPMENT

I'm very glad I took on this extra project, and I am intensely proud of what my colleagues and I have accomplished thus far. But, if the library is to see truly exciting and revolutionary results using this technology, it needs to devote serious resources to it. Because of my strong interest in the technology and my personal circumstances at the time, I was willing to sacrifice a great deal of my own time to making the project work and work well. I knew from the start that, if I was going to make it work, I'd have to do the lion's share of the work.

After initial implementation, when everyone could see the results and some had become more deeply interested in the project, I was able to get some help. Donna Goehner, dean of the university libraries, has allowed me to have a student work twelve hours a week on the Web for the past academic year. Since student workers are paid minimum wage, though, and since their plans change often, it has been difficult to demand much experience or to maintain consistency in this position. The workers have done a wonderful job and learned quickly, and I have learned things from them as well, but each required a high investment in training hours before there was a great deal of return. A permanent, more highly paid staff member would be a much better alternative to student work for this position.

As far as professional input into Web development and maintenance goes, to really progress much further, libraries will have to address their allocation of resources where the Web is concerned. The duties of Web manager/developer cannot realistically be accomplished by one librarian if that librarian already has full-time responsibilities in other areas. It would be better to have one person whose primary responsibilities would be caring for and developing the Web.

Having a certain level of unified editorial control helps to maintain a consistent feel for a library Web. Having one person primarily responsible for the entire Web presentation relieves the individual library units of the burden of keeping close tabs on details, resulting in more efficient Web management.

The Web manager/developer should not work alone. Developing a new group or groups of volunteers to work on the Web would tap local expertise and encourage consideration of a wider set of possibilities than could be thought of by one person. Also, maintaining some level of unit responsibility for unit content material would encourage involvement and awareness among library faculty and staff as well as perpetuate the sense of distributed ownership that is so vital to the library Web's image and its future support within the organization. However, facilitating groups effectively takes a great deal of time.

If the librarian in charge of the Web is working under a faculty model, this work needs to be evaluated accurately in terms of retention, promotion, and tenure. This type of activity, learning and using new technologies for library purposes, and the value ascribed to it call into question traditional methods of evaluating library faculty. If something is of high value to the library and its users, it should be given a high value in evaluating those responsible for it. Then, what about standards such as peer review? Are they to be dismissed entirely? If they are, how will library faculty be considered "real" faculty in comparison to teaching faculty? These are difficult questions indeed that need to be answered.

LOOKING BACK AND TO THE FUTURE

I would not change much in the route I took coordinating the development of the WIU Library Web pages. With this acquired experience, I can say what resources and time must be devoted to making a Web work, as well as what skills people would need to play certain roles in the development process. The Web pages themselves show just how much has been accomplished.

In the future, the real value of a library Web will be in offering actual services through use of forms for various purposes (along the lines of the ILL forms now available at WIU). Development of multimedia presentations that can actually teach users research skills and provision of direct access to "connected" information products in a wide variety of formats (as opposed to access to citations to printed material) will add to the library Web's value.

Libraries have a chance to expand their hours and their shelf space "virtually" using new technologies, and they have a chance to "acquire" products they could never have held in physical collections. They can also use the WWW to make their unique collections available in a wide variety of formats including images and sound. Technological innovations of the future will present countless other opportunities for libraries.

Libraries can play a strong role in this new information world, if librarians are up to the challenges. They are the ones with the most experience in handling the technical and ethical challenges of supplying information to the public. These institutions (whether they be physical or virtual) are now and will continue to be but one place of many places where people can seek information. Libraries and library staff will need to define what various roles to play in the future of information and to play those roles with vitality and conviction.

SPECIAL AND PUBLIC LIBRARY WEB SITES

Chapter 7

Goddard Library's Web Page

Robin M. Dixon

Coordinator of Information Services
NASA Goddard Space Flight Center
rmd@sun.gsfc.nasa.gov
http://www-library.gsfc.nasa.gov

The Goddard Library would be on the World Wide Web! At long last we had received verification of what the Goddard Library staff already knew, the library should be the focal point of a Centerwide Virtual Library for Goddard Space Flight Center. In the summer of 1993, the Goddard Library hosted a Visiting Committee, comprised of representatives of peer scientific and technical institutions, to help evaluate the services that were currently being provided by the library. One of the recommendations of the Visiting Committee was to "establish a Centerwide Virtual Library." As a means of implementing this recommendation, the library administration decided to have a World Wide Web home page as the core for the Centerwide Virtual Library. The staff's collective excitement could hardly be contained; finally we could begin to offer services remotely—something our customers had been requesting for some time. In addition, we would have the added bonus of having a way of providing open access to items of interest to the general public and a chance to showcase the depth of our Space and Earth Sciences Collection which is the library's strength.

The use of the World Wide Web for remote library services had promise in that it would be the solution to a number of problems, including serving users of multiple, unrelated computer systems. The nature of space and Earth sciences research conducted at NASA Goddard Space Flight Center (GSFC) necessitates the use of many different computer platforms, including UNIX, PC, and Macintosh. A Centerwide Virtual Library that would be productive and viable to this community had to be flexible enough to be accessed from whatever platform the researcher was using. In addition, it had to be easy to learn. Past experience has shown that our researchers are willing to use new tools, provided the information derived from the tool is worth the effort it took to find it. A home page was envisioned as the solution to providing library access from the predominant platforms currently in use. The research community, by and large was familiar with the Internet and its basic components, though familiarity with the WWW varied from in-depth to nonexistent. Based on our understanding of the community's Internet skills, the library staff believed that using the library's resources through the WWW would come as second nature to Goddard researchers.

GETTING STARTED

It was determined that the programming and maintenance of the home page would be added to the duties of the Goddard Library's support contractor. The contractor reconfigured its staffing pattern to create a UNIX administrator position to handle this task. The UNIX administrator had been another recommendation of the Visiting Committee in support of the Virtual Library. The UNIX administrator was required to be familiar with the hardware and software configurations needed to create a presence for the library on the World Wide Web. The support contractor recruited applicants, located a suitable candidate, and incorporated this person as a full-time member of the contractor staff.

To begin the effort and to support the Centerwide Virtual Library, money to purchase equipment and software was allocated to the Goddard Library by the center's Institutional Planning Committee (IPC), based on recommendations and a presentation to the IPC by the Visiting Committee. The initial hardware configuration was a Sun Sparc 10 IPC running at 20 megahertz with 48 megs of memory, 50 megs of swap space, with one 1 gigabyte hard disk internal, one 207 meg hard disk external, and a quarter inch tape backup (QIC-150). As of this date the library's Web page still runs on the Sun Sparc 10 using NCSA HTTPD software, although there have been some system upgrades.

The initial planning and production of the Web site was the responsibility of the Unix administrator, a member of the support contractor for Goddard Library. The library's contractor works onsite and its staff members are full-time contractor employees of the Goddard Library. Therefore, though technically it could be said that the work was outsourced because it was performed by contractor staff, it was not outsourced in the traditional sense, meaning employing temporary outside help and/or a contractor located in a separate facility such as the contractor's corporate headquarters. It was important that the UNIX administrator, or Webmaster, be someone who worked with the library staff on a daily basis.

Later, after the home page was up, an Internet Steering Committee, consisting of volunteers from both the civil service and contractor staffs, was convened. The staff members, by job position, were the UNIX administrator, senior LAN administrator, two information desk librarians, reference librarian, technical information specialist, engineering librarian, management analyst and junior librarian, with the branch head and contractor project manager serving as overseers. All members volunteered because of personal interest in the WWW and the Internet and because each had job-related functions such as technical expertise, library promotions, outreach or user education responsibilities that would involve the Web site. The Internet Steering Committee became involved in the design of the home page as the content and structure became more complex. Though the Internet Steering Committee members suggested sites for inclusion on the page and assumed the maintenance of one or two of the pages, the UNIX administrator performs the major updating and maintenance of the pages and WAIS databases available from the home page.

CHALLENGES

The first major problem we encountered was providing access to the library's DOS-based CD-ROMs from UNIX and Macintosh platforms. Though Goddard Space Flight Center Library has a very well-established and stable LAN (Local Area Network), it can only be accessed by those branches and/or divisions sharing the same network protocols. Networking the CD-ROMs in the traditional fashion, or solely by way of the library's LAN, would eliminate use of the CD-ROMs by a large percentage of the current and potential customers.

Research by the management analyst yielded a solution. A commercial vendor was selected—based on its assurances that this system would allow access to all the platforms in our specifications. What we discovered was that this was *not* going to be a turnkey solution. The system would definitely work with DOS machines, since it is a DOS-based system itself, and though it was designed to allow other platforms to access our CD-ROM towers, it was going to work a little differently than we expected when contacted by non-DOS platforms. In fact, it took our LAN administrator and UNIX administrator a few months to get our configuration to facilitate access to our CD-ROM towers from the home page.

Goddard Library's complete CD-ROM access system consists of a LS4500 CD-server with four CD-towers, two Logicraft 486Ware boxes, one OMNI-WARE box, and a SUN IPC. Once the CD-ROM option is chosen on the home page, the "behind the scenes" activity begins. After choosing the CD-ROM icon from the home page, a CD-Access Form appears, from which the user must choose the type of machine he/she is using. Once the selection has been made, the PC-DOS users access the system by making a direct connection to the CD-Server using Netbios. MAC and UNIX users access the system by making a telnet connection to the SUN IPC. The IPC uses a preprogrammed script to establish a DOS session on one of the 486WARE/OMNIWARE boxes. PC-DOS users who are not running Netbios can make a telnet session to the SUN IPC and establish a DOS session just as MAC and UNIX users do.

While all of this is seamless to the user, it took a great deal of thought and a bit of ingenuity by the Systems Department to get the system to work in the way we required. Fortunately, the Goddard Library has systems/computer support personnel dedicated to library functions. Configuring the Logicraft system without that support would have been extremely challenging and possibly quite costly if we were required to seek programming expertise elsewhere. The Goddard Library staff has come to the understanding that most turnkey systems will usually need to be "tweeked" in order to meet a library's specific needs. The important thing to look for is a system capable of performing the task well, but also to expect that any given commercial package will more than likely need a few modifications to function as the system the library staff originally envisioned. For example, the CD-ROM system works very well, but users typically see DOS commands issued just before a CD-ROM selection menu comes up. In a perfect situation, the customer would not see the DOS commands. The upside to this is that no customers have complained about viewing the DOS commands. Granted, they scroll by faster than the credits on a TV movie, but librarians have been known to receive complaints about less intrusive things than a fifteen-second scroll of DOS commands!

ACCOMPLISHMENTS

The desire to provide a database which contains citations and abstracts to information of interest to the Goddard research community resulted in the production of one of our more exciting offerings from the home page, the SCI/TECH Journals: Contents and Abstracts database, which uses raw Current Contents data purchased from the Institute for Scientific Information. The data is massaged using a filter program designed for the Goddard Library to allow the data to be read. The data is then indexed with WAIS (Wide Area Information Server), which is a commonly used search software on the Internet. At this point, a researcher can use our HTML interface to search and/or browse the data. Search/browse results, citations, tables of contents, and abstracts of journal articles are displayed on HTML formatted pages.

Goddard's SCI/TECH Journals: Contents and Abstracts database has the advantage of using WAIS search software, which is familiar to many WEB/Internet users, is extremely user-friendly, and provides good search results with a short learning curve. Some of the features of the SCI/TECH Journals: Contents and Abstracts database are the following:

- searching or browsing journal tables of contents
- searching author, title, subject, citations and abstracts fields
- ability to create stored searches allowing an easy way of keeping abreast of current research or a specific journal
- browsing the latest weeks of Current Contents data
- Boolean searching
- electronic request form available from the database (with citation information already filled in)

Due to our licensing agreement with ISI, the SCI/TECH Journals: Contents and Abstracts database is restricted to use by Goddard employees; however, a demonstration of this database is available clicking on the demo icon at the bottom of the SCI/TECH Journals page (http://www-library.gsfc.nasa.gov/DB/CC.html).

One of the Goddard Library's first electronic initiatives was GLOBAL Goddard Library's Online Bibliographic Access Locator. This database is essentially an electronic guide to the library and its resources. It provides information for locating information, databases, and other resources within the library and gives suggestions of resources to use based on the researcher's interest. Originally a PC-based application, it has been converted to HTML and is now available from the home page. The URL for GLOBAL is http://www-library.gsfc.nasa.gov/GLOBAL/ GLOBAL.HTM.

ESTABLISHING A WEB PRESENCE

In the initial stages, we were completely focused on getting the home page online, and though there was concern as to whether we should completely plan everything down to the last detail first, we ultimately decided to use a simple design, so that we could establish a presence on the Web as soon as it was feasible. The content was decided upon by library management and the design was centered around the idea of having a virtual representation of the Goddard Library. It was believed that clients of the physical library would be comfortable with the electronic version, and those who were not frequent visitors to the library would have an idea of the library's layout when they had the occasion to visit. The design also recognized the possibility of usage by those who did not have, or chose not to use, graphics capabilities and was worded to make sense to a text browser.

Since the purpose of the home page is to provide access to the library from remote locations around the center, we needed feedback from our customers to help assess how well these new services were being received. We had a number of functions to promote the home pages and to gather feedback. We placed notices in the centerwide publications, we had Poster Sessions, which were physically held in a building other than the library, and we had a library Open House. Comments ranged from "This is wonderful" to "I don't have a Web browser" to "I like the idea, but not the arrangement" to "Please place the library catalog when I can easily find it," along with ideas of how to improve the content of the page. From comments received and reactions to the publicity, we were faced with two glaring observations that a redesign was in order and that we had overestimated the base of installed technology.

THE REDESIGN

The Goddard Library home page debuted in October 1994. Almost immediately after that browsers other than MOSAIC became available, Netscape became "enhanced" and new and different types of Web Pages were being developed. Based on "new" things on the Web and incorporating comments from users, The Internet Steering Committee under the direction of the branch head, set about redesigning the Goddard Library home page.

The first decision was that the content of the library home page was basically sound and suited to our primary audience. The second decision was to have the existing pages restructured so that databases were together, the library catalog was easily accessible from several pages, and other library services were organized logically for our primary users, based on customer comments (see Figure 7.1).

MAJOR FEATURES OF THE GODDARD LIBRARY HOME PAGE

Both the library's ARIN Online Catalog and NASA/RECON are on the home page. The ARIN Catalog provides navigational access to the books and journal titles owned by the Goddard Library as well as all the other NASA libraries. The NASA/RECON database is a guide to information about articles, conference papers and NASA Technical Reports, and includes abstracts.

- *GLOBAL* is an electronic handbook to the GSFC library, complete with maps of the library and expert advice on how to research a topic in the GSFC library.
- *The Goddard Library Hot List* has hyperlinks to other sites, libraries and resources within NASA and the world that have information related to GSFC research
- *Points of Contact* for Circulation, Information, Reference and Journals assistance is available on the home page. Users may contact the library by e-mail or telephone for assistance in navigating the library's electronic and paper resources.
- *SCI/TECH Journals: Contents and Abstracts* is a database of citations and abstracts of over 2,500 scientific and technology journals. The database, customized by the Goddard Library using information from the Currents Contents database provided by the Institute for Scientific Information, is accessible by most WWW clients and therefore by many of Goddard's clientele who have Internet access. The database is a WAIS (Wide Area Information Server) database which allows both fielded and free-text searching.
- *NASA List of Acronyms* is a WAIS searchable database which allows the user to search on keywords to find a NASA acronym or to search for an acronym to find what the acronym means.

Welcome to the Homer E. Newell Memorial Library

Information Technology and Services Division
Library Information Services Branch
Code 252.0

In support of GSFC's mission, the Library Information Services Branch facilitates and promotes access to scientific, technical and management information to sustain research and development, foster creativity and increase the productivity and effectiveness of GSFC programs. The Library facilitates access to information needed by GSFC's scientists, engineers and managers, regardless of format or content.

The Library also supports participants in educational programs. Visitors may use the library by special arrangement. The Goddard Library is composed of two sites: Greenbelt and Wallops.

Try the *NASA Galaxie* Online Information System!

What's New, updated on Nov 8, 1996.

Databases.

Books, Journals, & Documents.

Pathways to Information.

Library Services & Policies.

Floor Plan (clickmap).

Handbook of the library. (GLOBAL)

Goddard Library Council.

On line request forms.

Visit the rest of the world (hotlist).

Software support.

GSFC library web pages.

Figure 7.1 The changed home page

- The *Wallops Flight Facility (WFF) Balloon Technology Library* is a WAIS searchable database of a unique special collection of materials related to scientific balloons and balloon technology. Copies of the papers described in the abstracts can be obtained from the Wallops Flight Facility Library.
- The *RECON Select* database is a WAIS-searchable form of the traditional NASA RECON database. RECON Select is easier to use but is limited to documents within the public domain. Articles, proceedings papers, and technical reports accessed here can be requested by Goddard users through the Goddard Library.
- The *Goddard Technical Reports Server (GTRS)* is a WAIS-based database, housed on a server in the Goddard Library and provides access to abstracts and citations of technical reports by Goddard authors printed in 1994 through 1996. The database is in a prototype phase but is slated to include not only citations and abstracts but the full text of Goddard documents. Users will be able to search for, retrieve, and read or print document from their desktop.
- *Goddard Library CD-ROM Access* includes multiplatform access provided to many of the CD-ROM databases subscribed to by the Goddard Library. Databases included are Computer Select, DataPro-Computer Systems Analyst, DataPro-Communications Analyst, DataPro-Client/ Server Analyst, GeoRef, Index to Scientific & Technical Proceedings, MathSci, and Science Citation Index.
- *Goddard Library Hot List* provides telnet access to other databases and sites of interest to the Goddard researcher. Some of the major databases which are accessible are STELAR Project WWW Server, NASA Technical Reports Server, NASA Astrophysics Data System (ADS) Abstract Service, Space Telescope Science Institute, Institute for Computer Applications in Science and Engineering, Geographic Information Systems—GIS United States Geological Survey—HTTP Server—home page, Cambridge Scientific Abstracts, The Library of Congress, Colorado Alliance of Research Libraries, Harvard University and John Hopkins University Applied Physics Lab.

The Goddard Library staff placed a great deal of time and effort into providing the Goddard Space Flight Center researchers with the tools most closely related to the work going on at the center.

THE BASE OF INSTALLED TECHNOLOGY

Once the home page was established and we had some feedback, we discovered that although a large percentage of the Goddard population was using the Internet in some capacity or another, mostly as e-mail, many did not have Web browsers or knowledge of how to obtain browsers. Others were waiting in a long queue within their departments for their computer personnel to install browsers on their workstations.

In response to customer comments, we established a program in which members of the library staff would go out to customers' offices to help them use the library's home page. We limited ourselves to helping with use of the page, or with accessing the page, but not with installing hardware or software. Though this service was a short-term project, specifically designed to help in our initial phases and not as as highly used as we anticipated, it was beneficial in helping clients understand that library services were available remotely and that the library is not just a quiet place to study.

Amazing, we thought, for once the library is ahead in terms of technological advances instead of trailing along behind as many people might expect. The effects of this were good and bad. Yes, we were out front with our innovations, but in some cases, we were so far out in front that there was no basis of understanding of what we had accomplished.

As is the case with many libraries, the Goddard Library is placed within the Goddard organizational structure in a service-oriented directorate. The library is a part of the Management Operations Directorate, which includes the Facilities Management Division; Safety, Environmental and Security Office; Institutional Procurement Division; Logistics Management Division; and the Information Technology and Services Division. The Library Information Services Branch (the Goddard Library) falls under the Information Technology and Services Division. Fortunately, the NASA Goddard Space Flight Center had a page established at about the same time as ours, and we were linked to that page. We could point to that page as indication that what were doing was in touch with the latest technology. Finally, we had a basis of understanding, and some appreciation for what we had accomplished, if not an understanding of the talent, resources, and patience it took to establish our Web presence.

WHO USES OUR PAGE

Statistics of Web use, including who uses it, and how many times it is used within the library versus outside of the library and off center are kept on a daily basis, with a report generated each month. Current statistics indicate that use of our page is high, the page is "hit" in excess of 70,000 times a month. The counter can be seen on our current home page; it was added in 1996 and is not a true indicator of use statistics from the first day the page went public. The counter gives an indication of the number of times the home page is first downloaded; therefore, it indicates only that, not how many times the page is used after it is originally downloaded. The statistics kept on Web use give us an indication of which services are being used regularly and which ones may need to be reviewed or publicized better.

LAST THOUGHTS

Though there is always room for improvement in a process, our experiences with putting up the home page were positive. In our home page we have the basis for our Centerwide Virtual Library, which will continue to change and be updated, reflecting the needs of our primary clientele. The focus of the Goddard Library home page has always been our customers, and with our home page we endeavor to provide timely and useful information through a technological infrastructure that supports the mission of the NASA Goddard Space Flight Center.

Chapter 8

THE AIR UNIVERSITY LIBRARY WEB SITE

Linda K. Colding

Air University Library
licolding@max1.au.af.mil
http://www.au.af.mil/aul.aul.htm

WHAT IS AIR UNIVERSITY?

This is a frequently asked question for staff members attending professional conferences or meeting with colleagues outside the Department of Defense. Air University is a major element of the United States Air Force's Air Education and Training Command. It is responsible for Air Force professional military education, professional continuing education, and graduate education. The students of Air University are primarily Air Force officers, airmen, and career Department of Defense civil servants. The educational programs include precommissioning programs such as Air Force Reserve Officer Training Corps, professional development schools, and training for senior Air Force officers. The schools include Air War College, Air Command and Staff College, Squadron Officer School, Officer Training School, and the College for Enlisted Professional Military Education to name a few.

The Air University Library (AUL) is the premier library of the Air Force. In addition to being the largest federal library outside Washington, D.C., it is the largest library in the Department of Defense. The library was founded in 1946 at Maxwell Field, now Maxwell Air Force Base (AFB), in Montgomery, Alabama. The collection is well-balanced but is especially strong in the fields of aeronautics, Air Force operations, military science, international relations, warfighting, education, and management. AUL houses over 450,000 books and bound periodicals, 2,000 current periodical and journal subscriptions, over 60 newspapers, 500,000 military documents, and 650,000 maps and charts. Nearly half of the sixty-eight-member staff are professional librarians.

The library is very much like a small to medium-sized academic library. Our university has its colleges and departments and the library must serve the information needs of the faculty, students, and staff. Like any library, the Air University Library has a mission, which is to support Air Force education by providing access to the world of information through quality library services. With advancing technology, this could be accomplished through electronic resources including the World Wide Web.

THE WEB SITE

The Air University's Web site includes links to all of the major schools, the Air University Library, and other important Air Force and Department of Defense sites. Construction of the initial site was coordinated by the research coordinator's office (RCO), an office directly under the Air University commander. The site made its debut in the fall of 1995.

As stated, all major organizations in the Air University have a site on the Web. Some of these pages are more technically advanced than others. The library's initial page was very basic and was designed with little direct input from the library staff. The rest of the library staff and I felt we needed control over the production of our page to better serve the information needs of our users both here at Maxwell AFB and at other Air Force locations worldwide. After lengthy discussions between library staff and RCO members, it was agreed that the library would maintain control of its site, although it would still be accessible through the Air University site. The staff understood that we were taking on a big responsibility and to begin the undertaking, the Web team was created.

THE WEB TEAM MEMBERS

In January 1996, the Web team was formed to redesign the library's Web site and insure that the needs of library users were being met. The electronic resources librarian was designated as the team leader. He had previously worked with the initial site and had the technical expertise required for the project. The selection of other team members was important because we needed technical expertise as well as a good understanding of the library and its users. It was also important to have members who wanted to be a part of this groundbreaking group. We did not want to draft members who may have looked upon this team as "just serving on another library committee."

The final team composition included the assistant electronic resources librarian, a reference service librarian, a periodicals reference librarian, a bibliographer, and a cataloger. While it may appear that most team members were from the reference services area, we were comfortable with the variety of backgrounds that each individual brought to the team. This variety proved to be invaluable in the redesign process.

The team leader and the assistant electronic resources librarian had more technical experience than the other team members. To even the knowledge base, all team members began surfing the Internet for information dealing with Web site construction. This electronically accessed information, as well as materials found in recent print publications, was exchanged among members. Most team members were also able to take advantage of off-site training courses on the construction and design of Web sites.

THE PLANNING STAGE

Once the team members were in place and on the road to being trained, weekly meetings were held to start planning the redesign of the library's Web site. Our first meeting focused on who our customers were going to be. We decided our primary customers were the faculty and students attending Air University at Maxwell AFB. While we considered Air Force members stationed worldwide to be potential customers, the needs of Air University faculty and staff have priority. However, this distinction is expected to blur as more distant education courses come online.

Next we had to decide what our primary customers needed and wanted to find when they arrived at our site. Some of the sites for the schools were very detailed and advanced. A decision had to be made whether the library would offer the same information or whether we would complement the existing information found at the school sites. We knew we wanted to highlight and showcase several items produced at the library. We also felt the information available through the library's site would complement information already existing at the school sites.

As part of the planning phase, a survey was sent through e-mail to staff and students of several schools within Air University. Of the forty-five surveys sent out, only three were returned—an extremely poor response rate for any survey. The three-question survey asked whether the current library site had been used, what information the customers would like to find at the site, and what links they would like to see added. Even the small response reinforced the team's perception that the original site offered little of what our users expected. This reaffirmed the library's desire to have control over what information was to be found at our site. Based on the survey results and discussions with other library staff members, we felt we were heading in the right direction.

The team concluded that the site should be divided into eight different areas or subdivisions. These were Services, Schools, Database Access, Online Catalog, Bibliographies, FAQs (Frequently Asked Questions), New Information, and information about the library itself.

The Services site would undoubtedly be the largest section. Here a customer would find information on reference service and policies, subject specialists, a request form for e-mail reference questions, circulation policies, support services available, and links to other reference sites. Another area found under the Services site was Interlibrary Loan (ILL). An order form was available at the site so that customers could directly request materials not found in our library. This area is limited to those customers with borrowing privileges at the Air University Library.

Periodical services would also be at the Services site. This section would include access to the library's Master List of Periodicals, ILL, and information about electronic indexes found in the library for access to periodicals. Plans to include an in-house product called Selected Acquisitions was discussed. Because it is uncertain that this product will be published for much longer, we were not sure we wanted to include it at our site. However, we decided that until we got definite word the product was going to cease, we would include it.

At the Schools section of the library's Web site, the team wanted to have more than just a link to each school's site. In other words, when customers click on the Air Command and Staff College site from the library's Web site, we did not want them to find the same identical information that they would have found going directly to the college's Web site. We wanted to stress the services and unique items the library could provide. With the assistance of the library's liaisons to each school, we accomplished this goal. The plan was to include information that would assist students with assignments that required use of library materials.

Another item the team planned to include was the Online Catalog. Technical difficulties would prevent this from happening when the redesigned page was scheduled to debut, but instructions on how to telnet to the Online Catalog would be included until the existing problems could be overcome. The same was true for the CD-ROM databases we wanted to have available for our customers. However, both of these capabilities were scheduled for implementation in the fall of 1996.

Another in-house product that the library is especially proud of is the guides produced by our bibliographers. They are unique due to their subject matter and because no one else in the Air Force produces such reference tools. They are used by Air Force personnel, not only at the Air University schools located at Maxwell AFB, but worldwide. However, with over 300 different titles available to our customers, we decided to include only those that were most frequently used or applicable to the school curricula.

The team members spent months redesigning and planning the library's Web site. Our goals were to insure that when our new site appeared on the Web, our users would find the information they needed and wanted and that the special items the library had to offer would be useful.

SITE PRODUCTION

When it came time to put the plans into motion, all team members were involved, and no outsourcing was done for the site. We found that our weekly meetings were not frequent enough to accomplish all of things that needed to be done so we resolved this situation by dedicating two afternoons each week exclusively to Web team activities. This meant that none of the team members would have reference desk duty on those afternoons. While this did not always make life easy for the reference desk scheduler, we knew this was the only way to accomplish our goals, and the library administration agreed.

The major problem in production, but certainly not a show-stopper, was the concept for the first page of the site. The idea was to make the page look like the cockpit of an airplane. An individual looking at the page was supposed to feel as if he or she was sitting in the cockpit ready to take off down the information runway. The instrument panel would have buttons to click to take the customer directly to those sites. The slogan would be: "Air University Library—Where You Are at the Controls."

With the help of the Maxwell AFB graphics shop, work began on finding a cockpit image to fit our needs. When we tried to make it fit into the page, it was too big and loaded far too slowly to meet our requirements. We were concerned that customers would be discouraged at the lengthy loading time and leave the site before getting to the information they needed. We fell back to a simpler design (see Figure 8.1). Our goal was to have a site with good information not pretty pictures. In the future, as technology improves, we may be able to go back to the cockpit design.

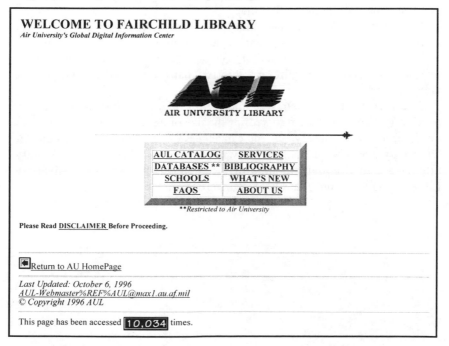

Figure 8.1 The logo for the Air University Library

The other production difficulty was cabling problems. The library was scheduled and rescheduled several times for new cabling that would provide faster data throughput. This project is scheduled to be completed soon but with budget limitations we can only hope that it is completed.

MARKETING PLANS

The reference services branch has monthly marketing meetings to determine what services should be marketed to our customers. Plans are underway to include the redesigned Web site in the marketing plan. It will include marketing the site through orientation tours and briefings to students and faculty as well as through local publicity and articles in the local base newspaper.

WORDS OF WISDOM

Having been through the planning and production stages of a Web site, I offer a few words of advice for friends and colleagues in other libraries. Do not to be afraid or reluctant to stop the planning or production phase to step back and see how things are going. Is the site really going in the direction the library staff wants it to go? Will the site really serve the needs of those you are designing it for? Do not be afraid to make changes so that your site will fulfill the needs of your customers. Your customers should be the reason you are designing the site in the first place.

We understood from the beginning that the site would always be "under construction" but we did not want to put up empty links. Like the library within walls, the Web site would always be adding new and valuable information our customers require and this is what we meant by being always under construction.

Please take a look at our Web site. While like other institutions, we do have certain areas that are reserved for the use of our affiliated users, most of our links are open to everyone. You can access our homepage through the Air University site located at http://www.au.af.mil or go directly to the library http://www.au.af.mil/au/aul/aul.htm. Remember at the Air University Library, you are at the controls of your information needs!

Chapter 9

THE INFORMATION NAVIGATION SYSTEM

Robert F. Skinder

Thomas L. Cooper Library
University of South Carolina
rskinder@tcl.scarolina.edu
http://lib2.jhuapl.edu/APL/ins/ins.html

This chapter discusses the Information Navigation System (INS), which my supervisor Bob Gresehover and I designed for the R. E. Gibson Library and Information Center of the Johns Hopkins University Applied Physics Laboratory (APL) as an aid to navigating the Internet.

THE WORLD BEFORE WEB

Because this is a book about Web sites and libraries, I assume that you, the reader, are familiar with the Internet and the sites or tools that affect your world, be it work, hobbies, or play. Let's imagine, however, that you know nothing of the Internet except what you have heard. Put the book down now, and try to remember back to D-Day minus 1, the day before you got on. If someone didn't take the time to show you the way around, what could you do? "Click" your way around the home page? Look for a search engine? Pray that you could find the famous Yahoo, whatever that is? At D-Day minus 1, what does the Internet look like? The advertisements conjure up fancy images, but they are pictures of lightening bolts and cars and highways and lovers who've suddenly found fulfillment by typing "Hello." We know that is not really what is there.

What is there is more information than has probably been published since Gutenberg invented movable type. It is not necessarily particularly good or useful information—there is just a great deal of it—and it is accumulating very fast. It sometimes seems as if sacks of information were being dumped onto a table without enough sorters. This glut of information presents problems to a brand-new user who cannot even imagine what is on the Internet. These problems, as they relate to our clientele, the scientists and engineers at APL, are the focus of the following discussion.

THE APPLIED PHYSICS LABORATORY

Founded early in World War II, the Applied Physics Laboratory (APL) has dealt with defense and space projects for many years. Recently, faced with government downsizing, the lab has expanded its potential customer base. New areas of interest include biomedical engineering, transportation, and several other areas where APL's core competencies can best be used. Timely information is of great value to its approximately 2,500 employees.

PROBLEMS WITH THE WWW

In the spring of 1994, Mosaic and the World Wide Web were introduced to our community of researchers. As librarians, we were interested in learning their reactions to this new form of information. With only a few exceptions, everyone we talked to (all of them APL professional staff members) had the same response: "It is too big and I keep getting lost."

Clearly, positive things were not happening for our researchers in cyberspace. To better understand a newcomer's difficulties, we attempted to analyze the problems and see what, if anything, could be done to solve them. The following questions and associated issues seemed to be central:

- How can I access the Internet? (access)
- How can I know what is on it? (knowledge of content)
- How can I know if the information is useful or correct (evaluation)
- How can I know if a tool is the right one to use? (validation)
- How do I keep from getting lost in this labyrinth? (guidance)

The terms in parentheses suggested we were seeing problems that fell within the realm of librarians. Eventually we were able to solve these immediate problems and add substantial value to the Internet for laboratory employees. The vehicle we used, which will be explained in depth, came to be known as the Information Navigation System or the INS, and it has also generated some interesting spin-offs. While it is not the definitive answer to harnessing the Internet, it is a reasonable attempt to implement some principles of librarianship and find order in an otherwise chaotic situation.

PREVIOUS EXPERIENCE

My experience with the Internet prior to the introduction of Mosaic was probably much like yours. I had e-mail and occasionally used it. Beyond that, the Internet was vague and mysterious. At the time, we had a supervisor of reference, Linda Kosmin, who was very interested in the Internet. She often gave workshops throughout the laboratory, generally of an introductory nature, and she would demonstrate searching with Archie and Veronica and the gophers. The class would get an overview of government programs which might provide funding and pointers on how to find a colleague's e-mail address. She taught how to telnet to library gophers and search their on-line public access catalogs (OPACs), as well as how to look at what other services might exist at a site, and explained how to FTP files. As far as I was concerned, and I believe this applied to most others at the laboratory, these were all dissimilar products, related only by the fact that they were not available via conventional channels such as the telephone or television or even print.

Now, suddenly there was the World Wide Web as well as Mosaic—an enormous change by any standards. The excitement was tempered by extremely long waits while clients tried to log on to a very limited number of servers. The first guides were the Virtual Libraries which originated at CERN (the European Particle Physics Laboratory), and to start out, there were two basic choices: locations or subjects. Either list could be logged on and worked through by clicking here and then here and then there. Perhaps a user would select Massachusetts and then Universities and then MIT and then the Physics Department or the library, and the user might end up in Singapore. It would be very exhilarating, but what was the result? Probably nothing. Like others, I continued to log on, fascinated by the technology but ultimately disappointed with the results.

RELEVANT PROJECTS

Just before Mosaic came online, I had been involved in two projects that would affect how the library coped with the Internet. One was a mandate that the professional reference librarians would no longer work at the reference desk. Our job was to streamline the flow of information between our sources, which were rapidly increasing, and our clientele, the scientists and engineers. The other was that, as a result of this new mandate, I was attempting to design a system (basically a hypertext scheme) that would guide our clients to the best resources based upon their needs at the time. The system included connections to our OPAC and other OPACs at Johns Hopkins, as well as connections and instructions for the new CD-ROMs that we were beginning to acquire. There were also provisions for library services and documentation in the form of a manual. I called this experiment "The Electronic Librarian."

BEGINNING

Given the problems associated with the Internet, these two projects became drivers of a thought process which suggested a solution that, at first, was far from clear. My previous hypertext experience led me to try and figure out how HTML worked. Soon I had a sample page and knew how to connect to other resources from it. I had also started collecting Hot Links, the forerunner of the Netscape Bookmarks.

Bob Gresehover, my boss, was also interested in the possibilities offered by the new technologies, and he and I spent quite a bit of time trying to define what was available on the Internet or, more important, what was on the Internet that our clients could use.

Our first thoughts of actually constructing anything originated with the idea of a home page for the library. The inherent intellectual challenge in this project was strong, but our central interest in designing a home page or any other type of Internet service for APL was the idea of enhancing the library's image. For many years, the R. E. Gibson Library had concentrated on delivering excellent service to the laboratory's researchers. In addition to the networked CD-ROMs, we also supplied Carl's UnCover, performed mediated searches, and set up accounts for those who wanted to do their own searching. The library also provided the utmost in document delivery; all of this was done in a quiet and efficient way. Times change, however, and it was becoming obvious that, with governmental down-sizing on the horizon, a bit more presence might be worthwhile. The laboratory staff has a high regard for technology and information, as do our customers. We decided that rather than designing a home page, we needed to create a tool: a central point of departure for exploring the Internet, for finding useful resources, and for returning effortlessly—none of which was really possible at the time.

A PLAN

As we searched for a structure, we examined the problems and questions a novice Internet user faces, which were listed earlier in this chapter, with one big difference: we were looking at it from a corporate rather than a personal viewpoint.

The issues of access, knowledge of content, evaluation, validation, and guidance certainly suggested librarians and an electronic library, but what to put into this library? Some answers were more apparent than others. Two items came to mind immediately because we had used them in the design of the Electronic Librarian: the connections to the OPACs and the CD-ROM material. We also thought that it made sense to put connectors to all of the search engines in one place. These items gave us a fairly general set of tools so that a user could connect to our own and several other libraries and use their OPACs. They could also use Archie, Veronica, and the gophers to search the different components of the Internet.

What we really needed, however, were specific APL-related sites and objects to which we could point our users. Early in our discussions we realized that our primary mission was not so much to find sites for the staff member as to eliminate or segregate those sites from the numerous irrelevant sites that distracted or led them down a twisting path. It seemed reasonable that subject collections would be a good place to begin. Since APL is a technical laboratory, we could fairly easily identify the twenty or so technical fields that would be of interest. In our earliest versions of the Information Navigation System (INS), our subject lists were little more than pointers to all of the lists of pointers of which we were aware. From the very beginning, we always felt that we would be able to mine and refine these lists to provide quality sites, resources, and tools. Now, eighteen months later, these lists (and others) are still there, but they make up only a small segment of the resources offered on the INS. They were the source of most of our present sites, tools, and resources.

Exploring these lists led to some interesting discoveries. Today they might seem insignificant, but the number of electronic reference works that I found was startling. Fortunately, others had done much of the collection development in reference materials so I was able to find material at sites as well as on the lists and develop the collection quite quickly; one page soon divided into several pages, which are still being added to.

Equally interesting but a bit more problematic were the electronic journals. There were many titles of interest, but inspection revealed that most of them were not useful; most were advertisements or carriers of administrative information, such as instructions to authors. Our clientele would not put up with having to open each entry in the hope of finding an interesting paper. Happily, we were able to identify enough of them with potential to organize a useful collection. First we established criteria for acceptance: a journal had to be on a topic related to the laboratory, it had to be free of charge, it had to have some type of search device, and it had to yield at least an abstract. We have made a few exceptions to these criteria and expect to make more on a case-by-case basis. One exception relates to subscription arrangements that the library has with two important physics journals. We have agreed to pay a modest surcharge over the regular paper subscription cost. In return, we receive the right to log on one person at a time per journal. There are alternate pricing arrangements for more ports.

Very closely related to the electronic journals are the preprints. These are particularly suited to our clientele dealing with physics, mathematics, and oceanography. They are also useful because they are very timely and are a bit of a consolation in these days of cost-cutting and subscription cancellations.

As with the reference collection, we also started collecting our e-journals and preprints by listing them and their URLs all on a page. We then alphabetized them. Later we separated them into categories, and finally we turned every category into a separate page. Incidentally, separating all of the reference tools and the journals added about twenty-five pages to the INS within a day or two.

At this point in its development, the INS had some components loosely arranged, and we saw that a system was slowly emerging. It looked like this:

I.   Library Tools
    A. Connection to our OPAC
    B. Connections to other OPACs
    C. CD-ROMs
    D. Electronic Reference Desk
    E. Electronic Journals and Preprints

II. Subjects
III. Search Tools
   A. Archie
   B. Veronica
   C. Gophers

We still made a few additions before we were ready to release our premiere model. There was also a deletion; we soon discovered that with so many different types of computers being used, it was quite difficult to use the browsers for the CD-ROMs. Instead we have networked them throughout the laboratory.

ADDITIONS

In narrowing down the subjects, we noticed that while there are many universities and laboratories, only a small number are similar to or share interests with APL. We felt that our researchers would be interested in these sites. We also added headings for companies, archives, and societies. These began life on one page but, like everything else, eventually grew until every heading or category became a page (see Figure 9.1). We called these "Important Locations" and due to sheer numbers made "Government and Military Sites" a subset of Locations. The locations were all hand-picked but the Government and Military Sites were merely pointers to several lists. Now, they too have expanded into lists of their own if they are of interest to the laboratory staff.

Our page used "satellites" as section headings. In an attempt to make the new system more appealing to the researchers, I named it the Information Navigation System. It seemed appropriate to provide some "navigation satellites" for guidance. This was a mistake. We used this terminology for several months and then realized that few users recognized or appreciated the analogy. "Navigation Satellites" eventually became "Useful Information Resources" and the "Command Satellites" were renamed "Search Tools on the Internet." (We are still using the satellite terminology on some of the internal pages of the system, however.) The lesson here is keep things simple and clear—clever analogies often just don't work.

INTRODUCTION OF THE INS TO THE LABORATORY

Thus far I've described the development of the INS up to the point of its introduction. It just so happened that the INS was ready for introduction at the same time that we had planned a library Open House at the end of September 1994. This worked out very well because it gave the developers an opportunity to demonstrate the system to a large number of the staff, to answer questions, and to listen to comments about the Internet. The entire Open House was very well received, and it demonstrated that the library was thoroughly committed to the new technologies.

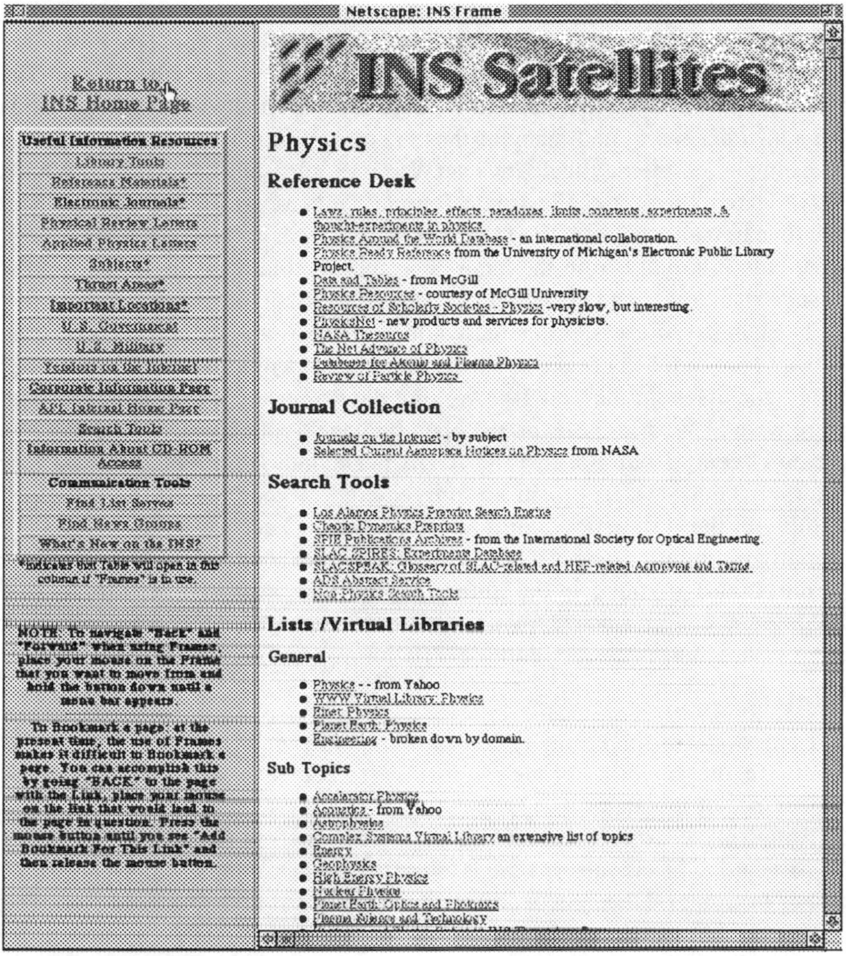

Figure 9.1 An example of the Physics page

Evolution

That introduction was about eighteen months before this chapter was written. Since then, there have been at least eight distinct revisions. We intended to do the revising monthly, but as the system grew, time slipped by, and eventually we were almost six months between revisions. At that point I requested and received access to the server and began making a few changes every day.

Growth

The system has grown steadily in size, in content, and in number of users. Version 1 consisted of approximately twenty-five files. Today's version has about 100 files. Two of the biggest increases in size resulted from the expansion of both the reference and the journal collection. The other was the addition of research "Thrust Areas," which will be described later. The system is relatively dynamic, and I would estimate that ten to twenty items are added per week, and many of these items go on more than one page. As an example, on the day that UnCoverWeb was released, I added it to What's New, Search Tools, and Electronic Journals, thus rewriting each of the files and then transferring each file to the server. Because we have a version accessible only internally from the laboratory and one that is accessible from the outside ("internal" and "external" versions), we transfer files twice.

The number of users has increased quite steadily, and there is a correlation between the number of users and the number of people who have taken our training courses. In the first 100 working days after the INS was introduced, there were about 1,000 hits on the opening page—roughly ten hits a day. We are now seeing from 800 to 1,000 visits per month from APL staff, but our external version has not been up long enough to generate accurate figures. Validity of these statistics is difficult to determine because we are constantly reconfiguring library pages while trying for the best combination. During one period, to use anything in the library required the user to enter through the INS; now there are several ways to get in. My particular tendency is to look at how particular pages are doing in relation to similar ones.

Quality

I am aware of three quality issues: the quality of the sites and resources identified, the reliability of the connections (whether the links work), and the appearance of the pages.

Almost all sites on the earliest versions were pointers to virtual libraries or lists for particular subjects and for various tools such as the communication and search tools. I have not rid the system of these completely, but in the best and well-used pages, such links are in a definite minority. Whenever possible, the intent is to get the users directly to a quality site or resource in the same way that the OPAC tells them where a text is (rather than giving them an arrow saying "Physics Books Here"). A lot of effort goes into adding new links, and none are added unless the sites have been examined for quality and relevance. If these sites have links, they also are checked to make sure that most are operable. Conversely, our most serious deficiency is not checking our own pages actively enough for nonlinking sites; consequently, we may soon go to a Web validator.

Visual Appeal

Appearance is a very touchy subject. I have kept all of our earlier versions and they are almost heartbreakingly poor. The indentations are all over the map, print is all different sizes for no apparent reason, and the pages are really difficult to look at. After about six months, however, a real improvement became apparent, primarily because we received some professional artwork, and I became more conscious of what I was doing. This was also about the time when we were adding many pages because of growth. When you add many pages you quickly learn to standardize, and that alone will make the new pages better than the earlier ones were. Until several months ago (month sixteen), there was nothing in the INS that was any more advanced than the simplest HTML 1 code. Since then we have adopted tables, colors, and frames, all of which really enhance our look and image. They also make the system much easier to use. The frames feature divides the page into two or more windows which permits users to have a table of contents in front of them at all times. The colors are coordinated so that users generally can tell in which section they are traveling: reference pages are blue, journals are yellow, and so on. One serious problem is associated with the frames feature. Not everyone has updated their computer to the latest version of Netscape, and not everyone even uses Netscape. That means that we must make two versions of several pages, and since we have an internal and external edition, the possibility of confusion does exist.

RESEARCH "THRUST AREAS"

The INS was approximately a year old when a new need was perceived. Our subject and location pages were maturing satisfactorily but they were not exactly on the mark. The laboratory needed more concentration on the areas that people were actually working in. People may be engineers or physicists but they do not necessarily work in a field as broad as engineering or physics on a day-to-day basis. At APL, they are most likely to be working on a particular project or an emerging technology that the laboratory management views as important. The newest of these are called Research Thrust Areas, and that is where the INS went next. As you might expect, the pages on Thrust Areas vary quite a bit in quality and amount of information available. Some areas, such as Modeling and Simulation, are very rich because so much relevant material is on the Internet; on the other hand, APL often has interests that few (if any) others are working on, and little or nothing is available for those areas. This is one direction in which we will continually expand.

TRAINING

Designing and building the INS required a certain amount of work, but that was not the end. Even though we felt that the system was relatively self-explanatory, we perceived a need within the laboratory for some instruction. The head of the training and development group called a meeting to request our comments and those of other interested parties concerning a curriculum to be presented to outside contractors for bid. In addition to librarians, trainers, a technical writer, and people from the group that oversees computer services throughout APL attended. After a few meetings it was determined that the needs of the laboratory were so specialized that no outside group could prepare such a course. In addition to a belief that we could design a good course, we also made a pleasant discovery when we realized that the INS, with its focused design, would serve as an excellent framework in which to teach the course. Amy DeBrower and I wrote a paper describing this course and its results (see "Additional Reading"). I believe that the course presentations had a significant effect on overall usage of the INS and the Internet. We also have learned a great deal about the Internet and its resources from our teaching experiences. We have now gone beyond the introductory classes and have given workshops and seminars dedicated to particular staff levels and disciplines. That specialized approach is expected to be the trend of future training efforts.

SPIN-OFFS

Given the structure of APL and of the INS, most of the work has been completed except for the addition of Thrust Areas and daily maintenance. Surprisingly, however, new opportunities based on Internet technologies continue to develop. One of the first that we saw was the ability to convert our focused INS to someone else's focus. This came about on a military project when the sponsor saw the INS but realized that it would not meet his needs exactly. It was not very difficult to modify the scope of the INS and create a custom system for the sponsor.

Another opportunity that recently emerged is electronic study rooms. Often the laboratory establishes a room where documents relative to a particular interest can be collected and where people can meet to evaluate, edit, and study them. When this work is completed, a consensus of some sort is reached. While APL is large and diverse, many projects share particular aspects such as navigation using the Global Positioning System. For this reason we felt that it might be advantageous if the key documents and conclusions from these study rooms could be electronically posted lab-wide. We are also able to supply forms capability so a reader can respond and make the response available to other participants. This program has just started but seems quite promising. Some groups are posting this type of information on their own. In other cases, instead of posting the information ourselves, we either will develop an electronic "room" or get the owners started with a framework and sample scripting and coding as well as assistance in scanning documents. This effort also serves to put the library into a position of managing and producing information as well as becoming knowledgeable about important programs.

CONCLUSION

I have explained what we have done and why we have done it and how it was done. Now comes the more important question: Should it have been done? I think that the answer must be yes.

One reason is that the Internet provides an enormous amount of information that is available in no other form. This wealth may be particularly apparent because of the subjects that we deal with, but I doubt it. We are constantly amazed at the currency and wealth of the information that we uncover every time we teach one of our classes or workshops. In a sense, we have expanded our collection enormously without a large expenditure.

Second, I think that this project allowed us a rare opportunity to reinvent the business of librarianship and to develop an expertise at the same time. I spend very little time at the reference desk, but am fairly confident of answering 75 percent of the questions received there by using the INS.

Third, a project like this portrays our library as progressive and customer-oriented. We are perceived throughout the laboratory as being knowledgeable about the Internet. The INS brings us into contact with many people who might never have dealt with us. They see that we are involved with many types of information and that we are competent, and they will come to us for other things.

It is too early to tell, but now that we have gone public, I hope that the system will reflect well on APL and the type of work that it does. For all of these reasons I would strongly urge anyone interested to develop whatever sort of system that they feel comfortable within their own organization and follow the opportunities that it will create.

ADDITIONAL READINGS

A. M. DeBrower and R. F. Skinder, Designing an Internet Class for a Scientific and Technical Audience, *Special Libraries* 87 (3) 139-146 (Summer 1996).

R. F. Skinder, The Information Navigation System: A Web-Based Reference Tool, *IRSQ* (Internet Reference Services Quarterly) 2 (213) (In Press).

R. F. Skinder and R. S. Gresehover, An Internet Navigation Tool for the Technical and Scientific Researcher, *Online* 19 (4), 38–42 (1995).

Chapter 10

Spinning a Corporate Site: Faxon's Adventures on the World Wide Web

Jodi L. Israel

formerly Product Manager, Internet Resources
The Faxon Company
jisrael@silverplatter.com

Dedication: In memory of Fritz Schwartz. His insight, foresight, and energy enriched our Web site as he did our lives. He is sorely missed.

IN THE BEGINNING

The year Faxon began its Web project was 1994, a momentous year for the company. Management and organizational changes presented exciting opportunities for personal and professional growth. Nowhere was this excitement more apparent than our work on the World Wide Web. Faxon was blessed to have the late Frederick Schwartz in a leadership role for this project.

Schwartz, a former academic librarian, strongly believed in the dissemination of information. As the manager of Electronic Resources and Standards, he wanted to develop a platform-independent means of sharing information. He was first attracted to Adobe Acrobat. He approached Roz Ault, then manager of User Support Technology. Ault, a former school librarian, was one of Faxon's principal Internet resources. She brought Mosaic to Schwartz's attention, and he was at once captivated and energized. He began doing research, consulting with Kim Schacher, another of our principal Internet resources, and making presentations. He became convinced that Faxon should have a presence on the Web.

He gathered together a small team of people, including Ault, Schacher, and Bob Boissy of Research and Development. Boissy and Ault began experimenting with a freeware server for the VAX but it was difficult to set up and maintain. Then Faxon discovered MacHTTP (now WebSTAR). We had surplus Macs available and it made sense to make one into a server with the added benefit of being a completely separate machine from those that were running our business applications. Also, MacHTTP was easy to set up and configure.

Although the software was free to educational and nonprofit institutions, there was a charge of $100 for registration of commercial use. This was the first money to change hands. Faxon also had the advantage of a direct link to the Internet as well as network personnel who understood the technical issues. These are normally rather large hurdles. That we didn't have to surmount those hurdles made it easier to focus on the content of the site.

Once the platform had been decided, Schwartz and others were able to concentrate on the site itself. He gathered delegates from the departments he anticipated would embrace this new project. Among the groups tapped for resources were Research and Development, Network Services, Client Technical Support, Technical Services, User Support Technology and Marketing. (Fully one-third of the team were librarians.) Faxon had always supported a team development environment and most of the players had worked together before in some fashion.

Although Schwartz directed the content effort, he did not do so randomly. A small team of people, consisting of Schwartz, Boissy, and Ault created a project charter. This fulfilled several purposes: the most important ones were to keep the group both on track and in focus.

THE RECIPE FOR SUCCESS

The team had a non-negotiable deadline of ALA Midwinter 1995, and several months of beta testing were included in the timetable. The team met weekly and members were assigned action items. Minutes were taken and e-mailed to everyone in the group. The phased structure of the charter gave people the needed guidelines to delay certain facets of the Web site until Phase II. One of the problems with content development is that there is rarely a natural stopping point. As more people buy into the Web concept, the more ideas flourish. Any brainstorming sessions quickly raged like wildfire, each idea giving rise to at least three more exciting ones. Schwartz applauded them all and then pointed to the charter as the definitive voice because if it wasn't in Phase I, it wouldn't happen by the Midwinter Conference. This didn't stop the flow of ideas, but it did force the group to focus more narrowly on the tasks that had to be accomplished by the deadline.

Another benefit to the charter was that it assigned responsibility for certain tasks to particular departments and resources. Reality, however, has greatly deviated from what was set down in the charter. These deviations will be discussed in detail later in this chapter.

Identifying Goals and Sticking to Them

The most important goal Faxon had was to reestablish itself as a technical leader among clients and publishers. Faxon had always been at the forefront of technical advancement. In many respects this is the principal reason why only about a third of the site is dedicated to proprietary Faxon information. Although we wrote much of the content and potential clients can find information about our products and services, we wanted to continue to build on our reputation as information managers.

We also wanted to expose Faxon to a much wider and perhaps nontraditional audience encompassing clients, nonclients, and our competitors' clients. Our statistics back up our success in this area. As I study the links to our pages from outside sources, it is interesting to see just how many sites agreed with our nonproprietary focus. A considerable number of links to our pages are from nonclient and nontraditional sites.

In addition, the Web site would permit more timely distribution of proprietary publications. At present we have made available *The Faxon Report*, our client newsletter; and PubUpdate Online, an electronic version of our print publication, which alerts clients to new publications and other special offers. The hypertext medium allows publishers to make available much more information than the traditional print environment.

Benefits and Other Decision Support Information

Included in the charter was a benefit analysis. Although we believed strongly in the medium, we wanted to use the charter as a basis for approval. We also wanted to use it to cement future commitment to the project. Some of the benefits listed were the following:

- *Competitive advantage.* At the time, no other subscription agency had a Web site.
- *Proven technology.* Though the Web was new to us, several of the Integrated Library Systems vendors were making use of WWW technology in their application.
- *Popularity in the library market.* Librarians and libraries as a whole showed avid curiosity about the Internet and have embraced, as the evidence now suggests, the Web technology.
- *Popularity in general.* Growth of the Web has been and continues to be phenomenal.
- *Acceptance of commercial applications.* It is becoming a distant memory but there was a time when commercial use of the Internet was severely frowned upon (only last year!). Obviously techniques like spamming (sending messages to multiple listservs or user groups) are still intolerable. However, since the Web is still very much a passive environment, meaning that one must go to a URL deliberately, commercialism has gone from being tolerated to being expected.
- *Marketing efficiency.* We anticipated using the Web as a marketing and client communication tool and it has shown itself to be a very effective one. We are able to make information available in a much more timely and cost-effective fashion.
- *New development area for the subscription business.* As librarians know, the traditional subscription business is changing. Electronic

journals and other means of communication have altered the playing field. Adopting the Web technology early would give us the opportunity to plan for the future using a live "test-bed" environment.

The Faxon Internet/Web development team fully expected the World Wide Web to become a part of Faxon's overall strategic corporate plan. The charter was a way to prove that we had thought everything through before engaging in a development effort.

Organization and Staffing

The project charter also contained information on organization and staffing. The three primary areas named were choice of content, provision of content, and technical administration.

Choice of content for Phase I was selected by committee. Although this worked for Phase I, the reality has been a little different. Of the four original members of the content committee, one is no longer with Faxon, one has been promoted to the highest level, and one has passed away. The fourth is still critical to the development of the site but on an advisory basis. The organization itself has changed. When the project was started, Faxon was a privately held firm; now it is owned by Dawson Holdings, PLC., a publicly held United Kingdom company. The Web site, since it was up and running well, was put on the back burner. As I write this, there is no official content committee. Decisions about content still keep the charter's goals and objectives in mind, but they are slightly more random. The charter has not yet been updated to reflect the changing Web world. It should be noted that as soon as the Web site went "live" we began work on Phase II. This fully detailed document was designed to follow the model of the first charter complete with staffing requirements and fully explained content expansion. The loss of Fritz Schwartz put that charter on hold.

The departments that created the information were supposed to supply and update the content. Unfortunately, several things have happened since the charter was written. Much of the nonproprietary content that was created in-house was written by a department whose resources have since been reallocated. Faxon's marketing department has been cooperative about supplying proprietary material; however, the Web is not a priority project. Further, there are few available resources in the company who have the time to create or validate content. Thankfully, this is changing. Though the new Web development team may not mirror the charter's specific descriptions, they will certainly mirror the intent. A variety of departments are becoming eager to include their expertise on this dynamic platform.

As for technical administration, when the project began, Faxon had a Webmaster who was responsible for encoding and mounting all new content. In addition, before the site was rolled out, she also created much of the content. It was also her job to periodically validate all external links. That was fine when there were fewer than 300. Now there are well over 800 external links on a single page. (We have purchased software to make this task more manageable.) When our Webmaster left, the void was covered by Roz Ault who had already had a full-time position. When the Webmaster role was reassigned to marketing, I was assigned the position. This was a good fit since I was a member of the Internet development team from the beginning.

I am now responsible for all of the above tasks, as well as choice and provision of content and technical administration. Although I am a librarian and have had significant experience with the Internet, it is still daunting to be responsible for a corporate site. Unlike personal sites, Faxon is trying to project a corporate image that clients and nonclients alike can trust and respect. Thankfully I am still able to draw on Ault's expertise, her considerable talent for technical writing, and her understanding of issues affecting libraries. In addition to being responsible for content, she was principally responsible for the design of Faxon's initial Web site. Although the role of Webmaster was designed for a single full-time employee, the role of product manager was intended to be a separate role. We are again heading toward that model.

LESSONS LEARNED (PART ONE)

What are the morals of this story? Those involved in designing/creating Web pages should bear in mind that personnel changes. This is particularly true in the corporate arena but the trend is beginning to spill over into other areas. Content should be determined by committee. When the committee is being developed, concentrate more on the areas of the organization that should be determining content rather than on specific individuals.

Get real buy-in from all the areas that are supposed to produce content. One of the mistakes we made was in not including our Client Service Department in our discussions. It is difficult to get cooperation from departments that believe they have been slighted. Make certain it is clear what their responsibilities will be for updating that content and be sure that the content creator is not the single island of knowledge. Again, personnel changes.

With an estimated four new Web pages a minute, the World Wide Web is very volatile. What this means is that many sites are reinventing the same wheel. If the site's information is not current or new, people will go elsewhere. When we lost our Webmaster, we had someone who could handle maintenance, but without a dedicated resource, very few truly new things were added. Even when I took over the role, the learning curve was high enough and the backlog long enough, that though our site is extremely useful and becomes more so daily, it is not where Phase II of the charter intended that it should be.

CONTENT IS KING

Developing the content was not an action done blindly or even hastily. Having quantifiable goals also meant we had a target audience. Although our site is accessed by many nonlibrarians and many no-library sites, it is geared toward serial librarians.

Our initial site was divided into four principal sections: Faxon, Internet, Publishers, and Standards. We chose this approach because we wanted our home page to reflect the company's organization. Although we have added sections dealing with our sibling and parent companies and have plans to add even more content in the future, our basic structure has not changed.

We started with a proprietary Faxon area. Pages in this area revolve around Faxon's people, products, and services. It has been well-documented that the Web is a great marketing tool and a communication vehicle that enhances and develops client relationships. With that in mind, we made available names, phone numbers, and now "mailto" addresses of key sales contacts and executives. In addition we included brief biographies of each of those individuals. We fully anticipate adding all personnel who have dealings with external clients. Feedback to this electronic phone book has been uniformly positive.

Faxon is the only Dawson North America subscription agent to have its own Web server. As such, we also maintain information, under a separate link, for Faxon Canada. Faxon Canada continues to be responsible for the accuracy and timeliness of the content in this section.

Another section is aimed at serials and acquisitions librarians. We included our price projections and PubUpdate Online. The Web has enabled us to make those price projections available to librarians faster than traditional print publications and the United States Postal Service. PubUpdate Online is the Web-based version of the print publication that alerts readers to serials titles that are new, changed, or have special pricing offers. The first online issue was a mirror of the print publication but that has not been the case since.

PubUpdate was a good example of something that appeared to translate perfectly to the Web medium but in fact has not. Although the Web allows potential advertisers to include tables of contents and add hyperlinks to their own sites, many advertisers have not known how to take advantage of the opportunity. We are currently rethinking our strategy for approaching advertisers. We have also realized that, in fact, we have two separate publications: the print version reaches one set of librarians while the hypertext version might reach an entirely different audience. This has been a slow lesson to learn because it seemed so easy to recreate the print version. In fact, that has not been the case. The print publication has a variety of graphics and other design features that have not been practical to recreate online. The real trick will be to create an online version with as much vitality as the print version. Hypertext is no longer considered a special effect!

We created another section for Internet information and links. Our first Webmaster wrote a fairly comprehensive guidebook to the Internet called "The Librarian's Guide to the Internet." This hypertext document has been very well-received. Written for both the beginner and the expert, it not only covers the basics and include links to additional information, but it also includes information on some of the lesser known Internet tools. Faxon also created its own list of links of interest to the library community. Unfortunately, since Schacher's departure, this resource has not been updated in a consistent manner. Although all external links are regularly verified, new material has not yet been added. The guide is still useful and accurate but it does not reflect the changing Internet tools. This should be remedied by midyear 1997.

Perhaps the most successful page on our site falls within the Internet section. Faxon's "Publishers on the Internet" debuted with links to over 200 publishers who had some Internet presence. The list now contains over 800 links which are verified biweekly. We actively search out publishers to include, and publishers query us regularly. This has had an interesting by-product in terms of e-mail. Because we actively solicit new URLs from visitors, we include a "mailto" link to webmaster@faxon.com. I regularly receive requests from people who want to find publishers that are not listed. Wherever possible I attempt to unearth this information, though primarily through traditional reference sources.

LESSONS LEARNED (PART TWO)

Creation of Web pages implies responsibility for the information on them. In other words, before you become the repository for information not of your creating, be certain you know who will be responsible for answering the questions that information will generate. In our case, since working with publishers is a principal part of our business, we have the knowledge in-house to answer the questions. However, we recently removed information about a product because we were not the creators of that product. Instead we added a direct link to the supplier's home page.

STANDARDS

Another important section of the Web pages is standards. Faxon has always been a leader in promoting standards, particularly X12 and Z39.56. We wanted to create and provide resources and links to resources that anyone would find useful. We wrote in-house guides and provided links to the major resources in those areas.

Updating the information in this area has also fallen prey to lack of resources. Although the outside links are verified regularly, concentrated resource time has not been spent to qualify new links or update in-house created information. However, as the Web is given a higher profile, this area will also be regularly reviewed and updated.

BETA TESTING: BROWSERS ARE NOT ALL ALIKE

Almost all of this content was available for the grand opening of the site. Prior to making the link generally accessible, Schwartz approached colleagues at a variety of library sites and asked them to beta test the site. We gave our testers two weeks to review the site and comment on presentation and content.

Overall the comments were positive but they were able to point out details that the rest of us could no longer see and in some cases could not see at all. (We reviewed our pages using Netscape, Mosaic, MacWeb and Lynx but there were and are a lot of other browsers available, each one displaying the same information a little differently.) They were very pleased with the organization of the page (see Figure 10.1) and found it very easy to navigate. We have since approached our Client Advisory Board and asked for their further input.

DESIGN DECISIONS (PRETTY OR USEFUL?)

The Web team also focused on design. As mentioned previously we had an in-house expert who had designed all of our documentation. We were also conscious that many, and at the time most, of our clients would be reaching us through Lynx, a text-based browser. This meant we could use a minimum of graphics and no image maps. Our real goal, from which we have not yet wavered, is that our pages should look almost identical no matter whether one is using Lynx or Netscape. We deliberately chose not to adopt Netscape enhancements so as not to block clients inadvertently. It was also an internal issue. Most internal employees at Faxon have access only to DEC terminals. If we had created a graphics-intensive site, our own people would not be able to view it. In terms of looking toward the future and creating an intranet, this remains an issue.

We didn't implement forms for the first six months. This was partially a resource issue. More importantly, however, we wanted to wait until we had an actual requirement. We developed our first Web service, Faxon FlashTOC, and released it at the ALA annual conference in 1995. This service enables users to search the title list from our Faxon Finder Table of Contents database and order tables of contents. This service has been well-received. As a result of this success we have plans to implement more forms in almost all areas.

THE FUTURE

The site has been available for about two years and it is time to do a detailed statistical analysis. We do track what sites "hit" our site and where they are hitting on our site. As a commercial site we have a mission to make the Web into more than merely a marketing tool. Before we do that we have to have a crystal clear understanding of what is happening. We average approximately 1,000 hits per day which translates roughly into 650 individual sites. The hit rate is not a direct correlation to individuals because each page includes one or two small graphics. Each graphic counts as a hit. However, not everyone loads graphics so we do not incur the extra hits on all visitors. We have not been promoting our hit rate because we understand how ambiguous that number really is. Our publisher page receives slightly less than a third of those hits. We have a disclaimer on our default page that alerts viewers of the page that we do track their actions. We do not track individuals, merely site addresses.

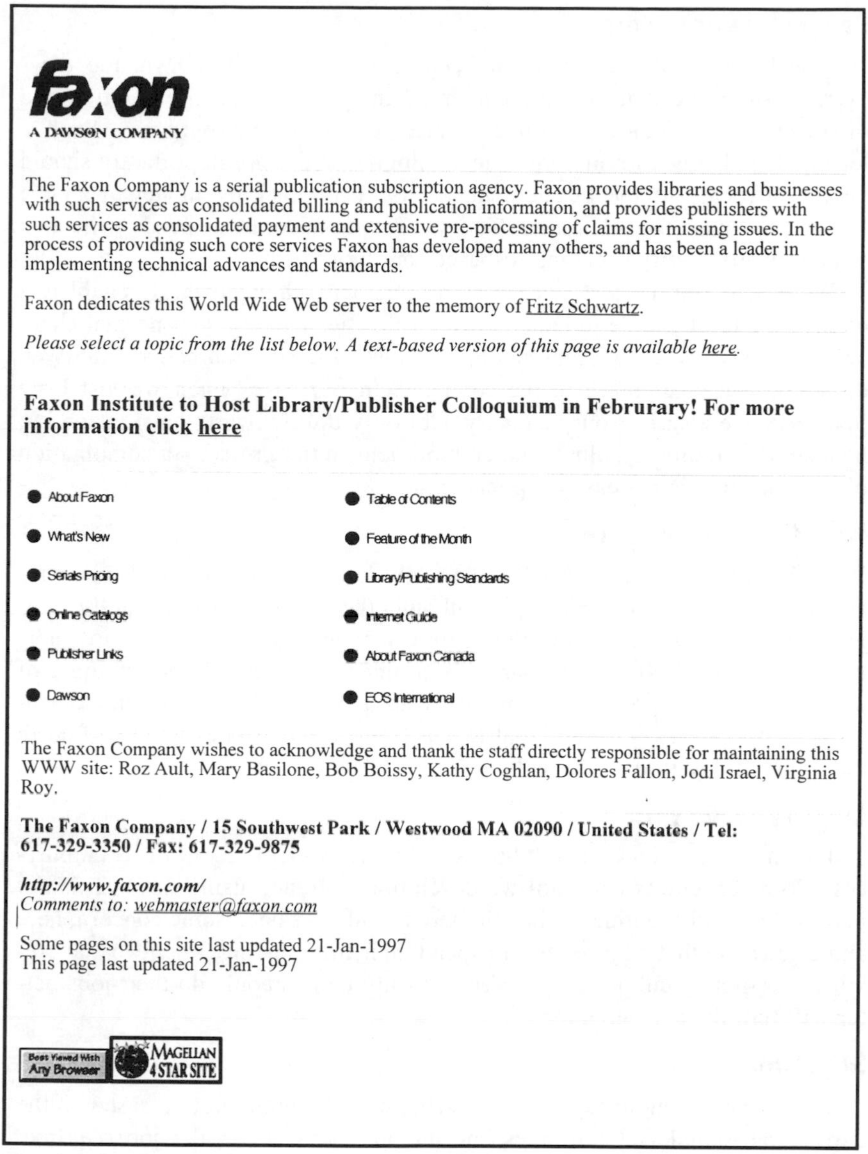

faxon
A DAWSON COMPANY

The Faxon Company is a serial publication subscription agency. Faxon provides libraries and businesses with such services as consolidated billing and publication information, and provides publishers with such services as consolidated payment and extensive pre-processing of claims for missing issues. In the process of providing such core services Faxon has developed many others, and has been a leader in implementing technical advances and standards.

Faxon dedicates this World Wide Web server to the memory of Fritz Schwartz.

Please select a topic from the list below. A text-based version of this page is available here.

Faxon Institute to Host Library/Publisher Colloquium in Februrary! For more information click here

- About Faxon
- What's New
- Serials Pricing
- Online Catalogs
- Publisher Links
- Dawson

- Table of Contents
- Feature of the Month
- Library/Publishing Standards
- Internet Guide
- About Faxon Canada
- EOS International

The Faxon Company wishes to acknowledge and thank the staff directly responsible for maintaining this WWW site: Roz Ault, Mary Basilone, Bob Boissy, Kathy Coghlan, Dolores Fallon, Jodi Israel, Virginia Roy.

The Faxon Company / 15 Southwest Park / Westwood MA 02090 / United States / Tel: 617-329-3350 / Fax: 617-329-9875

http://www.faxon.com/
Comments to: webmaster@faxon.com

Some pages on this site last updated 21-Jan-1997
This page last updated 21-Jan-1997

Best Viewed With Any Browser | MAGELLAN 4 STAR SITE

Figure 10.1 The Faxon home page

LESSONS LEARNED (THE FINAL CHAPTER)

Putting together a Web site created quite a number of revelations and an equal number of lessons. Although several of those lessons have been covered above, they bear repetition.

Project Leadership

A Web site should be dynamic in keeping with the medium. Dynamic, however, means more than just the content. It may also mean presentation and organization. A dedicated project leader serves several purposes. Such a leader should stay current on new technologies, and more importantly should be the advocate to the business managers. Until making money from the Internet becomes the rule rather than the exception, someone needs to be able to continually justify spending resources on the project.

We began our project during a management changeover. It enabled a diverse group of people to take on responsibilities outside their normal channels. However, when we returned to our normal business practices, the Web didn't have a clear place in the company. In our case, when we lost Fritz Schwartz, we also lost our visionary. Not only did Schwartz have vision but he also had credibility, clout, and commitment to the project—a combination of qualities that is not easily replicated.

Management Buy-in

I touched on this only briefly, primarily because we presented our management team with a fait accompli. Although they were informed that this project was underway, it was not their primary concern. Now we have to determine where the Web fits into our daily business practices. Although those of us involved in the project are committed to it, we need to spend time developing justifications for additional resources—time that is difficult to find in the midst of day-to-day demands.

Employee Buy-in

Faxon chose to make a Web browser (Lynx) available to all of its employees. However, unless and until we develop an intranet, using the Web is not part of their daily routine. Although there has always been some concern, here and elsewhere, that employees will spend their time surfing, I believe that creating a corporate culture where Web use truly helps people do their jobs better will turn the toy into a tool.

Staffing

It bears repeating to say that the staffing model should not be based on the current personnel and resources but should be based on the job required. When we lost key personnel involved on this project, we were slow to pick up the pieces. Not everyone understood what the tasks were. Consequently the tasks were simply reassigned to the next available resource rather than the most appropriate resource. (Only occasionally are they the same person.)

Design and Content

I cannot stress enough that while you should not wait until your site is perfect, you should wait until you have completely thought through your purpose for its creation. If you cannot say why you are creating a Web site, then you probably are not ready to create one. Too many sites, corporate and otherwise, are falling victim to the media's hype. Creating a Web site is an important task that should not be downgraded simply because tools have made page development easy. Here are some suggestions:

- Determine your image. Don't be afraid not to appeal to the masses unless they comprise your client base. We chose a very corporate image because that was how we wanted clients to see us.
- Focus on your audience. Ideally do market research to determine the type of equipment and connections they will be using. It is not productive to create a site that your users cannot view as you intended.
- Links are important but do not and should not take the place of in-house developed content. Unless you are a clearinghouse, you will want people to be using your site for more than a gateway. On the other hand, your site will be held responsible for the information on it. Be prepared for questions.
- If you are going to be completely proprietary, beware of what will appeal to your competitors. They will visit, probably under an unresolvable IP address.
- Review your site regularly. And have others do so as well. Update information as often as possible. There is a perception about the Web that information should ever be new. Old or dated information may relegate your site to a back burner. Making changes "on the fly" is one of the benefits of the medium, take advantage of it.

GOALS

Review your long term plan often. What sounds terrific now may well be outdated in six months. Or it may have been done elsewhere already. Do not waste time reinventing the wheel unless you believe you really can design a better wheel and also have the resources to maintain it.

CONCLUSION

Creating Faxon's Web site was an enriching experience. Working with a spirited team on a dynamic project was energizing for all involved. Although it took months of planning, creating the site was the easy part. Keeping up the momentum is another story entirely. Dire predictions about large numbers of Web sites collapsing from neglect are probably understating the case. Until the Web fully evolves from a toy to a tool, underdeveloped Web pages will continue to proliferate. Meanwhile, those of us who have committed to providing information and services over the Web are still searching for the best model to use.

NOTES

URLs for areas mentioned in the text:

http://www.faxon.com—Faxon's Home Page
http://www.faxon.com/Internet/Publishers/pubs.html—Faxon's Publishers on the
    Internet
http://www.faxon.com/Internet/LibGuide/LibTOC.html—Faxon's Librarian's Guide
    to the Internet
http://www.faxon.com/Serials/pubupdate/pubupdate-menu.html—Faxon's PubUpdate
http://www.faxon.com/Faxon/Company/finder/finder_search_profiling.html—Faxon's
    FlashTOC service

Chapter 11

DEVELOPMENT OF PRACTICE-AREA-ORIENTED INTERNET RESOURCES

Margareta S. Knauff

Technical and Online Services Librarian
Dickstein, Shapiro, Morin & Oshinsky
Washington, D.C.
KnauffM@dsmo.com
http://www.dsmo.com

BACKGROUND

The law firm of Dickstein, Shapiro, Morin & Oshinsky (DSM&O) consists of over 200 attorneys. Information Services (IS) at DSM&O consists of both the library and the MIS department. The head of the IS department is a librarian by training. The library itself has a staff of twelve: five professionals, four paraprofessionals, and three part-time employees. At many institutions the library and MIS often disagree over who will provide equipment and services, but at DSM&O they work in unison to provide information resources to the firm.

The IS department decided to implement firmwide access to the Internet in April 1995. The decision came about because a particular piece of equipment was needed to link the firm's UNIX-based time and billing system with the PC/Windows-based network. This piece could also be used to allow the firm access to the Internet. The IS department seized the opportunity and began planning for firmwide implementation, with a start-up date of mid-June.

While the MIS department would handle the purchase of the hardware and software necessary for the site, the library would be responsible for handling the content of the site. The original domain name—dsmllp.com—was registered by the systems administrator, and the software/hardware selection began. Because we were just learning about the Internet, we did not want to invest a great deal of capital only to find we did it all wrong. So, with that in mind, the systems administrator located inexpensive software such as freeware or shareware; however, no expense was spared in the security software. We did not want people to be able to break into our internal network. For our grand experiment, we selected server software by EMWAC and used the Nov*IX package for access to the Internet with Mosaic as our browser.

DEVELOPMENT

In the early stages of site planning, it was not clear how the promotional needs of the marketing department could be meshed with the library's desire to provide informational resources to the attorneys within the firm. The simplest solution seemed to be to have two separate World Wide Web pages. The official firm page, known as the external page, would contain the firm information and other promotional materials as designated by the marketing department (see Figure 11.1). The internal page would contain hypertext links to informational resources for the attorneys. Both these pages would be created and maintained by the library. The director of the IS department felt that as librarians had the training in locating, sifting, and disseminating information, librarians should be the ones to create and maintain the Web pages.

At that time, the only person in the entire firm who knew HyperText Markup Language (HTML), the language for coding documents for the Web, was the systems administrator. He got the site started and set up a preliminary external home page, using information from the marketing brochure. Now it was time for the library to take over. Of the library staff, I had the most interest in learning HTML. I had already had some experience on the Internet from a dial-up account, and I loved it. Using the *Beginner's Guide to HTML* (http://www.ncsa.uiuc.edu/General/Internet/WWW/HTMLPrimer.html), I taught myself how to mark up documents, using the firm's internal page as my test page. To my surprise, I found HTML very easy to learn, one of the best kept secrets of the Web. If everyone knew how easy it was to use, all those people who make their living out of coding with HTML would be out of work!

I started construction of the internal page using the Notepad function which is shipped with Microsoft Windows, simply typing in all the codes in addition to all the text. Later, the director of IS purchased *Using HTML, Special Edition* by Tom Savola, Alan Westenbroek, and Joseph Heck (NY: Que Corp., 1995) for me, and it contained a CD-ROM with many shareware and freeware programs. I tried out several of the HTML programs, including Hot Metal, but ended up using HTMLWriter. I use HTMLWriter to insert all the HTML tags in their appropriate locations instead of typing them all in by hand. HTMLWriter can insert all standard HTML 2.0 tags. It does not support the proposed HTML 3.0 tags or the tags created by Netscape and Microsoft for frames and tables. Those codes still need to be typed out. It is probably not the best program available on the market, but it is relatively flexible, easy to use, and almost free.

Initially, the internal page contained the following: general help information about the World Wide Web, hypertext links to search tools, a few fun places to go; and general legal resources on the Internet. The attorneys in DSM&O, however, are organized into practice sections, each specializing in a particular field of law. I felt it would be useful to them if we could create pages of Internet

DICKSTEIN
SHAPIRO
MORIN &
OSHINSKY
LLP

2101 L St. NW
Washington, D.C. 20037
(202) 785-9700

598 Madison Ave.
12th Floor
New York, N.Y. 10022
(212) 832-9100

Firm Information

- Firm Profile
- Practice Sections
- **Attorney Biographies**
  - Alphabetic List
  - Practice Section List

Think....Think Again!

You may have seen our highly successful appearances in the legal and business press recently featuring a number of challenging puzzles. We invite you to view the solutions.

DSM&O NewsBase

- *Firm Articles & Publications*
- *Upcoming Speeches, Seminars and Activities*
- *DSM&O In the News!*
- *DSM&O's Analysis of Significant Legal Developments*
  This Month's Topic: The Nuclear Regulatory Commission Calls For Comments On Its Draft Policy Statement On Electric Industry Restructuring And Divestiture

DSM&O InfoBase

Our Information Center has developed and maintains exceedingly useful topical collections of Internet legal and business resources. Our attorneys find them valuable and we are happy to share them with you. If you have comments or recommendations for resources to include please feel free to contact Margareta Knauff.

- Energy Law Resources
- Government & Legislative Affairs Resources
- Government Contracts Resources
- Intellectual Property Resources
- Legal or law-related Resources
- Tax Law Resources
- Each week the DSM&O assembles a short list entitled New on the Web, which features new legal and business related Web sites, and usually one or two entertaining places to visit.

On October 18, 1996, Margareta Knauff spoke at the American Association of Law Libraries 3rd Annual Northeast Regional Conference. During the Internet in a Day session, she discussed Law Firms and the Internet: Beyond Marketing. Following the paper are a number of useful resources, both print and online, which further explore issues (recruiting, communication and ethics).

About DSM&O Home Page

Figure 11.1 The home page of DSM&O

resources specifically geared to each practice section. As a librarian I also felt obligated to "give something back" to the Internet community. Sure, we were using the Internet to market our law firm, but we should also provide something beneficial and of potential use and interest to researchers.

The library at DSM&O already had Internet access through a dial-up connection to a local provider since 1993. There was one account for the entire library, and I became responsible for monitoring several e-mail discussion lists for the entire staff. During the course of this monitoring, I began collecting addresses of useful Internet resources as they were mentioned on the various discussion lists. I ended up using a spiral-bound notebook to organize the various addresses. I used glue-in tabs to separate the book into subject-specific areas, such as Federal Government, Courts, and one for each practice section in the firm. From my notebook of resources, I was able to begin to assemble subject specific lists of Internet resources.

To supplement these skeletal lists, I began conducting searches on the World Wide Web, using simple phrases, such as "real estate law" or "intellectual property" in order to locate sites which I thought might contain useful resources for our practitioners. I also scanned archives of the *Legal Automation and Internet Review* (LAIR), a seemingly now-defunct electronic newsletter assembled by librarians at the University of Texas Law Library. At the time I began creating these resources, LAIR was a reliable source of the latest and the best legal sources available on the Web. It was through searching their archived electronic newsletters that I was able to locate more useful sites.

As I was plugging away on my Internet research, every now and then attorneys who were familiar with the Internet would notify me of sites that they had found useful. I would usually add these sites to the page I was creating for that particular section. I found the input of these attorneys so invaluable that I actively sought out attorneys in other sections to be my "Internet buddies." What this would entail, I told them, was letting me bounce ideas for the site off them, mentioning potentially interesting Web sites and requesting that if they found anything really useful on the Web, they would let me know about it. While I did not get an Internet buddy in all sections, I did get one for most of them. Their input has been inestimable, and it shows in the pages created for each particular practice section.

The general format of the pages consisted of a link to the resource, followed by a brief explanation of what could be found at the particular site, and on the following line, the actual Internet address of the site, for example:

Telecom Information Resources: Over 900 links to a variety of sites affiliated with telecommunications, from policy and regulation to broadcasters. *http://www.spp.umich.edu/telecom/telecom-info.html*

This format allowed the pages to be used online, to be printed out and used as handouts for training purposes, or be given to clients. If I had enough resources on a particular subject, I would try to subdivide them topically in order to organize the sites a little better. In some practice areas, I just did not find enough useful resources on the Internet to merit subdivision.

THE ATTORNEYS GET INVOLVED

When I began compiling lists of Internet resources by practice section, I was skeptical as to whether individuals outside the firm would really be interested in them. My primary objective was to create something useful for the practitioners at DSM&O. The attorneys themselves saw the real value these resources might have to the Internet public, and they began to work actively with me to improve the resources list for their particular section.

The two practice sections in DSM&O with the most computer proficiency are those that deal with high technology matters on a regular basis: Intellectual Property and Government Contracts. Of all the practice sections in the firm, these two quickly grasped the need for creating comprehensive Internet resources in a particular subject area. They wanted potential clients to visit our site. People would not visit our site unless we provided something of interest to them, and the chances of people visiting our site would improve dramatically if we could offer links to Internet resources geared towards a particular audience (e.g., Figure 11.2). In addition to suggesting sites to link to, attorneys began sending me copies of published articles that they wished to have added to our Web site.

In many cases, the attorneys submitted a photocopy of their article, a printed version, or just told me where it had been printed. While I did not mind doing the HTML coding, I had no intention of retyping an article. Moreover, it seemed none of the attorneys were clear on whether or not they had reprint rights for their articles, and just exactly what those reprint rights were! This led to some interesting experiences which included spending three days on the phone with a publisher, trying to figure out if a particular partner had reprint rights to his article. Eventually, these circumstances led to the establishment of an informal policy. Anyone submitting an article to be reprinted on our Web site must submit it to me in electronic format, make sure that they have reprint rights, and let me know exactly what those rights entail, so that I may make appropriate notations on the articles. In addition to adding links to these articles from the firm's external page, I also created a section for legal articles on the subject resources page and began including links to the articles.

While the Government Contracts section was content with an Internet resources page containing only links to articles and to other resources outside the Internet, the Intellectual Property section presented me with a grand plan for their page. In addition to links to outside resources, they began creating their own resources to be added to their page. The first of

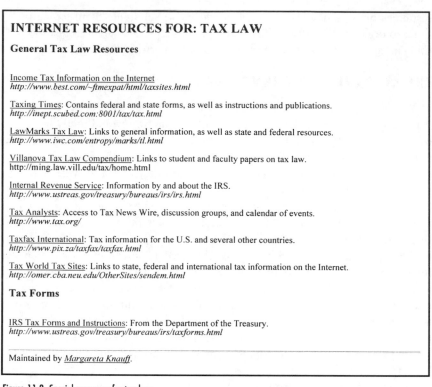

INTERNET RESOURCES FOR: TAX LAW

General Tax Law Resources

Income Tax Information on the Internet
http://www.best.com/~ftmexpat/html/taxsites.html

Taxing Times: Contains federal and state forms, as well as instructions and publications.
http://inept.scubed.com:8001/tax/tax.html

LawMarks Tax Law: Links to general information, as well as state and federal resources.
http://www.iwc.com/entropy/marks/tl.html

Villanova Tax Law Compendium: Links to student and faculty papers on tax law.
http://ming.law.vill.edu/tax/home.html

Internal Revenue Service: Information by and about the IRS.
http://www.ustreas.gov/treasury/bureaus/irs/irs.html

Tax Analysts: Access to Tax News Wire, discussion groups, and calendar of events.
http://www.tax.org/

Taxfax International: Tax information for the U.S. and several other countries.
http://www.pix.za/taxfax/taxfax.html

Tax World Tax Sites: Links to state, federal and international tax information on the Internet.
http://omer.cba.neu.edu/OtherSites/sendem.html

Tax Forms

IRS Tax Forms and Instructions: From the Department of the Treasury.
http://www.ustreas.gov/treasury/bureaus/irs/taxforms.html

Maintained by *Margareta Knauff*.

Figure 11.2 Special resources for tax law

these was an Intellectual Property Frequently Asked Questions (FAQ). The FAQ contained basic questions about copyrights, trademark, and patents. Later on, I was presented with a list of fees for the United States Patent and Trademark Office. This list was offered both in tables format for those browsers that could read tables, and as a regular text document. I then sat down with one of the attorneys in the Intellectual Property Section, and we began discussing what other features we could add to the page. In addition to the Internet resources, the attorney wanted to feature a graphic—called "Patent of the Month," which would be changed on a monthly basis. As many of the articles written by the Intellectual Property section referenced specific cases, he wished to include a full text of the cases, linking to and from their articles. Equally important, the attorney felt, was to feature the cases in which DSM&O attorneys participated and won. However, some of the features suggested by the attorney are still waiting to be implemented. These include a section entitled "Check it Out!" which would discuss the latest events in the intellectual property field; and "Pleadings and Memoranda" which would link to attorney work product.

The most important part of the page is the other Internet resources to which it links. These include general intellectual property information, information specific to either patents, trademarks, or copyrights, foreign patent and trademark offices, and links to tools useful for conducting searches on existing patents and copyrights. Although I did much of the preliminary research, the creators of the Intellectual Property section took this project to heart, and located many of the resources. This is as it should be since I am not a practitioner in any legal field, and I can only guess what might be useful to the attorneys. The attorneys, however, know what is useful to them, and, therefore, what would be useful to other attorneys and in particular those in the intellectual property field. Because my responsibilities still include management of the Technical Services department of the library, and other technical services' responsibilities such as cataloging, I am not able to devote as much time as I would like to locating resources for various practice sections. Consequently, attorney involvement in location of resources has been of great help to me.

The resources pages for both the Government Contracts section and for the Intellectual Property section also contain other information about their respective practice areas, including attorney biographies. In addition, at the bottom of each page is a link to the main firm home page, in case visitors wish to find out about the rest of the firm. There has been some discussion within the IS department about setting up subdomains for each of these sites (such as http://www.ip.DSM&Ollp.com or http://govcon.dsmo.com) and letting them stand on their own, as representative pages for their whole section.

PUBLICITY

I did not want to advertise the Government Contracts or Intellectual Property pages while they were still in development. I did not want visitors coming to the pages while they were still experiencing growing pains. I first advertised the pages within the firm and asked the practitioners if they had any suggestions or comments for improvements. I evaluated their responses and implemented the ones which I felt were valid and achievable. I then began to advertise the pages, submitting their URLs for indexing to a number of different search engines, and this has met with some success. I know that the URL was added to at least a few of the search engines, but I don't know how many. I do know that Yahoo only has one entry for DSM&O, the main firm page. I also submitted the Government Contracts page for evaluation by the Government Contractor Resource Center (http://www.govcon.com). The GCRC is an Internet resource which contains links of interest (both to resources and to services) to the government contracting community. The page was presented with a Top Sites award from the GCRC. Furthermore, the GCRC now also contains a link to our Government Contracts Resources page.

WHERE ARE WE NOW AND WHERE ARE WE GOING?

Over a year has passed since we first implemented the Internet firmwide, and we have made a great deal of progress. Currently, I still manage our Web site, except for the issues dealing with the hardware and software. We have recently switched servers from EMWAC to the Netscape Fasttrack Commerce server, because the Netscape server is easier to maintain and more flexible than EMWAC. We are looking into use of Communication Gateway Interface (CGI) in order to make our pages more interactive, and we hope to add user-friendly features, such as a tool for searching the site.

Over the course of this year, I anticipate a complete overhaul of our entire Internet site. Not only would we be looking at the way the files are stored on our server, but also at the aesthetics of our Web pages. I foresee a greater use of the frames tag, which will allow division of our Web pages into multiple scrollable regions. As not all browsers yet support this tag, just as all browsers do not support graphics, we will continue to offer frameless versions of our Web pages in order to keep them accessible to all users.

Looking back, I think the best step I took was when I asked the attorneys to get involved. They know their area of practice as well as I know mine and could tell me which resources were really useful to them, and which were not. One of the difficult points to get across is how much work is involved in maintaining a good Web site. Good Web sites should not be static, they should always be growing, changing, and improving. I had the best success when I began to concentrate on a few particular subjects instead of trying to create resources that ran the gamut of the legal practice world. Focusing on a few subjects allowed me to channel my time and energy into creating quality Internet resources.

When I started creating the Internet Resources by practice section, I did not have much of a plan, just a vague idea that I wanted to put some links together organized by subject area. In the future, I will not attempt anything of this sort without having a careful plan first, meeting with attorneys if necessary to develop the plan. I have found their input invaluable, and they have often come up with ideas which would not have occurred to me. After all, the attorneys in the firm are going to be the primary users of these resources, and only they know what is useful to them. Outside in the Internet world, I imagine that the primary users of our site are other attorneys or those practicing in a similar field.

In the course of the coming year, we are also going to begin to promote our pages of Internet Resources a little more actively. In addition to requesting reindexing of our site by the various search engines, we will also be posting information about our new pages to relevant discussion lists and newsgroups, in order to make sure that those who would be interested in such sites will be able to find them. At the moment, users can only find our pages of Internet resources if they know where to look. We hope to make access easier during the next year.

I hope to keep up attorney involvement in our Web site, but I think that may be one of my more difficult goals. While some attorneys are aware of the value of assisting in the creation of Internet resources, it is not a universal trait. Many do not feel they have the time to devote to something of this sort. To give them credit, they are not hired to work on Internet development, they are hired to litigate. However, as use of the Internet expands and perhaps more business is generated through the Internet, I expect more attorneys in different sections will be interested in assisting with the development of quality Internet resources.

Indeed, the creation of the various pages of Internet resources by practice section began, for me, as a personal effort. Yet, through the course of a year, collaboration with individuals in other areas of the firm have improved these pages dramatically. I did not wait for approval or direction from above to begin work on the resources, I just started them. I asked for help from the attorneys, and when I received it, I used their input to create useful online guides to Internet resources. Even when I did not receive their input, I still did my best to locate and evaluate Internet resources. After the resources had been developed and advertised within the firm, people began to take more notice and to offer suggestions. Now that they have taken on a life of their own, their existence and usefulness are being recognized by the upper echelons of management. The fact that these pages were created and maintained by the library, adds more cachet to the IS department as a whole.

Chapter 12

THE OCEAN CITY FREE PUBLIC LIBRARY HOME PAGE

Janice Painter

Technical Services Librarian
Ocean City Free Public Library
oclib@acy.digex.net
http://www.acy.digex.net/~oclib

"The time has come," the web-weaver said,
"To talk of many things:
Of hyper-text—and space shuttle—
Of virtual gardens—and Web rings—
And why the sea is boiling hot—
And whether pigs have wings."
(Apologies to Lewis Carroll, here and following)

DOWN THE RABBIT-HOLE

Like Alice, I was spending the afternoon in routine pursuits, on duty at the reference desk, when the call came: a woman posed an innocent enough question. "How can I find the names of local and municipal officials in Virginia?" As my reference interview proceeded, the purpose of the question was refined. The library patron wanted to pursue her ex-husband to collect back child support payments. She had tracked him from Pennsylvania to California and finally to Virginia. She wanted to contact public officials and begin a letter writing campaign and legal proceedings in the region before he moved on again.

We located the town on a map and checked the printed directories of municipal officials. I took the patron's name and phone number, told her I'd log onto the Internet, and let her know what else I could find online to help her.

Using Veronica and gopher searches, I soon found that Virginia had a well-established public information network. Checking the legislative gopher, I learned that Virginia was also home state to a Congressional Representative who had been active in supporting proposed "deadbeat dad" legislation. Bingo! I had found the bottle "with the words 'Drink me' beautifully printed on it in large letters" (Carroll, 9), the small cake "on which the words 'Eat me' were beautifully marked in currants"(Carroll, 12).

Here was my first live Internet reference question. Down the rabbit-hole I went.

Ocean City Free Public Library is a single-branch municipal library in southern New Jersey on the Atlantic coast. The library is not affiliated with any larger county or municipal library system. We are located in a resort area where the population swells from 15,000 year-round to over 200,000 in the summer months. Our daily checkout count surges from 300 to 500 items daily to routinely over 1,000 items per day during peak tourist season. In 1996, we have a total of 22,000 patrons, and a collection of 81,000 volumes. The staff consists of eleven full-time and fourteen part-time employees, including five full-time professional librarians (counting the director and assistant director).

The library runs a Novell local area network (LAN) with twenty-five IBM-compatible personal computers, four networked laser printers, one networked dot matrix printer, eight local dot matrix printers, thirty-five networked CD-ROM drives, and eleven local CD-ROM drives (eight are installed on staff workstations; three on public access PCs). Eleven PCs are public access workstations: of these four are DOS Online Public Access Catalog (OPAC) workstations for the library's Winnebago Online Catalog; three PCs run Windows-based applications and networked and stand-alone CD-ROM databases/programs; and four PCs run DOS-based networked CD-ROM applications including Infotrac and Newsbank databases. Three PCs are dedicated Winnebago circulation system workstations for staff use. The remaining eleven PCs handle Windows and DOS business applications run by staff (Winnebago, Geoworks, Lotus SmartSuite, graphics and publishing tools).

ADVICE FROM A CATERPILLAR

"Who are *you*?" said the Caterpillar.
This was not an encouraging opening for a conversation. Alice replied, rather shyly, "I—I hardly know, Sir, just at present—at least I know who I *was* when I got up this morning, but I think I must have changed several times since then." (Carroll, 49-50)

In 1995, the Ocean City Free Public Library received an LSCA grant (federal funding for the development and improvement of public libraries in the United States) from the New Jersey State Library. Grant funding was to be used to contract with a mid-level Internet provider to establish accounts; pay telecommmunication costs; install telephone lines; or purchase modems, telecommmunication software, and reference materials on the use of the Internet and its resources. The Ocean City Free Public Library established an Internet account with a local Internet Service Provider (ISP) to evaluate the use of the Internet for reference services. After the grant period ended, the library absorbed the cost of maintaining this ISP account. The following factors were considered in our decision: whether the provider had a reliable, proven track record, network support sufficient in terms of hardware and telecommunications infrastructure, and end-user support for software, UNIX, and Internet services. Other concerns were whether there were multiple local dial-up numbers available, sufficient dial-in lines to avoid busy signals, and additional Internet services available (for example, UNIX shell account, storage space on provider's server for e-mail and a library Web site, and usage reports on Web pages). As project manager and technical services librarian, I became the resident Internet librarian and de facto guru. Initially, I focused on learning basic Internet services: e-mail, telnet, FTP, gopher, WAIS, Archie, and Veronica searches, using a text-only interface (Lynx) and UNIX shell account. After three months I installed a graphical browser (Netscape) and a PPP connection and support software (Internet Chameleon). I began exploring the World Wide Web, and I was hooked!

We realized that the library was not yet in the position to support a full-blown Internet server in-house—we did not have the staff time, expertise, or financial means to accomplish such an ambitious project. Our ISP provided our library account with disk storage space for a Web site on their server and urged us to take advantage of this feature as an outreach tool. We realized that we could offer patrons, and potential patrons, Internet access and a finding guide to online information via the Ocean City Free Public Library home page on the World Wide Web. As we experimented with using the Internet to try to answer reference questions, we saw the need for pointers to useful online information and recognized that organizing and categorizing these pointers would add value to our Web site.

A MAD TEA-PARTY

> There was a table set out under a tree in front of the house, and the March Hare and the Hatter were having tea at it: a Dormouse was sitting between them, fast asleep . . . The table was a large one, but the three were all crowded together at one corner of it. "'No room! No room!" they cried out when they saw Alice coming. "There's *plenty* of room!" said Alice indignantly, and she sat down in a large armchair at one end of the table. (Carroll, 76-77)

The technical services librarian collected links to Web addresses (Uniform Resource Locators or URLs), file transfer (FTP) and gopher sites, and Web-based search tools. Yahoo, Magellan, PointCom, and other subject-oriented Internet guides and rating tools were departure points for exploring the Internet's ever-changing resources.

The basic approach to designing the library's Web site was to try and incorporate pointers to the kinds of information that our library patrons asked for when they called or came in to our reference desk. Local information and news, community, and tourism information available on the Internet were another focus. We also wanted to spotlight the unique and exciting character of the Internet and the World Wide Web, and to direct users of our Web site to information about the culture of the Net.

Input into potential links came directly from reference staff, patrons, various Internet-related periodicals, and indirectly from online peers in online discussion groups and workshops such as Stumpers-List, Web4Lib, Back2 School, and the South Jersey Internet Users' Group. As the Ocean City Free Public Library home page on the World Wide Web became more visible, the input and enthusisam from users and potential users grew.

Stepping back and looking at the links that had been collected, I was able to organize the pointers I wanted to present on the library's Web site into several basic categories:

- Internet Reference Libraries (online "libraries" and library materials)
- Internet/Web Search/Finding Tools (ways to search the Internet by subject of content keyword)
- Education Resources (K-12, school, distance learning, and college, preparatory subjects and resources)
- Consumer Information (including general consumer information, automotive, health, medical, employment, and business sources)
- United States government information resources
- About Books (online book-related information and texts, including periodicals)
- Regional Information for the southern New Jersey and Philadelphia area
- Current Events (including news, weather and local news resources)
- The Internet Universe/World/Community (space and the solar system, the world on Earth, Internet cities, locations featuring museums and the arts, and libraries)
- Internet/Web Search Tools (a mixed bag of sources for Internet and Web information)

Each category (see Figure 12.1) was designed to have an associated graphic hypertext "button" to represent the category visually. The graphic chosen for each category was a visual and mnemonic clue to the information being presented (URL:http://www.acy.digex.net/~oclib/index.html).

The library's Web pages were structured as individual subpages accessible from links on the Ocean City Free Public Library's home page. Each category above had its own HTML (HyperText Markup Language) document. This modular approach made the task of building the Web site manageable. I worked on collecting and organizing links to online information in all

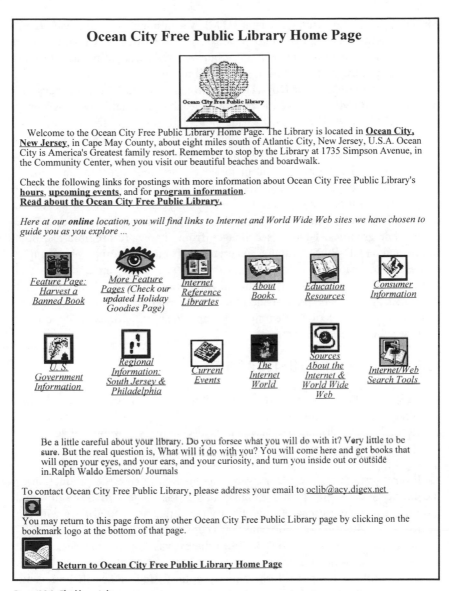

Ocean City Free Public Library Home Page

Welcome to the Ocean City Free Public Library Home Page. The Library is located in **Ocean City, New Jersey**, in Cape May County, about eight miles south of Atlantic City, New Jersey, U.S.A. Ocean City is America's Greatest family resort. Remember to stop by the Library at 1735 Simpson Avenue, in the Community Center, when you visit our beautiful beaches and boardwalk.

Check the following links for postings with more information about Ocean City Free Public Library's **hours**, **upcoming events**, and for **program information**.
Read about the Ocean City Free Public Library.

*Here at our **online** location, you will find links to Internet and World Wide Web sites we have chosen to guide you as you explore ...*

Feature Page: Harvest a Banned Book

More Feature Pages (Check our updated Holiday Goodies Page)

Internet Reference Libraries

About Books

Education Resources

Consumer Information

U.S. Government Information

Regional Information: South Jersey & Philadelphia

Current Events

The Internet World

Sources About the Internet & World Wide Web

Internet/Web Search Tools

Be a little careful about your library. Do you forsee what you will do with it? Very little to be sure. But the real question is, What will it do with you? You will come here and get books that will open your eyes, and your ears, and your curiosity, and turn you inside out or outside in.Ralph Waldo Emerson/ Journals

To contact Ocean City Free Public Library, please address your email to oclib@acy.digex.net

You may return to this page from any other Ocean City Free Public Library page by clicking on the bookmark logo at the bottom of that page.

Return to Ocean City Free Public Library Home Page

Figure 12.1 The library's home page

categories at the same time, but having several smaller documents to edit seemed preferential to working on one long running HTML page. Graphics are kept in a separate subdirectory on the ISP's UNIX machine.

While I had no previous background in HTML, I had worked extensively with various text processing and publishing packages. I found that compiling and writing the library's Web page was conceptually similar to using these computer tools.

My primary reference for self-taught HTML was a book, *Netscape and HTML Explorer* (Scottsdale: Coriolis Group Books, 1995), written by Urban LeJeune, the president of my local Internet user's group. All of the design and markup work was done in-house by the technical services librarian.

Initally, I used the Hot Dog HTML editor, a graphical "word processor" program for HTML. However, I was not pleased at the quality or consistency of the HTML code generated by Hot Dog, and now I prefer to create my HTML pages as ASCII text using my favorite text processing program, Lotus AmiPro. I find that I can "cut and paste" HTML markup commands easily between several open pages, and maintain a consistent structure and "look" for my Web pages by manually coding them myself. I use WebLint (http://www.unipress.com/weblint/) and Web Tech (http://www.webtechs. com/html-val-svc/) online HTML checkers, to scan my Web pages for HTML errors. For graphics, I have used images from shareware art libraries, both online and on CD-ROM, graphics generator tools on the Internet, photographs processed to graphic files, and scanned images. I use Paint Shop Pro and Lotus Freelance graphics for graphic manipulation. Both products are easier to learn and use than some of the more high-powered professional graphics programs available, offer flexible file import/export options, and perform basic graphics editing tasks.

THE QUEEN'S CROQUET GROUND

"Why the fact is, you see, Miss, this here ought to have been a *red* rose-tree, and we put a white one in by mistake; and if the Queen was to find it out, we should all have our heads cut off, you know. So you see, Miss, we're doing our best . . ." (Carroll, 90)

Several pitfalls and problems were encountered during the production of the library's Web site. In my enthusiasm for the project of designing and building an online presence for the library (read that as inexperience with the genre), I initially did not anticipate that keeping up a Web site was an ongoing task. First, the time it took to build pages was longer than anticipated. There was the initial learning curve for HTML, as well as mastering the process of checking page formatting, graphics, and links off-line (with Netscape), and online using a text-based bowser (Lynx) and America Online and CompuServe. (This is done for each new page design to be sure that the different browsers display the pages satisfactorily).

A second problem was that checking and updating links, constantly adding new pointers to sites, and coming up with fresh material to keep patrons coming back to our pages involved what seemed to be an exponential amount of time. One solution I found helpful was to use the services of a library volunteer to help check links. My volunteer assistant spends two hours per week "surfing" the Web, verifying the URLs on the library's pages and new sites being considered for updates. I also spend about ten hours compiling each semi-monthly special focus page, and roughly another eight to twelve hours per month collecting, compiling, and updating links to the main subject category pages.

A third problem, that of negotiating UNIX, learning file structures and organization, and figuring out the most effective way to set access permissions for the library's growing collection of Web documents, was a daunting task early on in the project. My ISP's support team and local Internet user's group were invaluable resources in these areas.

I use in-house equipment and software to implement the library's Web site whenever possible. I type and edit HTML code using Lotus AmiPro, and save Web pages as ASCII files. Where there is an exisiting page model, I copy basic HTML commands and structure from a previously mounted page. Initially, I used the Netscape feature to "View HTML source" code from online pages and used these working documents as models for my own HTML. I edit HTML documents by working in multiple windows, cutting and pasting links from my online Web browser (Netscape) into AmiPro. I often have several copies of different library Web pages open at the same time so I can add links to various categories and compare or cut and paste HTML formatting commands between pages. To keep hypertext links accurately typed, I find that it is best to cut and paste them directly from my Web browser's window.

Using Netscape local files options to preview page formatting and check for HTML coding problems involves pointing my Web browser to a file on disk on my PC, instead of a URL on the World Wide Web. When a HTML page is complete and tested in Netscape, I use Netmanage Internet Chameleon for a PPP connection and FTP services to transfer files from my local drive to the library's public FTP directory on our ISP's machine. I also use Internet Chameleon telnet services to assign UNIX permissions which make the HTML pages accessible to the public. The library acquired copies of Netscape and Internet Chameleon specifically for this project.

THE MOCK TURTLE'S STORY

> Then the Queen left off, quite out of breath, and said to Alice "Have you seen the mock Turtle yet?"
> "No," said Alice. "I don't even know what a Mock Turtle is."
> "It's the thing Mock Turtle Soup is made from," said the Queen.
> "I never saw one, or heard of one," said Alice. (Carroll, 109)

Mounting the Ocean City Free Public Library's home page on the World Wide Web immediately increased the visibility of the library in the local community and beyond. Because the library was the first public agency in our town to provide an in-house Web site, we found that our communication with other municipal agencies improved as we reached out to include information from outside of the library. For example, Ocean City's BeachWalk program, PTA and New Year's First Night programs have been publicized via the library's Web site. Members of these community groups attended library Internet orientation sessions and demonstrations of the Ocean City Free Public Library's home page and talks about including their information on the Web spiralled off informally. Communication lines opened up quickly to local Web weavers, site designers and maintainers, often via the local Internet user's group, the South Jersey Internet Users' Group (http://www.acy. digex.net/~sjiug). The library's visibility in professional library communities also increased. I have been in touch by mail, phone, and e-mail to librarians who are implementing similar projects and have been asked to participate in professional programs and workshops about libraries and the Internet. As a result of discussion group correspondence, the Ocean City Free Public Library has contributed to columns in *American Libraries*, and we have assisted in reference queries from across the country, and even internationally.

WHO STOLE THE TARTS?

> "I wish you wouldn't squeeze so," said the Dormouse " . . . I can hardly breathe."
> "I can't help it," said Alice very meekly "I'm growing."
> "Don't talk nonsense'" said Alice more boldly: "you know you're growing too."
> "Yes, but *I* grow at a reasonable pace," said the Dormouse: "not in that ridiculous fashion." (Carroll, 133)

As our Web presence grew, we began to market our site. We used several (free) avenues for publicity: local press coverage, our community cable TV channel, computer clubs and users' groups, the PTA and schools, and word of mouth in the community. I registered our site in online finding tools and Web crawlers so that users and potential users could find it doing keyword searches. The simple act of using the library's URL in e-mail communications and on staff business cards publicizes our Web site. We welcome other Web sites to share links, and encourage cross-linking to and from our site (by schools, a real estate Web site, the Chamber of Commerce Web site, the local community college, various South Jersey resources pages, the South Jersey Internet Users' group, and other libraries in the area). This Web ring concept markets our site well.

The library offers training about the Internet regularly. We use the Ocean City Free Public Library home page as a launching point for training sessions and live Internet demonstrations. We anticipate expanding our public Internet training to include guest teachers from the South Jersey Internet Users' Group.

Coincidentally (certainly independent of my design), the library's Web site was publicly unveiled at a meeting of the local Internet users' group in the fall of 1995. Our site was featured in the monthly program and Internet demo as the first local library to mount a Web page, and as a starting point to use to search for online information. Soon afterwards, an article in the *Atlantic City Press* weekly feature column about the Internet was devoted to the Ocean City Free Public Library's home page. These two avenues of exposure got the word out to the local community and our page was off the back burners and into the frying pan.

Our objective to keep the online information we present fresh and to keep people coming back led to the compilation of semimonthly special focus pages. Each page serves as a Web bibliography for a topic or theme. Web pages featuring Halloween, holiday seasons, African American history month, Ireland and Irish resources, gardens and gardening, and a Logon At the Library Internet tour page were mounted over an eight month period. These special focus pages are publicized in the local press and on public access cable TV.

We have had a great deal of constructive feedback from our home page patrons. Two examples follow:

> Hi. I live in California, but I graduated from OCHS, Class of '59. I was surfing the Net and found the library's page. It's great to be able to read about my home town. I remember pleasant days I spent in the old library. (e-mail message from a former Ocean City resident, received in February 1996)

> I just checked out the gardens and gardening page and I'm glad you included my orchid page in your links. The virtual garden is really cool. I think I'll go and plant something when I get a free moment. (e-mail message from the owner of a page of links cited in the Ocean City Free Public Library Gardens and Gardening on the Web Page, http://www.acy.digex.net/~oclib/gardens.html, received in May 1996)

Aside from online and live feedback from patrons, we needed to keep track of who uses our Web site and which sections and how often it is used. We are currently in a beta program to receive daily usage statistics log reports from our ISP. We anticipate using daily and weekly reports to analyze and report on the number of accesses to our Web pages, which areas are most popular, which areas need more work, the number of repeat visitors, and which browser programs are being used to access our pages.

ALICE'S EVIDENCE

> "If there's no meaning in it," said the King, "that saves a world of trouble, you know, as we needn't try to find any. And yet I don't know," he went on, spreading out the verses on his knee and looking at them with one eye; "I seem to see some meaning in them after all." (Carroll, 144–145)

In retrospect, I would urge any library or public agency to pursue developing a Web site and mounting it on a commercial ISP's Internet server. Look for people with expertise and experience in your community. I found many talented and willing volunteers who continue to help me as I maintain the Ocean City Free Public Library's Web site. Realize that you must devote resources and time to the project, and be willing to learn and work after hours—the job of implementing new technology must coexist with, as well as enhance and add value to, the more traditional business and services of your library.

As for the ending of my first reference foray into the wilds of the Internet Wonderland, way back in the days before I even realized that the World Wide Web existed, the library patron who was searching for her ex-husband used the contact list I had found from online searches for her letter writing campaign. She communicated with several womens' assistance organizations, followed legislative developments, wrote and called Congressional representatives. About six months later she came into the library to tell me that she'd gotten a new court order for child support in Virginia, and that her husband was facing prosecution. She'd gotten her first back child support payment, and felt that she'd done "all that she could do" to help her children. She was most optimistic and grateful for the fact that the library's new online research tools brought her information she would not have gotten otherwise.

REFERENCE

Carroll, Lewis. *Alice's Adventures in Wonderland.* NY: Random House, 1946.

Chapter 13

CREATING THE CHICAGO PUBLIC LIBRARY WWW SITE

Marcia Dellenbach
Online Services, cplcarc@interaccess.com
Kathleen Ryan
Neighborhood Services, cplns@interaccess.com
Ellen Starkman
Computer Services, starkman@interaccess.com

BEGINNINGS

Creating a World Wide Web site was not the initial goal of the Chicago Public Library (CPL) when we started exploring the Internet in 1992. It was two committees, two years, one grant, loads of good advice and countless hours later that our Web site was born.

We first approached the Internet as the equivalent of another online service that could supplement the commercial databases that we subscribed to, such as Dialog and Nexis. By the middle of 1993, we realized the potential was much broader and a committee was formed to investigate the uses of the Internet and its impact on library services. This committee was much like a user group: it was very informal with a great deal of discussion and was open to anyone. It provided a good format for exchanging ideas and generating interest.

Commissioner of the Chicago Public Library, Mary Dempsey, soon realized that to take full advantage of the Internet's usefulness in a public library, a more structured and organized approach to the relatively unstructured and poetically chaotic Internet was needed. Another committee was formed in early 1994 to function as a working committee. Eighteen librarians were named to this committee and they represented all subject divisions in the central library and all geographic areas of the library's extensive branch system, as well as the library administration. It was stressed that these people were representatives and should involve others from their units as much as possible. Members were chosen by the co-chairs mainly based on their computer expertise or Internet interest, but there was still a wide disparity in knowledge and experience. Nonetheless, this committee was the backbone of the Internet project and all planning and work was done by these eighteen people. The learning curve for many people was steep. Many were Internet novices who needed to immerse themselves to become familiar with the Internet resources in their assigned areas. As the work of the committee progressed, members were able to devote varying amounts of time to their individual areas which resulted in some subjects having comprehensive coverage and others with coverage that was uneven. Most of the committee members remained very enthusiastic and worked extremely hard. The committee benefited greatly from the diversity of the members' backgrounds and interests.

While this committee was forming, the library applied for and received a grant from the Illinois State Library to offer Internet services to the public. Looking back, it is amazing that we had the temerity to take on a task like public access before we had *any* idea about what we were attempting. Very few librarians in the CPL system, not to mention our committee, even had Internet access. We were soon going to set up eight Internet workstations for the public.

A very fortuitous acquaintance early in the project turned around the whole enterprise. At an Internet Fair, we met Nancy John, assistant university librarian at the University of Illinois at Chicago (UIC). She asked the right questions which compelled us to examine exactly what we wanted to accomplish and to learn what we were capable of doing. From the outset we knew that we wanted to structure access to the Internet in a way that best benefited our patrons. We already had a very good understanding of who used the library and what type of information they were seeking. We simply wanted to organize the Internet in such a way that it would be easier for our librarians and patrons to use. This could be as little as making a list of recommended sites for all of our librarians to use or it could be a text-based gopher, an undertaking we considered monumental at the time. Everything was changing very quickly on the Internet at this time and UIC librarians convinced us that our goal was too narrow. They suggested that by creating a Web page we would be able to meet that goal and also be able to highlight other services the library offered. We would, in effect, be able to weave the Internet into the traditional library services and collections that the Chicago Public Library had been building and provide our librarians and patrons with the best informational sources. Commissioner Dempsey and the rest of the library administration quickly realized the vast potential of having a Web site and were very supportive. Since no in-house expertise existed, we set out to create it.

PRODUCTION

When we began working on this project, we used our own Macintosh Performa 636 CD with 20MB Ram, 250MB HD, and running WebSTAR server software, AppleSearch, Eudora, and AppleScript CGI, and we expected that the library would soon have a direct connection to the Internet. Since this did not happen as soon as we expected, we had to modify our plans. Thanks to Sharon Hogan, the university librarian at the University of Illinois at Chicago (UIC), we were able to make arrangements, as part of UIC's Great Cities Initiative (http://www.uic.edu/depts/cuppa/gci/), to be taught how to create and maintain our own server and pages. Through the Great Cities Program, UIC directs its teaching, research, and service to address human needs in Chicago and in metropolitan areas worldwide by becoming a partner with government and public agencies, corporations, and philanthropic and civic organizations. Tom Jevec, electronic services librarian and assistant professor, guided us in developing our style and scope. He created an awareness of what we were indicating to users through our selections and emphasis.

Our partnership with UIC has opened up wonderful opportunities for us. We are able to concentrate on developing our server independent of building our own network. Once our own connection to the Internet is in place, we will move our server to it.

The greatest advantage of locating our server at UIC is access to the expertise of professional librarians who have been working on the Internet since its beginning. It is an arrangement we can suggest to any library which has a similar opportunity. Since we were using local Internet providers for our staff and public access, we explored using them for our home page too. However, we seized the opportunity to work with colleagues who had interests similar to ours. We were also lucky to be able to use UIC's sophisticated graphic software and hardware before acquiring our own.

Creating a style we could build on in years (and platforms) to come was important. We try to use simple graphics that alert visitors they are within our site. Though it took time to create pages that logically interlinked and always pointed back to our home page (see Figure 13.1), it was well worth the effort. This design became even more important once other sites began linking directly to pages within our site rather than to our home page. One of the wonderful things about the Internet is that there is no control over who links to which pages on your site. We know from our server statistics that many of our visitors are not coming through our front door, so our design provides an invitation to them to explore our entire site. Our simple graphics can easily be replaced with new improved ones as they are developed. The underlying structure will support new graphics and whatever new technologies become available.

We structured our server and its contents with the public's informational needs in mind. We have, when possible, offered the choice of text instead of

Figure 13.1 Home page of the Chicago Public Library

images. This works well for people without graphics capability or with slower modems. For items where graphics are essential, we developed clickable images that present the information attractively; for example, click on a map of the library system showing our 79 neighborhood locations click on pieces of the Chicago flag to learn about the parts of the flag, or click on a picture of

City of Chicago Information

Listed here are references for information on the City of Chicago. Some of the sources are ones the Chicago Public Library and Municipal Reference Library have gathered, others are links to Internet based information systems.

| CPL Chicago Information | Chicago Mosaic | Other Chicago Spots A-Z |

City of Chicago Information compiled by the librarians at CPL, the Information Center, Municipal Reference Collection, and the Municipal Reference Library, City of Chicago.

- Chicago History Information at CPL
- Chicago History Timeline 1673-
  Chronological history of Chicago that will help with school assignments -
  Look here to find out more about Jean Baptiste Point du Sable, Thompson Plat, Chicago River reversed, Chicago River straightened, Haymarket Riot, street level change, Century of Progress Exposition, histories of the fire and police departments, and much more!
- Chicago's Mayors, a Chronological List
  - Mayors (with clickable photographs)
  - Mayors (text only version)
- Chicago's Symbols
  - Chicago Charter
  - Chicago Corporate Seal
  - Chicago "I Will" Figure
  - Chicago Motto
  - Chicago Municipal Device (Y-Shaped Figure)
  - Chicago Municipal Flag
    - Chicago Municipal Flag (clickable flag)
    - Chicago Municipal Flag (text only version)
  - Chicago Name Origin
  - Chicago Flower
  - Chicago Nicknames
  - Chicago (Unofficial) Song
- Facts about Chicago
  Find out what the tallest buildings are, how many visitors pass through Chicago airports, how many parking meters, and much more.
- Frequently Requested Telephone Numbers
  Chicago area telephone numbers most frequently asked for by patrons of the CPL Harold Washington Library Center's Information Center.
- Printers Row Book Fair
  Sponsored by the Near South Planning Board, this annual book fair (third largest in the United States) also sponsors children's programs at CPL during the year.

Links to Chicago Internet-based information systems

Chicago Mosaic - City of Chicago and NCSA, UIUC, UIC
Send email to the Mayor, find out about the City departments and services they offer, the parks, the City Council, road construction, Chicago's most wanted criminals, missing persons, and community policing. The Electronic Tour Guide has the free summer festivals, parades, calendar of events, and much more!

Figure 13.2 Important city information

one of the past mayors to find their party, who they ran against, terms of office, inaugurations, birth/death dates.

As a public library, our production is driven by the type of information that we know people are looking for: local information (see Figure 13.2), home-work help, job and company information and government-related material. One challenge is combining Internet information sources with information about

CPL's resources for patrons doing subject research as well as for children doing homework. One of the first things we concentrated on locating and adding to our home page were resources which would lead to answers to the typical types of homework (see Figure 13.3) and reference questions that our librarians are

Early 19th century portrait from the collections of the Pulaski Museum in Warka-Winiary

CASIMIR PULASKI 1747 - 1779

CPL Celebrates Casimir Pulaski Day March 4

| CPL Resources | Homework Help | Other Internet Resources |

CPL Resources

Polish Language Collection at the **Portage Cragin Branch Library**

Foreign Language Collection at the **Harold Washington Library Center**

Casimir Pulaski Bibliography

Bibliography prepared by the Portage-Cragin Branch Library of titles owned by CPL.

Selected Bibliography on General Pulaski

Additional titles prepared by the Foreign Language Collection.

Homework Help: Casimir Pulaski 1747 - 1779

A Short Biography

Courtesy of the Polish Museum of America and John J. Kulczycki, UIC.

A Shorter Biography of Important Dates General Casimir Pulaski's Life in America

Courtesy of the Polish Museum of America

Memorials to Casimir Pulaski

Compiled by CPL librarians. Find out about memorials in Chicago, the Illinois law making Pulaski's birthday a holiday, Congress' 150th anniversary of Pulaski's death, and the poem by Longfellow honoring Casimir Pulaski.

Picture and Signature of Count Pulaski 60K

Courtesy of the Polish Museum of America

Other Internet Resources

Figure 13.3 A frequent homework assignment

asked on a regular basis. For our subject pages, we included as many of these resources as possible, hoping that both children and adults who found an answer, or something else that interested them, might be likely to begin their information searches there again. We used a similar approach in developing the original Chicago information we added to our home page.

Another challenge, one everyone on the Internet faces, is copyright and currency. This led us to develop areas such as our Chicago information section, which could continually be enhanced with a new entry, additional information or photos, but did not require constant updating. Our Chicago history timeline is one example. The librarians of the Municipal Library of Chicago had produced a pamphlet in 1975 and gave us permission to update and use it for the Internet. We scanned the text, and our reference librarians updated entries and found pictures for us to scan from older materials and our own special collections. Once again, the results were well worth the time and effort. We worked with many city departments seeking the information we wanted, and learned a lot about converting graphics and text from obsolete versions of software, uncommon fonts, and advanced page layout programs. As a result, our site provides unique information on the history, art, and architecture of Chicago, as well as information on the Chicago Public Library.

The co-chairs represented Online Services and Computer Services, a union which meshed well; while one concentrated on organizing subject sources and in-house pathfinders, the other concentrated on converting information to electronic formats, and designing and creating HTML documents. Consulting, technical support, and troubleshooting were performed by the UIC Library Systems group.

Initially all documents were created by one person. Now several other staff members have been trained in HTML markup and our standard format. We have over 4,000 files on our server, and our server software logs over 150,000 connections a month from outside the library. We receive many comments from all over the world via our e-mail form. At present we are unable to answer reference questions via the server, but this is something we will be doing when we move the server to CPL, and all reference staff have access. Access to our online catalog, via telnet from our home page to the CARL system, is very popular. Visitors to our site are eagerly waiting for both e-mail reference and patron-placed holds from our catalog.

MARKETING THE HOME PAGE

Our aims in marketing our home page have been to build support for what the library is doing, to serve as an example for what could be done by others, and to generate interest and use among the public. Of course, an ancillary benefit for us is that as people become aware of what we are doing, they often make suggestions that help us expand and improve our home page. While in the developmental stage we targeted three specific groups as well as the general public: staff at the Chicago Public Library, other city of Chicago departments, and Illinois librarians.

It was most important that the staff at the library understand and support the work that was being done. They were often in the best position to promote usage of the home page, offer suggestions for improvement, and add their own material to it, e.g., subject pathfinders. A consequence of marketing to the staff was that the library administration was able to communicate what their future Internet plans were and receive recommendations from staff. With that in mind, a number of formal demonstrations of the CPL server and home page were given. These included discussions of how this could be used in reference, encouraging people to submit material to add to the home page and asking for hard-to-answer questions that could possibly be answered through the Internet. At this point, we were not using software for canned demos—everything was live. It was nerve-wracking trying to time our spiels to how long it might take to connect to various sites and load images. Only once were we unable to connect at all and staff used the time to ask questions instead. There were also many informal demos, given by all members of the committee to staff in their units or districts. We created written material for staff including articles for in-house publications and handouts with our Web address and basic server information.

Reaching out to other city departments was important for the library to gain financial and moral support. We were able to promote the library as a leader in the city's quest for Internet access and as such we were asked to participate in a number of Internet-related projects. Our home page was always used as the example of what could be done. The crowning glory for all of our long hours and hard work came when we were asked to give a demo of our server and home page to the mayor of Chicago and his staff. Mayor Daley was impressed enough to use our home page at a press conference held the following month to announce Chicago Mosaic (http://www.ci.chi.il.us/). Our WWW site was at least one reason that the library's budget has been increased to expand our Internet access.

We were fortunate that ALA was being held in Chicago the summer we announced our WWW site. This gave us a wonderful opportunity to promote it among librarians. We were able to develop special Web pages for the convention which gave library and city information, and we demonstrated our server at both the CPL and Apple booths at the convention. In addition, the home page appeared in the convention's Internet Room. While CPL held the ALA Gala Opening Reception at our main location at the Harold Washington Library Center, we held an "Internet Flow-by" showing our home page to many of the 8,000 librarians who attended. We attended a conference sponsored by the Illinois Association of College and Research Libraries

Creator of Electronic Information."

This was our first experience with demo software and showed us the distinct advantages of having everything already loaded and ready to go. One-on-one instruction for the public was done at all of the public access sites by members of the committee or staff at those locations. Sometimes this was part of an organized program, sometimes it was on-demand. This was truly the best way to promote our home page, but was also the most time-consuming. If we had more time and staff, we would welcome the opportunity to have public Internet training sessions that feature our home page. A number of articles and features on the home page appeared in local papers and on local television news programs. Committee members from the public access sites wrote articles, took pictures, etc., to promote the server locally. A brochure was created for the public explaining the Internet and our home page. This easy-to-do, low-tech marketing tool was still one of the best ways for us to get our message across. More difficult but certainly more fun were the special home pages we created for events around town. We created pages for the Printer's Row Book Fair (http://cpl.lib.uic.edu/PRBF.html) held in downtown Chicago. We attended the Today's Black Woman Expo and had a home page specially made for that event, too. Vitner's, a local potato chip producer, allowed us to sit at their booth and munch chips while we showed off our home page. There was the added bonus here of allowing us to have our pictures taken with Chris Zorich of the Chicago Bears.

Since the initial developmental stage, we have done less formal marketing of our home page. We continue to demonstrate and promote it when the opportunity arises. Librarians on the front lines still talk about it and demonstrate it. The creation of it has served us well. Bill Gates' staff at Microsoft was impressed with our WWW page and encouraged him to make a donation worth over one million dollars to help the Chicago Public Library extend its Internet services.

Our Web pages have truly become a community resource. Through a combination our our dedication and the accessibility of resource people, we have created home pages that serve not only the patrons of our library, but also the city of Chicago. As we say again and again to colleagues from libraries of all sizes, if we could do it, with the right help, so can you!

INSTRUCTIONAL MATERIALS, UNIQUE RESOURCES, AND COMMERCIAL DESIGN

Chapter 14

INSTRUCTIONAL MATERIALS AND HANDOUTS

Elizabeth A. Dupuis

Head, Digital Information Literacy Office
Undergraduate Library Services Division
University of Texas at Austin
beth@mail.utexas.edu

In part, the long-range plan for the University of Texas at Austin General Libraries, entitled "Libraries and Information Skills for Students: Support through Computing and Information Technology," states the following:

> In pursuit of its primary mission to support and enhance the University's instructional, research, and public service activities by providing access to information and resources for learning and scholarship, the General Libraries continues to follow its strategic plan of using computing and information technologies to enhance and extend library information sources and services to the UT Austin community.

Throughout this decade, library instruction and user assistance at our institution has involved the use of computers and the Internet as both a conduit for information resources and a media for instruction. Many libraries are using the Internet, especially the World Wide Web, to expand their hours of service and the locations from which assistance can be found. At the University of Texas at Austin, there are a number of these Internet-based initiatives including a publications collection, Web pages created for specific classes, a hypertext calendar of classes, and an instruction clearinghouse for librarians.

OUR ENVIRONMENT

The University of Texas at Austin campus is the intellectual home for approximately 50,000 students; nearly 35,000 of those are undergraduate students. Computing is an integral part of our academic environment, including incentives for faculty to incorporate new technologies in classroom instruction, large networked computer labs for student use, provision of more than forty databases via the Internet from the General Libraries, participation in distance education courses, and dial-up access provided by the Computation Center. On such a large campus, requiring students to use one particular facility for conducting research, writing papers, or seeking help is neither efficient nor realistic. Many students converge on the 198-workstation Student Microcomputer Facility (SMF) and the Electronic Information Centers (EIC) to fulfill their computing needs. Some students use personal computers to search for information from their apartments or dorm rooms through dial-up access; a number of residence halls are being wired for Internet connectivity in each room.

Since an increasing number of classes require students to utilize newsgroups or listservs for class communication, students seek out computers wherever possible. E-mail and the World Wide Web are very popular resources. Additionally, some professors not only encourage students to search for and evaluate Internet resources, but also expect them to develop a Web page around a class topic. Many of the students and faculty are either growing interested in computer-mediated instruction and communication or are already computer-literate. A number of electronic classrooms on campus expose students to this new world of information.

One of the popular classrooms for library instruction is a hands-on training room, located on the second floor of the Undergraduate Library within the Student Microcomputer Facility. The training room is shared equally by the General Libraries and the Computation Center. This room offers fifteen Macintosh workstations and a trainer's station with both a Macintosh and PC. Each of the computers in the room has a direct Ethernet connection and a full suite of Internet, word processing, spreadsheet, statistical, presentation, and graphics software. Other lecture and demonstration classrooms are available in libraries across campus; those rooms range in capacity from twenty to seventy seats.

Library instruction at the University of Texas at Austin is a mix of course-integrated sessions and prescheduled, free workshops called the Electronic Information Classes. The Electronic Information Classes program was initiated in the summer of 1992 by librarians who realized the potential of the Internet and other electronic information systems brought directly to the end user. Since its inception, the program has thrived largely due to the volunteer spirit of librarians and library assistants across campus. Each class is team-taught. The team approach allows staff to work with a variety of staff members, to learn new topics, and to share the roles of speaking and assisting students during the class. Topics include general introductions to electronic information, demonstrations of specific databases, and lecture and hands-on experiences with the Internet and Web publishing. Throughout the past four years, the General Libraries has reached over 11,000 attendees in approximately 1,100 classes. The program was initiated when the Internet was command-based and largely accessible only to universities and government entities. Students, faculty, and staff members at the university have greatly expanded their knowledge of the electronic resources available to them. We are finding less interest in the introductory classes and more interest in advanced classes such as HTML Basics, Advanced HTML, and Searching the Internet.

Since many students feel comfortable with the Internet, librarians can be particularly helpful by teaching sessions within courses. Course-integrated sessions allow us to bring our expertise directly into the classroom and to work with faculty in helping students with specific assignments or goals. Many studies (and personal experience) find that students gain more from sessions which relate directly to their coursework and which allow them to experience the resource you are discussing. Hands-on sessions and collaborative assignments are helpful ways to ensure that students benefit. On our campus, one dilemma is how to accommodate some of the larger classes; it is not uncommon to hear of an undergraduate class having more than 100 students. Currently the only hands-on training room we have available for library instruction has a maximum capacity of thirty.

To accommodate these large numbers of students as well as our goals, we have created a number of Internet-based instruction materials to complement our programs and courses. Using the Web, we can create class pathfinders and handouts. These resources can be accessed by all students during or after class, at any hour of the day (or night), at no extra charge, and has reduced the library's expenditure for paper supplies. It is easier for us to update our handouts and pathfinders and make that new information immediately available without having to redistribute new pages. Most of these projects grew from our realization that we needed to reach out to the university community and offer our services in a more widely accessible way.

The instruction materials highlighted in this chapter include a handout collection, class-related Web pathfinders, a calendar of Electronic Information Classes, and a clearinghouse of instruction materials. Each of these projects focuses on a different user group and has a unique goal.

A SPECIFIC INSTRUCTIONAL PROJECT: THE PUBLICATIONS GUIDE

One of the most common resources produced by libraries is the handout. Every library probably maintains a number of user aids to assist students in searching databases, utilizing print materials, and learning to do research. Since the General Libraries offers electronic databases via the Internet, it is a natural decision to simultaneously offer the handouts that accompany those databases through the same medium. The Publications Guide (http://www. lib.utexas.edu/Pubs/guides/) on UT Library Online (see Figure 14.1) presents

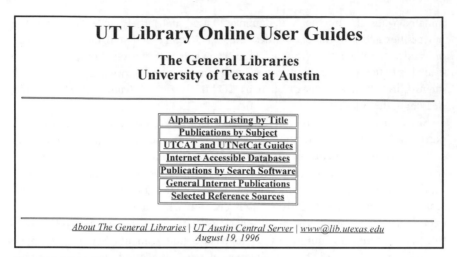

Figure 14.1 An introductory page to the General Libraries publications

approximately 130 handouts related to the Internet, databases offered through the Internet, and some CD-ROM titles.

At the time this project was initiated, the Electronic Information Services Office (EISO) supervised the conversion and organization of many of the handouts that the General Libraries now offers via the Web. EISO was the communication link for public service staff to keep abreast of the library's electronic resources and digital library initiatives. Since then, the EISO mission and staff have merged into the Collections and Information Resources Division. The coordination of this publications project is now incorporated in the Reference and Information Services Department of the main library, the Perry-Castañeda Library (PCL). Most of this project was done by one library assistant, though one librarian and one office assistant helped with organizational issues and conversion of some documents. This was a special project for which money was found from saved clerical assistant wages. I imagine librarians from any type of library can relate to lack of funds and the necessity for creative management to get the job done. After two months of ten hours a week, the first phase of the project was complete.

When conceptualizing this project, a small SWAT team of librarians and library assistants, from a variety of units and libraries, met to brainstorm and gather ideas for inclusion and layout. An image map of a handout rack was one idea that gave way for the current layout which is a simple table with basic links. Small group collaboration, for a project which impacts all units, is a wonderful way to gain new perspectives and be encouraged about the benefits and relevance of the project. The group mainly communicated via e-mail and some real-time meetings. From these discussions they chose the front page and the secondary page design for the project. The group thought of various ways users would approach a database and tried to organize the handouts in each of those categories. The chosen sections include the following:

- Alphabetical Listing by Title
- Publications by Subject
- UTCAT and UTNetCAT Guides
- Internet Accessible Databases
- Publications by Search Software
- General Internet Publications

Additionally, they chose to offer the handouts both as HTML pages and as PDF (Portable Document Format) files; some older handouts are still available in plain-text (ASCII) format.

One important initial decision was the scope of this project. The sections listed above reflect a collection of handouts for databases and Internet resources available in all units of the General Libraries. The goal was to provide user aids in support of the databases offered via UT Library Online and the Internet. Each unit and library has other handouts, such as the Selected Reference Sources (SRS) series and library research handouts, that are not part of this initial project. I believe it is the General Libraries' intention that most handouts will be available electronically in the future. The involvement of library staff from other units in the early stages of this project was an important step; now they can take their expertise back to their own units and help to provide more handouts electronically.

Once the layout was agreed upon and the process outlined, the handouts were taken from their Word formatting, converted to HTML, and converted to PDF. Finally each of the handouts were linked to the Web pages. Each handout presented new information and arrangements to deal with in HTML, though an average handout conversion would take between fifteen and thirty minutes. Of course, the more experience the user gains, the quicker the process becomes. Since many of the handouts had already been created in Word, the group chose not to use an RTF converter, rather they chose to tag the HTML pages by hand. Staff keep the masters on one computer in the Reference Office at PCL; to update a handout, they correct to the Word file and the HTML file, then create the PDF version.

One philosophical concern came from this creation of separate files and file types. Each medium has its own advantages and limitations. Links to the databases themselves, longer explanations of features, links to related handouts and other Internet resources, and rewording of some text may be included to make the most useful HTML handout. The creator of a PDF file is limited to the same space restrictions as on paper. Once an HTML and a PDF handout are created, a decision must be made if those handouts will be inherently the same or adapted for the new medium, and if they are different, whether they should have different names.

Some problems arose with this project. Since the electronic presence of libraries is fairly new to the Internet, so too are the administrative resources less well-developed. One difficulty was finding enough copies of the Adobe Acrobat software used to covert the files to PDF. Once those copies were purchased and placed on computers and became easy for staff to access, the process went smoothly. When other branches choose to PDF their handouts, this problem may again arise.

Another challenge was organizing this project when no distinct administrative structure and Web publishing procedure had been formed. Although the project was completed after only a few months, another few months passed before all the details were arranged concerning which server to place the files on, where to link the page from, whom to seek approval from, and how to request the pages be mirrored to the production server. With time we will learn more from experiences like this. I can't emphasize enough how important it is to outline procedures and guidelines for the Web publishers in any library. Those guidelines help establish what is expected as well as assist new publishers with the basics for successful project completion.

WEB PAGES FOR SPECIFIC CLASSES

Web Pages for HTML Classes

Web pages can be designed for many types of presentations and training. At the University of Texas at Austin, we use Web pages for trick dog and pony shows, tutorials, subject-oriented pathfinders, research toolkits, and class outlines. The purpose and possibilities of these pages are inherently the same, although the process of creating them and the layout or features may be different. The Electronic Information Classes program offers a number of Internet-related classes which utilize or demonstrate how to design Web pages. Some classes are hands-on; some are demonstrations. Two of these classes are HTML Basics and Designing a Personal Research Page.

One of my personal favorites is the HTML Basics class. This is the most introductory of the Web page classes offered by the library. Included in the discussion is an explanation of HTML, tags, absolute and relative URLs, and the basic publishing process. The model page (http://sawfish.lib.utexas.edu/~beth/Class/HTML/1996/) for this class is constructed like a personal Web page, which is a wonderful example for the hands-on class. After completing this page, students learn the following:

- basic document structure
- headings
- logical and physical styles, such as bold and address
- horizontal rules
- lists, such as ordered and unordered

- inline and thumbnail images
- links, including relative, absolute, and various protocols

In the hands-on class the attendees can type in their own information in certain sections so their final page reflects their personal interests and style. Although the classes do not often require an accompanying handout, many students prefer to have take-home materials when they are learning HTML. I have found that the right combination of handouts for us is one that shows the Web page via the browser, one that shows the source code for the page, a brief list of basic HTML tags and their functions, a short explanation of URLs and, for the hands-on class, a list of the links that will be added to the page.

A more advanced, but related, class focuses on the students' designing their personal research page. This class is the brainchild of a librarian who was interested in teaching students how to select and organize resources they find on the Internet. Beginning from a page that explains types of information, he walks them through each of the groups of sources; students use a topic that relates to their studies and search with keywords that are relevant. When they find a useful source in each area, they bookmark it. They have a small collection of bookmarks that they can reorganize and then save as a Web page. With some basic explanation, students learn to tailor that page, annotate sources, and clean up the HTML. Obviously this class is more aligned with the mission of libraries than HTML Basics. Besides the basic goal of teaching students how to make a Web page, they also learn to distinguish between types of resources; to evaluate, save and organize resources; and to add value to their findings.

Class Pathfinders

The General Libraries also offers course-integrated classes. As mentioned earlier, courses at the University of Texas at Austin often integrate electronic assignments and involve large numbers of students. To accommodate these two circumstances, we have be designing Web-based class pathfinders (http://sawfish.lib.utexas.edu/~beth/Class/). These pathfinders fill the following purposes:

- outlining and guiding the class presentation
- presenting both examples and links to the resource
- providing an enduring resource to which students can return after class
- exposing students to resources they can follow along with in a hands-on session
- offering exercises for students to use in a self-paced format
- collecting important resources to help students with class-related assignments

Each of these class pathfinders is designed as a joint venture between a librarian and instructor and is available and maintained only for that semester. Once a faculty member or teaching assistant chooses to have a library instruction session, they meet with the appropriate subject librarian. If the instructors are interested in having their students learn about electronic resources available via the Internet, a class Web pathfinder may be a useful resource. Often instructors will suggest specific Web sites, newsgroups, or topics to be included in the pathfinder and class discussion. The librarian then collects all relevant sites and designs the Web page.

Creation of these types of pages is certainly not mandatory. Just as each librarian is responsible for deciding how to teach a class or which handouts to create, the production of class pathfinders is just another option. I believe these pages can be useful to students. Pathfinders, especially paired with instruction, can assist students with their studies and enhance their ability to distinguish between types and quality of electronic resources. I talk to the faculty personally and suggest topics and protocols which might be useful to their students. Each page is different since faculty members have different goals, different lengths of time to devote to library-related instruction, and students with various levels of experience. I make most of my pages myself, sometimes just a few days before the class; thankfully changes can be made up to the last minute before presentations. Often a complete page will take less than four hours including finding the resources to link and creating the page in HTML. Experience makes the process quicker each time.

A basic template for the pathfinders makes the creation process very simple. With the template, other people can easily follow an example and save the time of selecting an appropriate layout. Occasionally, I will ask a library assistant to help me choose resources or add the links. A sample page is created with the basic sections; those sections include

- general guides to the subject
- collections related to a particular topic
- databases
- newsgroups
- listservs
- searching, evaluating, and citing information

Some of the courses that have used these pathfinders are Introduction to African American Culture, Astronomy, Media in Eastern Europe, Soviet and Post-Soviet Media, Rhetoric and Composition, and French Literature. After the discussion with the faculty member, some standard areas of the pathfinder may be excluded and new areas added. For instance, the astronomy professor requested a class which would focus on information on the Internet about black holes. For that particular assignment we included most of the sections above and also added a new section for images and movies.

After teaching many classes that utilize Web pages, I find that students are very interested and attentive. Not surprisingly, the participation from students and faculty increases when the page directly relates to a particular class or assignment. One pleasing benefit of these classes is that the professors are willing to attend every class, suggest keywords, relate concepts to other class discussions and even ask questions. This model has strengthened the relationship between faculty, librarians, and students. From my experience, I would recommend it for any library with interested faculty and an Internet connection.

Some necessary ingredients to make this recipe work include easy access to server space, link checkers, and robust Internet connections. The General Libraries operates a number of development production and training servers. The combination allows librarians to distinguish between Web pages created for long-term projects, those created for a semester-long course, and those designed for one session. At a minimum, access to one server is needed, in order to FTP files and manipulate them without having to use an intermediary. Often the projects require some maintenance and adjustments that would be difficult and time-consuming to explain to another person.

Another important tool is a reliable link checker. Often this software is designed to be installed on the server and run at certain intervals. As its name implies, its function is to connect to each Web link and detect if it is valid, redirected, or dead. We use MOMSpider. It is configured to run every other night and return an HTML report of all links, with a separate section for broken links. This tool is an enormous time-saver and an easy way to maintain pages. Unfortunately that link checker only checks http links and not other protocols.

Finally, these types of training pages will only be acceptable if they are reliable, responsive, and reachable. To ensure this, there must be a strong network connection. People must be able to depend on access to both the server and an Internet-connected computer. My only challenge with these pathfinders is the enormous demand for more from professors and students.

Calendar of Electronic Information Classes

One of my first Web projects was a calendar (http://www.lib.utexas. edu/cgi-bin/calendar/) for the Electronic Information Classes which would display all classes offered that semester. Enlisting the hypertext nature of the Web, people could easily jump from one piece of information to another. I wanted an image of the calendar for each month. Users could then click on a particular day and see a list of all classes for that date, including times and locations. They could also access a brief description of that class and see all the other times that class was offered throughout the semester. We also wanted people to be able to access the entire list of classes chronologically and categorically.

Though we had handouts which listed the classes by date and by subject, there was no exact model to base this project on. I proposed this project to Ladd Hanson, a programmer who thought it would be an interesting challenge. With his support and comments, I determined what each layout would look like and which field would link to what other pages. Our final list of fields included title, group, date, beginning time, ending time, location, and class description. All our organization was done by storyboarding the sections and drawing arrows from section to section. Hanson is insightful and knowledgeable; his perspectives about user needs, visual design, and technical constraints were invaluable.

Once we had an idea of the layout we considered how to present items so they would be accessible and clear in both a graphical-user interface (GUI) such as Netscape and with a character-based browser such as Lynx. A number of students and staff at UT are visually challenged so it is imperative to me that our pages are functional for them. We decided to keep the calendar image and at the bottom of the page have three text links—one for the classes on that day, a chronology for the semester, and a subject listing. In this way, the page works for anyone who might view it.

Our next project was to locate a calendar program to generate the images for each month. We chose Almanac on the PC for the source of the images and HiJaak Pro as the software to capture the screens. The images from that software are clear and well-sized. Once we saved each month, some time was spent with Adobe Photoshop cleaning up the images. For example, removing the blue box that highlighted the first day of each month and saving the images as GIFs. Once we determined the set of coordinates for each square on the calendar, we could easily just shift the coordinates to match the correct dates for each month. This makes the process of image mapping very simple.

The first version of the calendar was created in the summer of 1994 and consisted of handwritten HTML pages for each class, list, and category. The process was extremely tedious and prone to errors, since all information from the handouts was retyped into this new layout and coded. Some new information was incorporated, such as more detailed class descriptions and an integration of the group name. Although the project was laborious, feedback was positive. Support for this project was the only thing that kept me from cringing when I thought of having to re-create it three times a year!

Needless to say, we instantly began plotting ways to make this process more efficient. Instead of writing each HTML page, the programmer suggested writing a script which would process a tab-separated file of information and generate all the HTML pages on the fly. To organize the information we would use a FileMaker Pro database using the same fields as we needed for the final pages. Once the information was input into the database, we could choose in what order to export it, save that file, transfer it to the server, run it through the script, and—in seconds—all the pages would be generated. Using this system is much more efficient especially if we decide to add a new class or change the time of a class. Instead of remembering all the pages which listed that information, this program will make all the changes at once. To streamline the process even more, the handouts and the Web pages are all generated from one FileMaker Pro database and the margin of error has been dramatically reduced.

Each semester we update the database with new class titles, descriptions, dates, times, and locations. Although we still have to do this once a semester, it is a great relief to be handling both the handouts and Web calendar at once. Many people call looking for this information in electronic format and hoping they can access it at home. Some departments link to the calendar or even particular classes and topics from their home pages; others save the listing and post it to their newsgroups.

After nearly two years it is easy to think this has all gone smoothly and to forget about all the obstacles along the way. With some deep concentration I can remember some of our problems and offer the solutions. We did have some trouble locating the best software for our needs. It was difficult to locate a useful calendar program but we did not want to design an image for each month freehand. Almanac has proven to be quite useful. We try to save a year's worth each time we go through the process; sometimes it is difficult after a year to remember all the steps for accessing, saving, and editing those files. Additionally we must adjust the image map coordinates, so the dates on the calendar image link to the appropriate page.

Creating the script which generates the Web pages was not a small task. Each semester the only constants are the five category names. I was fortunate to find a programmer willing not only to write the script but also to help me determine what that script should do. Some small bugs in the script were found along the way. For example, the script determines the correct month and date each day to display that month's calendar. Everything was fine until October. The script was written to look for the first three letters of the month. October was read as "oct" which the computer interpreted as "octal" keeping it from finding the October image. With some small changes to the script, we were back in business. The only hazard in this arrangement is that the programmer must have time to respond to changes quickly. In our organization, his skills are in increasing demand and his time is scarce.

My most important lesson with this project was the idea of choosing the most efficient means to create a project. For example, if the information could be entered into a database and used for all purposes from that database then we could save an immense amount of time. There are some trade-offs. The initial time to write and perfect the script was longer than it would have been to write all the pages individually; however, in the long-run I save over fifteen hours a semester.

INSTRUCTION CLEARINGHOUSE FOR LIBRARY STAFF

The instruction clearinghouse is our newest project. Designed to assist librarians and library assistants who participate in the Electronic Information Classes program, this collection helps instructors share information, outlines, handouts, Web pages, and Power Point demonstrations with each other. Each of our classes is team taught and the combination of instructors changes to keep everyone interested in new topics. With over fifty staff members involved with the program, it can be difficult for instructors to keep track of which group taught the class last or even find time to walk to that part of campus and pick up previously used materials. There is an easy temptation to reinvent new exercises, handouts and presentations each time. Although some rooms are commonly used for the instruction sessions, there is no good central physical location for everyone to access and store these instructional materials. Instead, we chose an Intranet for distribution of these materials, which would allow all library staff access to the repository without placing these items on the main library home page.

This decision was easy for us since we wanted to make the distinction between these class materials, created as one-shot instructional items and which may become outdated quickly, and our publications, designed for public use and updated on a regular basis. Simply, we wanted to enhance our internal sharing without making the materials internationally available.

This project was completed by one librarian and a half-time library assistant. Since it is designed to compliment the Electronic Information Classes program, its organization is similar to the calendar. The most appropriate method of providing this service was the creation of an FTP site. We considered both anonymous FTP and user FTP. One benefit of anonymous FTP is that instructors would not need to remember another password just for this service. We did have a small setback; the original server chosen for this project did not have updated FTP software or a compiler. Other ideas were explored with EIPO (Electronic Information Programs Office) and Library Systems and we settled on using an existing staff Web server. The library has one server specifically designed as a staff Web server. It is wrapped by IP address and is designed for information about committees, procedural documents for units, and other professional development pages. "Wrapped by IP" address simply means the server only allows access to those computers making a connection from the "lib.utexas.edu" domain and therefore is an internal network or Intranet.

Storyboarding helped us outline what directories and subdirectories we would need. We chose a simple structure of four initial directories: incoming, introductory, Internet, and databases. The incoming directory allows instructors to put new files on the server for us to rename and place in the correct directory. Each of the other directories does not allow staff to upload, though they can download anything they wish. These three directories have subdirectories. For example, the Internet directory has subdivisions for general, publishing, and subject. Intentionally, the subdirectories have generic names, since our class titles are altered a bit each semester as the program grows and evolves.

Originally, we planned to create separate directories within each class title for outlines, handouts, and powerpoints. Since there are already approximately three levels of directories and there is not an overwhelming number of files, we decided to put all the files for one class—regardless of type—together. As new files are placed on the server, we change the names to reflect the content of the document, instructor's initials, and approximate date of creation. Hopefully, this will help new instructors know whom to contact with additional questions and to ask how current the materials are.

We wanted to make the process of maintaining the site fairly easy. One of the main tenets of this project was that we just offer these materials in a central location. We do not want to alter the format of the document; we will not convert these materials into HTML or PDF or even from Microsoft Word for the Macintosh to Microsoft Word for Windows. Since many, if not all, library staff members who participate in the instructional program have a Macintosh as their primary workstation, our desire to preserve materials in the format they were submitted in is workable.

Another goal of mine was to make the site easy to access. Most of the staff use Netscape and are familiar with its features. Fewer of the staff use an FTP client, such as Fetch, on a regular basis, to access information resources. In order to reach the largest numbers of staff, we wanted staff to be able to access it using Netscape and be able to upload and download files via the browser. Ordinarily, it is not a problem to access FTP sites via Netscape. Oddly enough once we had created our initial directories, we found that Netscape could not complete the connection or show the directories. Some research via newsgroups uncovered a problem others had had with certain servers and some versions of Netscape. I discussed these problems with the programmer from Library Systems who was maintaining the FTP server. Within a day, he had contacted one of the people from the newsgroup posting and had fixed our problem. With the newest version of Netscape it is possible to choose "Upload File" from the menu bar and allow people to submit instructional materials via the Web browser.

Once we had the Web browser fully functional, we created a Web page which links to Web pages made for these Electronic Information Classes. Some of these pages have become official pages on UT Library Online, others were only used once. It is easy for us to link to these pages, regardless of what server they exist on, and also to link to the Instruction Clearinghouse on the FTP server.

This project has just recently been completed. We have announced the site and are still collecting more materials from instructors. It is difficult to tell how often the site will be used, but with time we hope more instructors will add and update their materials. We also hope to know how to maintain the site more efficiently. In the beginning we will check the drop box a few times a week for new submissions. Once the clearinghouse has been in existence for a semester, the group of demo instructors can discuss what our policy should be for removing items. As a group we can determine when materials are too old to be useful and what to do with documents created in older versions of software.

I sincerely believe this project will help instructors by giving them multiple examples of ways to explain resources and samples of projects to use or remodel. The idea of an Intranet is particularly useful as a way to share information and still make a distinction between internal and public documents.

ANALYSIS OF RESOURCES

One of the most important resources for any Web project is the computer-related infrastructure. This would include the computers, hardware, software and Internet connections. At the University of Texas at Austin many library units have their own personal computers with basic word processing software, Internet software and Internet connections. Some of the more expensive items are housed in the Electronic Information Programs Office (EIPO) and are available for any staff member to use. These items include scanners, PDF software, graphics software and more. There is strong support from the administration for library-run servers for offering access to information resources to the university community, as well as for training and publication purposes for library staff. It is easy for any staff member to obtain an account and password which would allow them space to design Web projects related to work.

EIPO also manages many of the servers; therefore, library units often refer to them for technical support. To date they have been very effective at finding the tools that will make Web publishing most effective. One of the main resources for me is MOMSpider which generates reports after checking the links on all my pages. In about ten minutes each week, I maintain almost 2,000 links. Among other responsibilities, EIPO staff assist with PDF, scanning, creating CGI scripts, offering suggestions for streamlining projects, and answering questions about Web publishing options.

Many librarians and library assistants have taken advantage of this office and other training resources to increase their skills. TeamWeb is a campus-wide initiative of the General Libraries, Computation Center, and Data Processing to assist anyone with Web publishing skills for departmental and class pages. Additionally, the General Libraries offers some professional development classes to help library staff get started with Web publishing, to organize resources, and to conceive of new projects. In the end, it is left to each staff member's initiative to take part.

CONCLUSIONS

Web publishing has affected departmental relationships in many ways. Completion of a Web project requires teamwork, willingness to learn new topics, independent exploration, and creativity. It requires support from administration and staff working on the project. A successful project can strengthen a library as a whole. The end result, if useful and accessible, can positively affect the way students and faculty view the library and its mission. Many students, faculty, and staff are thankful for the helping hand when getting started. Now that people can access the information resources from home, they will be looking for user aids to help them use those resources and learn from them informally. The dynamics have changed, and it is clear that the lines between public and technical services are growing less defined each day. The distinction between print and electronic sources is also growing less defined. Our students, faculty, and staff welcome all resources they can access conveniently and repeatedly for free—whether it is in our building or through our network.

Some of our pages are useful for training, some for publicizing, some for instruction, and some for self-help. We have chosen not to conduct any special surveys before creating our projects. They seem to grow from our perceived demand and experimentation which is a luxury of academic environments. We do announce our Web projects in classes, point them out on printed handouts, and advertise in library computer labs. Our staff hear about new projects through e-mail, newsgroups, and meetings. Our response has been overwhelmingly positive on all counts.

To summarize, my top ten suggestions are to do the following:

- Create Web publishing policies and procedures.
- Organize your human, electronic, and financial resources.
- Plan your site with a goal and theme before beginning to create it.
- Determine who your primary audience is.
- Assess your free time for creation, maintenance, and improvement of the site.
- Minimize the repetitive work when possible.
- Be realistic about the willingness of others to embrace new technologies.
- Train your staff in new concepts and skills.
- Cooperate with other departments and units on campus.
- Always look for new ways to do standard things.

Chapter 15

Instruction and the Web: The Development of a Library Research Tutorial

Michael O. Engle

Reference, Instruction and Electronic Text Librarian
Olin*Kroch*Uris Libraries
Cornell University
moe1@cornell.edu
URL: http://www.library.cornell.edu/okuref/research/tutorial.html

"Computers don't just do things for us, they do things to us. . . ." —Sherry Turkle (26)

IN THE BEGINNING

The growing importance of computers and the Internet in college and university education is an unparalleled opportunity for librarians to extend instruction beyond the traditional geography of the classroom and the library. In the networked environment of the World Wide Web, teaching and learning happens twenty-four hours a day, wherever the network is available. This chapter is about the creation of a hypertext tutorial on library research that uses the interactive, relational nature of Web documents to encourage self-directed, self-paced learning.

I saw my first Web page in June 1994. A colleague in the Cornell University Library, Tony Cosgrave, invited me into his office and showed me NCSA's home page, displayed on an early version of the NCSA Mosaic Web browser software. Tony clicked on a few links and we visited several Web sites in the course of a few minutes. I was so excited by what I saw that I went back to my office, downloaded Mosaic, and began my first tentative exploration of the World Wide Web. A few months later, I realized that I could use the Web to teach library research. Although the construction of a Web-based tutorial on library research became a personal project, the basic materials from which it was built were created by many people at Cornell working together for more than two decades.

THE INSTRUCTION PROGRAM

The Cornell University Library began a bibliographic instruction program for undergraduate students in the fall of 1962, at the opening of Uris Undergraduate Library. In the early years, the instruction program consisted of a fifty-minute lecture and tour for first-year students. Later, in the 1970s and throughout the 1980s, Joan Ormondroyd elaborated on this simple beginning and developed a strong and highly visible program of course-related and course-integrated instruction.

Joan and the staff in Uris Library developed three types of printed instructional materials that we still use and revise today: information guides, skill guides, and reference guides. Information guides supply students with practical details about library services and collections: how to charge out a book, where to find books and periodicals in the stacks, and the history of the building, for example. Skill guides teach students how to think about research, how to evaluate library materials, and how to use periodical indexes, library catalogs, and other bibliographic tools. Reference guides provide annotated subject bibliographies of major reference titles in two dozen academic disciplines.

The keystone of the skill guides is Skill Guide No. 1: Research Strategy, a step-by-step outline of the library research process (see Figure 15.1). Using the research process as the central organizing concept, the guides expose students to the specific tools and skills necessary for completing their coursework, from the initial work of identifying their topic to the final task of properly citing books and periodical articles for papers. For each class, librarians prepare bibliographies of reference titles tailored to the topics the students are studying. These individualized, course-specific bibliographies are usually laid out in roughly the same order as the research process: they begin with background sources—encyclopedias, dictionaries, and handbooks—and move through catalog searching, using periodical indexes, and evaluating the sources to the final step of selecting and applying a style for the bibliography. Librarians supplement these class bibliographies with a selection of skill guides relevant to the research tasks of that specific class.

COMPUTERS AND THE INSTRUCTION PROGRAM

In 1990, when I inherited the instruction program, my main task was to adapt it to the changing needs of students and to make good use of the new research tools that were becoming available: computers and electronic resources. At that time, we were using computers to assemble and publish instructional handouts. Initially, work-study students formatted skill guides and bibliographies using WordPerfect. From a template marked up by one of the librarians, students prepared a draft version of a guide or a class bibliography. After the librarian reviewed and edited the draft, the final version was printed from WordPerfect. Later, when we realized that PageMaker offered more versatility and power for

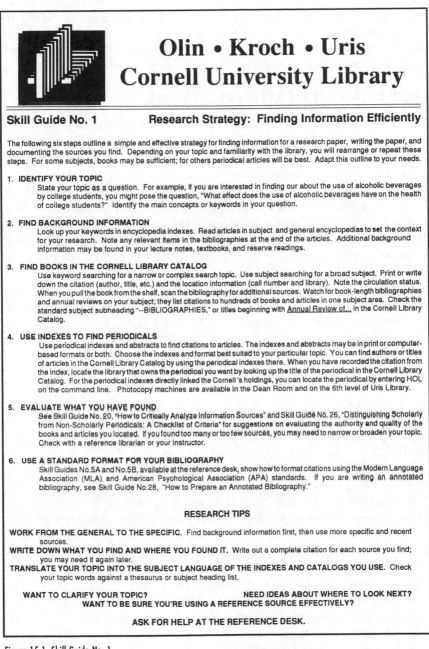

Figure 15.1 Skill Guide No. 1

designing and publishing, we exported the WordPerfect text to PageMaker for additional formatting before it was laser-printed, copied, collated, and stapled.

In our classes, we began to use computers more and more frequently to demonstrate the ever growing number of online resources, beginning with Cornell's online catalog and a few networked periodical indexes. We started producing PowerPoint presentations for instruction in 1994.

DEVELOPING WEB-BASED INSTRUCTION

During the first few months of my exploration of the World Wide Web, I gradually realized what a powerful teaching tool it could be. Students clicking on hyperlinks in Web pages could follow their specific interests and locate information on their own, whenever they needed it. Using the text from the existing skill guides as a base, I built an instructional Web site for Cornell students. The outline of library research strategy in Skill Guide No. 1 served as the organizational backbone of the site and the starting point for the tutorial. At each step of the research process, I linked skill guides into the structure provided by the outline to create a self-directed guide to library research.

The timing was right for building a Web site. An Ethernet network was already in place at Cornell. I had a networked a Mac LCII in my office, which was soon upgraded to a PowerMac 7100/66. I had access to a large database of instructional material in machine-readable form that had been constructed and honed over many years. I had technical support from Tony, who was always one step ahead of me in the computer world. I had the organizing principle for the Web site. In addition, one reference paraprofessional and several work-study students were already trained in the process of moving data from templates prepared by the teaching librarians into WordPerfect and PageMaker, a process that could be adapted to convert instructional materials into HTML.

To create the tutorial, I needed to learn how to mark up new documents and translate existing documents into HTML. By the fall of 1994, a few colleagues at Cornell had already learned HTML tagging and were willing to teach it; I went to their training sessions. At first I used SimpleText, a minimal word processing program that comes with the Mac, to write, tag, and edit a few Web pages. I soon switched to an early version of the HTML editing freeware, html.edit, that incorporated instructions on HTML tagging as part of the software. The design of html.edit was clever: while editing I could click anywhere in the text and access the instructions on HTML tagging. By clicking anywhere on the instructions I returned to the document I was editing. It was easy to move back and forth between the document and the instructions, and the reinforcement of my learning was almost immediate. I have since switched to another freeware editor, BBEdit Lite 3.5, that offers more robust editing tools (Information on these and other Macintosh HTML editors is available at http://www.com vista.com/net/www/htmleditor.html).

Web Site Organization

Complex Web sites benefit from organization around a process or a conceptual framework that is clear to the user, so I began by writing and tagging a page of links in which each link represented one step in the research process outlined in Skill Guide No. 1:

- How to Develop Your Research Topic
- How to Find Background Information
- How to Find Books
- How to Find Periodical Articles
- How to Find Internet Resources
- How to Evaluate What You Have Found
- How to Cite What You Have Found.

At each of these links, I began building the Web pages that would guide a student through each step.

The first two steps have no corresponding print skill guides. I usually offer students advice about how to perform these preliminary steps of the research process as part of my class presentation. The first step of the research process is to identify the topic and pose it as a question, then isolate the key concepts in the question and begin testing them against a catalog or index to see how they work. I decided to write the Web pages on topic development as if I were talking to the students in class or helping them at the reference desk. I didn't want to present a comprehensive explanation of what to do, because I suspected students would not read it all. So for the introductory steps I offered a series of tips and suggested that the information could be supplemented with personal help from a reference librarian if needed. As I wrote the pages, I remembered that students often need help coming up with and clarifying topic ideas, so I wrote another Web page suggesting sources for topic ideas and linked to it near the beginning of the Develop Your Topic page (Figure 15.2). I used a similar approach when I wrote the page for the second step, Finding Background Information.

Converting Existing Instructional Material

The integration of the text from the existing skill guides into the Web-based tutorial required a different approach. Our online catalog skill guide describes how to search for books but, since not all of our records for monographs are retrospectively converted to machine-readable form, a student first has to know that searching the online catalog is only one way to find books in our collections. So I wrote a page outlining how to decide to look in the remnant of the card catalog or to search OCLC and RLIN. This page serves as a preface to the Web page on using the online catalog. Conversion of instructional handouts intended for classroom use to Web pages requires writing additional pages to create the context that would normally be constructed by the teacher as part of the classroom presentation.

As with the writing of new pages, I used SimpleText at first to mark up the text from the existing skill guides, but we soon switched to using an early WordPerfect-to-HTML conversion macro that worked inside WordPerfect. There was still a lot of cleanup to do on the macro-ed text, but editing machine-converted text was much faster than adding the tags one-by-one in SimpleText. The Web format allowed us not only to add links to other relevant

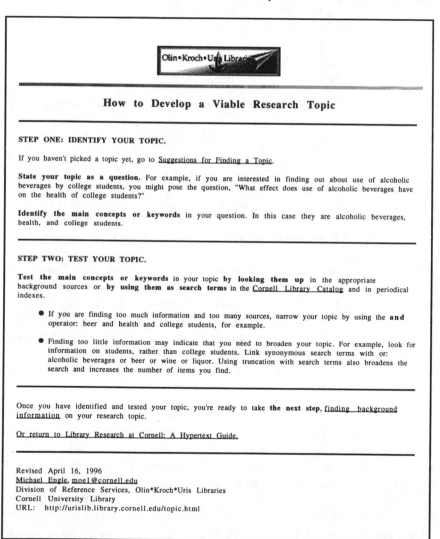

Olin•Kroch•Uris Libraries

How to Develop a Viable Research Topic

STEP ONE: IDENTIFY YOUR TOPIC.

If you haven't picked a topic yet, go to Suggestions for Finding a Topic.

State your topic as a question. For example, if you are interested in finding out about use of alcoholic beverages by college students, you might pose the question, "What effect does use of alcoholic beverages have on the health of college students?"

Identify the main concepts or keywords in your question. In this case they are alcoholic beverages, health, and college students.

STEP TWO: TEST YOUR TOPIC.

Test the main concepts or keywords in your topic **by looking them up** in the appropriate background sources or **by using them as search terms** in the Cornell Library Catalog and in periodical indexes.

- If you are finding too much information and too many sources, narrow your topic by using the **and** operator: beer and health and college students, for example.

- Finding too little information may indicate that you need to broaden your topic. For example, look for information on students, rather than college students. Link synonymous search terms with or: alcoholic beverages or beer or wine or liquor. Using truncation with search terms also broadens the search and increases the number of items you find.

Once you have identified and tested your topic, you're ready to take **the next step,** finding background information on your research topic.

Or return to Library Research at Cornell: A Hypertext Guide.

Revised April 16, 1996
Michael Engle, moel@cornell.edu
Division of Reference Services, Olin*Kroch*Uris Libraries
Cornell University Library
URL: http://urislib.library.cornell.edu/topic.html

Figure 15.2 The Develop Your Topic page

guides but also to establish links within the same document. To visually group similar information together, I divided the text of each document into sections using horizontal rules. Beginning each section with a horizontal rule provides an excellent place to link to from tables of contents. Inserting linked tables of contents is an important way to summarize the information available in longer pages and allows students to move quickly to the section they want to see. To further enhance users' mobility in longer pages, we added links back to the table of contents from each section.

Locating articles in periodicals is more complicated than finding books; the corresponding Web page in the tutorial is more complicated, too. To find a periodical article, students must select and use an appropriate index for their topic, then search the online catalog to locate the periodical title at one of the seventeen Cornell libraries. Meryl White from the Management Library developed a searchable list of the electronic periodical indexes at Cornell that became a key part of the periodicals section of the tutorial. A link to her list from the periodicals page allows students to search online for an index appropriate to their topic. Then they can access and use the networked indexes from their list of search hits. The print and CD-ROM indexes that turn up on their list of hits still require a trip to a physical library. The resulting Web page on periodical searching is quite long. Although an added table of contents provides fairly good access, breaking it down into a series of shorter, linked pages would improve it further.

Instructional materials with lots of text benefit by being reorganized into sections and lists in HTML. The process of converting text from word processing software into HTML provides an opportunity to make other changes to structure, format, and content. The instructional text can be updated and edited for clarity. The order of presentation of the main ideas in the print version can be changed in the Web version. Links to related resources can be added in the text. I considered adding targets to each entry in the vocabulary list and linking every occurrence of the word in the tutorial to the definition, but the magnitude of the task dissuaded me. Furthermore, it is impossible to link from the definition directly back to every occurrence of the word in the text, so sending students to the vocabulary list would lead to confusion unless students remember to use the back function in the browser to return to the tutorial. In addition, reading text littered with highlighted, underlined links is troublesome. The nature of HTML favors highlighting key concepts, however, and a selective version of this idea could work.

Reformatting instructional material into HTML should take advantage of the strengths of the Web to navigate within each page, to access related pages locally and around the world, to highlight key information, and to guide users with simple, colorful graphics.

Consistency: Color, Style, and Templates

Consistent use of color and layout helps users identify the individual sections of a Web site as parts of a larger whole. Early in the development of the library research tutorial, I adopted a yellow line—a 600 by 4 pixel GIF image from the division home page—as the main identifying element for tutorial pages. The distinctive color and shape near the top of each page remind students that they are in the tutorial. Consistent return links near the bottom of each page and clear identifying information in the footer (last revision date, author of page, division and library name, and page URL) also help orient users to the site and give them a sense of being inside a discrete entity.

If more than one person contributes finished Web pages to a particular site, it is well worth developing a simple style manual and an accompanying template to illustrate the style. The template can be a Web page with all the headers, returns, and footers in place and a blank space for the page content. Such a template can also include a basic outline for organizing the content. (An example of a template for individual class presentations can be found at http://www.library.cornell. edu/okuref/instrtem.htm). Each contributor may develop a full-blown Web page that is marked up in HTML and ready to link to the larger structure. Alternatively, one person might act as the general editor and paste individual contributions into the template, adding or correcting the markup as needed. Even with a clear template and style guide, however, someone will have to edit the pages for consistency. As staff members gain computer editing expertise and text markup skills, the work can be more widely distributed.

WHO USES THE TUTORIAL?

An unscientific review of the log file on my WebStar server shows that people from a wide variety of Internet sites around the world access the tutorial. I can roughly identify access points at Cornell by domain name server or IP address. The residence hall network has an identifiable address, as do the library's public terminals and the dial-up modems for off-campus users with SLIP connections. Local use of the tutorial appears to be evenly distributed across library sites (reference desks and public terminals), student computer labs, and the residence hall network. A significant number of commercial sites also appear in the log, and robots check in from time to time to index the site. A few other academic libraries have linked to the tutorial, and their users appear regularly. It is not unusual to have fifty or sixty sites access the server in a twenty-four hour period; the tutorial files are regularly accessed in the late night and early morning hours as well as during the day.

I suspect that librarians account for a large number of server accesses from non-Cornell educational sites. A half dozen academic librarians have e-mailed to ask permission to adapt the documents in the tutorial for use at their own institutions. It is easy to capture the HTML tagging using View/Source in

Netscape and then rewrite and edit the Web pages to fit local circumstances. This is an appropriate use of the instructional material, I think, and most librarians have been careful to check with us before proceeding. When they do, we ask them to acknowledge the source of the material prominently, to clearly state that they have adapted it for their own use, and to send us the URL of their version. I believe a spirit of cooperation is one of the hallmarks of librarianship; we learn more, and more quickly, by sharing our work.

Originally, I expected to use the tutorial as a teaching tool in freshman writing classes. Cornell has a required, two-semester freshman seminar program to develop the writing skills of new students. Each seminar is limited to seventeen students and focuses on a specific subject. Librarians teach a session on library research in 30 to 40 percent of these classes each semester. However, the tutorial is really too text-intensive to be useful during such a class. Combining PowerPoint modules to highlight the main points with live demonstrations and hands-on segments has proven much more effective. The tutorial is an adjunct to the class, a place where students can follow up on their own. I often describe the tutorial as the distilled wisdom of many reference librarians. To encourage use of the tutorial outside the class, I hand out colorful paper bookmarks with the URL printed on one side and "Learn library research on the Web" on the reverse. The wide availability of the Web on many library terminals, in all computer labs, and on the networking software supplied to students for use with their own computers means that the tutorial is also widely available to Cornell students who want to use it.

KEEPING THE TUTORIAL UP-TO-DATE

Now that the basic text and structure is in place, updating and expanding the tutorial is mostly a one-person job. One of the advantages of being the main person responsible for the development of this site is my thorough understanding of its history and function. I have a good idea of how much work a global change will entail and which parts need to be rewritten or reformatted over time. Much Web editing is work that can be fitted into the odd time slot in my office, at home, or even at the reference desk on a slow evening, anywhere a computer is at hand.

The part of the tutorial that is conceptual in nature is fairly stable and needs little updating. The how-to sections that deal with specific tools require more frequent revision. I try to review the entire site twice a year. Since the tutorial is relatively self-contained, there are not a large number of links to be checked for viability. Keeping all the pages consistent in format has been the largest portion of the updating work so far. A minor change like reducing the font size in the footer can require hours of updating by the time it is implemented across the entire tutorial. This is an obvious place to employ student help in the future.

PROBLEMS

Converting print materials to HTML is fairly straightforward. Editing the resulting Web pages is easy and addictively pleasurable at times. Feeding these updates in the Web text back into the printed version of instructional publications is more difficult. One way to complete the loop is to organize and train Web-knowledgeable, work-study students to incorporate the changes in the WordPerfect files we keep for the print version of the tutorial documents. To date we have not accomplished this task. Documents are created on word processing software, converted to HTML, and updated in HTML. The updates do not find yet their way back to the print version.

The text-to-HTML converters I have used produce sloppy markup, inserting multiple paragraph tags, extra lines, and some unwanted forms of tags. The cleanup work on these conversions that I now do should be transferred to the work-study students who support Web document production.

The biggest frustration I met when setting up and serving the tutorial was an obscure hardware problem. It plagued the Power Mac 7100/66 that I used as both a Web server and my office machine for nearly a year. The computer worked fine as long as I did not use it too much for my own work; when I did use it heavily, it froze too often. Then the Web site was down, and sometimes I lost what I was working on at the time. We eventually had the RAM memory chip reseated and that helped somewhat, but the problem has never been completely solved. I spent too much time on the phone with technical support people trying to solve this problem. The solution seemed always just around the next bend and that was very frustrating. The eventual solution was to substitute another, similar computer from a less demanding location in the division.

BENEFITS

The excitement of making instructional material available to students and librarians around the world has been a pleasure in and of itself, and it provided the motivation I needed to learn hypertext markup language. The rewards for learning HTML markup were immediate, since the Web page I write and the changes I make appear on the screen almost immediately. I have taught students, faculty, and staff how to write Web pages and watched them experience the satisfaction of creating something new, colorful, and interactive.

My experience with HTML has also led to work on the library committee that sets design guidelines and standards for library Web pages. A significant part of this work is maintaining a Web site of information for Web page designers and consulting with individual Web authors on changes and improvements to their pages.

THE FUTURE

Sometime over the next few months, the tutorial will be moved to a new server set up by the Cornell University Library for Web sites and maintained by library system staff. The move will require readdressing a large number of internal links. I have generally used relative links within the tutorial wherever possible, and this certainly reduces the number of changes that need to be made after the transfer. However, since some of the Web pages reside on another office computer that is currently doubling as a server, there are a fair number of absolute links to readdress.

Local use of the tutorial will grow as more students do their research on the network. At the moment, Cornell students more often use computers for writing papers and e-mailing friends and relatives. Use of the network for coursework is growing, however. In the spring semester of 1996, more than 100 Cornell course Web pages, containing syllabuses, lecture notes and drawings, old tests and quizzes, and reading materials, were available on Cornell servers. Students and faculty communicate by e-mail more, and each semester a new group of students learns about the library research tutorial in freshman writing classes.

One of my goals for the next year is to learn the server administration tools that allow the analysis of server log data. I now review the log to look for the error messages that might indicate an incorrectly addressed hypertext link or a misleading instruction in the text. An analysis of who uses the tutorial and how they use it will help with future planning.

Changes in HTML, new browser capabilities, and increased network bandwidth will offer additional ways to make the tutorial more lively. I hope to add images of screens and, later, animations illustrating aspects of the research process. Plug-in applications that extend the power of Web browsers may offer new instructional capabilities in the future. Web-based catalogs and indexes could be used to integrate teaching and searching tools on the library's public terminals and on the network. Point-of-use tutorials are much more powerful and attractive than today's unintegrated versions that are awkwardly linked to catalogs and indexes by a telnet or TN3270 connection. Creating a live component to the tutorial in which reference librarians work side-by-side with students in a MUD (multi-user domain)-style virtual reference room to use digitized full-text resources is another possibility. As we move from what Turkle calls a culture of calculation to a culture of simulation (19), one of our reference rooms will be a three-dimensional construction on a computer. Driven by the expansion of hardware, software, and network capabilities, the development of more powerful, interactive environments on the WWW and its successors will open up multimedia, multidimensional, instructional possibilities that we have not even imagined yet.

REFERENCE

Turkle, Sherry. *Life on the Screen: Identity in the Age of the Internet*. New York: Simon & Schuster, 1995.

Chapter 16

EthnoMed: A Medical Anthropology Work in Progress

Ellen H. Howard
Head, K. K. Sherwood Library
Harborview Medical Center
University of Washington
ehh@u.washington.edu

Martha L. Means
Information Management Librarian
Health Sciences Libraries and Information Center
University of Washington
means@u.washington.edu

OVERVIEW

Health care professionals in the greater Seattle area are seeing increasing numbers of non-English-speaking refugees and other immigrants, many from non-European cultures. The care provided to these patients may be less than adequate, since the majority of health providers are not trained in cross-cultural medicine and must try to bridge language and cultural barriers during brief medical visits.

To meet the needs of both patients and providers, EthnoMed was started in the autumn of 1994. Its objective is to make electronic information about culture, language, health, illness, and community resources directly accessible in clinical areas to providers who are seeing patients from several Southeast Asian and East African refugee groups (see Figure 16.1). The project is a joint project of the University of Washington (UW) Health Sciences Libraries and Information Center (HSLIC) and Harborview Medical Center's Community House Calls Program. HSLIC was fortunate in that the UW Health Sciences Center (HSC) was involved in an Integrated Advanced Information Management System (IAIMS) implementation grant from the National Library of Medicine (NLM). As stated in the UW HSC IAIMS *Factsheet*, "IAIMS is a National Library of Medicine Program to assist health-related schools, organizations, and libraries in planning, developing, and implementing computer systems that make it possible for health care workers to gain access to the information they need for problem solving and learning." This meant that once EthnoMed was accepted as being related to the goals of the UW Health Sciences Center, i.e. adopted as a UW IAIMS project, EthnoMed could benefit from what was being developed and achieved by the IAIMS staff. Harborview Medical Center, a teaching hospital of the University of

---

EthnoMed

Ethnic Medicine Guide
Harborview Medical Center, University of Washington

EthnoMed Home Page

Harborview Medical Center, University of Washington, Seattle, Washington

These files contain information about cultural beliefs and medical issues pertinent to the health care of recent immigrants to Seattle, many of whom are refugees fleeing war-torn parts of the world.

Clinical Pearls in Cross Cultural Medicine

Current Pearl and Past Pearls

Ethnic Groups Included in EthnoMed:

East Africa, including Ethiopia, Eritrea, and Somalia

Amharic	Cultural	Symptoms	Health/Illness	References	Patient Ed
Eritrean	Cultural	Symptoms	Health/Illness	References	Patient Ed
Oromo	Cultural	Symptoms	Health/Illness	References	Patient Ed
Somali	Cultural	Symptoms	Health/Illness	References	Patient Ed
Tigrean	Cultural	Symptoms	Health/Illness	References	Patient Ed

Southeast Asian

Cambodian	Cultural	Symptoms	Health/Illness	References	Patient Ed
Vietnamese	Cultural	Symptoms	Health/Illness	References	Patient Ed

The general section by geographic area includes health related information common to several groups and links to other Web sites. The profile of each ethnic group covers cultural topics, symptoms, health and illness, community resources, and patient education materials, as well as further reading and links to other Web sources.

Current Information related to Community Issues

[News Flashes] [Local News]

Topics in General Cross Cultural Health Care:

Guidelines for Interpreted Visits - Information on doing an interpreted visit.
Beyond Medical Interpretation: The Role of Interpreter Cultural Mediators (ICMs) - A manual describing the work of Community House Calls in building bridges between ethnic communities annd health institutions.

Related Projects at the University of Washington and Selected Links to External Sites

Cross Cultural Nursing Bibliography
Voices of the Community - Cross Cultural Health Care Program community profiles.

Information about EthnoMed

Figure 16.1 A list of ethnic groups

Washington located in central Seattle, serves a diverse population which includes recent refugees and immigrants. The Community House Calls Program, a demonstration project initially funded through the Opening Doors Initiative of the Robert Wood Johnson and Henry J. Kaiser Foundations, with matching funds from the state and Harborview, tries to enhance two-way communication between patients and physicians through interpreters and cultural mediators. This program generated information about health practices and established links to the community. (For more information see Voekler, R. "Speaking the languages of medicine and culture," *JAMA* 273 #21: 1639-41.)

While Harborview and HSLIC staff began and will maintain the EthnoMed files, in the long run we expect input from users. We have tried to make it easy for members of the targeted ethnic communities and primary care providers using the information to make comments to the editors via e-mail or bulletin boards. This information will be incorporated into the files as appropriate.

ORIGIN

EthnoMed (http://www.hslib.washington.edu/clinical/ethnomed) grew out of needs recognized by professionals who worked at Harborview Medical Center. Several health care workers with in-depth knowledge about specific ethnic groups and/or cross-cultural medicine knew that they had information which could improve service to patients if it could be more widely shared. The health care professionals associated with the Community House Calls Program realized that information being generated by that project needed to be disseminated. Also, the Harborview librarian was being asked questions about the cultural practices and medical concerns of various groups of patients served at Harborview. As a consequence, the librarian and several physicians began discussing ways that this specialized knowledge could be disseminated including, for example, developing a bibliographic management program to create and maintain a file of abstracts of materials related to cross-cultural medicine.

When the UW began to support broad-based access to the Internet and space on servers became readily available, the librarian and two physicians at Harborview considered using a computer file as a way to share the cross-cultural information held by some but needed by many in clinical settings. About the time we put a prototype up on a gopher site, World Wide Web developments began to explode. We rapidly changed our plans. Putting information on the Web allowed us to create what we really wanted—an interactive format which was convenient to consult in a busy clinic and which allowed comment from health care users and from members of the target communities. This project could be used to empower members of ethnic communities as well as to inform health care providers.

PLANNING

EthnoMed represents the efforts of a multidisciplinary team. The original group involved in planning the site consisted of two physicians involved in the Community House Calls Program, the head of the Refugee Clinic and the director of the Children's Clinic, and the Harborview librarian. We invited two chief residents to join us. One was from pediatrics and very interested in medical informatics, and the other was from the Ambulatory Care Clinics. Soon a library school student involved in informatics at HSLIC was hired to do the HTML editing of EthnoMed World Wide Web documents. The student and the pediatric resident became the technical experts who kept up with the quickly changing nature of the Web.

After some discussion, the EthnoMed team decided that we wanted to create a useful clinical tool, not just a file for cross-cultural comparisons. We felt it would work best to create a file for each cultural group. The files would be identical in structure so that once familiar with the organization of one file representing one population, a clinician could quickly navigate others. For each group there would be a brief cultural description which would include information that might be useful to a health care provider needing to relate to a person from the culture, a section on health and illness, information about community resources, patient education materials, and an area where users could communicate with the team. We envisioned that some information would be shared between files, for example, descriptions of diagnostic tests commonly used with various refugee groups. Additionally, we expected to put documentation about our project (e.g., who we were and our standards) on our site since team members would change, new writers would be recruited, and users could evaluate the information provided. Because we wanted this to be a clinical work site rather than a research site, we decided not to include many cross references to other Web sites nor to include extensive bibliographies with each document.

THE ETHNOMED TEAM

We established the following roles for the different team members as follows:

- The faculty members would guide the parameters of the project including the content and format of the various types of pages in the file, oversee standards, recruit local writers and help seek ongoing support and funding for the site.
- The chief residents would recruit writers, review the content of the documents submitted by them, help implement and evaluate the use of the tool in various settings, and write documents for the site.
- The editor/support person would track documents from creation to production, keep archives of materials put on the site, review the

documents and other input for consistency of format and style, add HyperText Markup Language (HTML) tags, work on the look and function of the pages, put materials on the construction site, and move documents from the construction to the public site.

• UW IAIMS and other HSLIC staff would provide technical advice and support.

• The Harborview librarian would coordinate work among team members and between the team and the UW IAIMS/HSLIC staff, keep archives documenting team decisions and progress, manage communications from the Web site to the team, keep up with general Web technology, handle or assign miscellaneous tasks arising out of the project, and help seek ongoing funding.

The writing would be done by volunteers recruited from the faculty, house staff, interpreters, and other UW staff and students, as well as by team members, providing they had the appropriate background. Unfortunately, issues related to copyright and tenure have become stumbling blocks. While it is clear that copyright owners can allow adaptations of their work to be produced, the issue as to what an editor will accept as not being previously published if the some of the information has been presented on a Web site is far from settled. Also, how faculty will look at Web publishing in relationship to tenure and promotion still needs to be clarified. Until these two matters are resolved, we anticipate barriers in receiving original information in a timely fashion. Currently faculty may decide to first publish the information in journals, and then the EthnoMed team would apply to the copyright holder for permission to adapt the content for our site. At one point we discussed paying some authors, but we abandoned that idea because we are an academic institution and would like the contributions to be related to work and research at the institution. If we paid some but not all authors, we would constantly need to worry about being fair and equitable.

PRODUCTION

Initial production problems arose owing to inexperience with HTML editing and with computers and computer software. Project management was also a problem because the participants were geographically distributed and busy with other aspects of their jobs. The librarians participating in the project played a crucial role in ameliorating these difficulties.

The library school student, who was initially involved in the HTML editing, accepted a position as an HSLIC librarian upon her graduation and continued in her new job to do the HTML editing of the EthnoMed files. Some difficulties arose at this point because of technical problems involved with using Microsoft Word to create HTML-coded files. As a result, she wrote documentation on the process of creating files for EthnoMed, which was made available via the Web for others on the team.

None of the EthnoMed team members had experience with Web page design at the conceptual phase of the project, but everyone had strong opinions when faced with some actual pages. The initial design of the Web files underwent considerable revision when options were developed and presented. Since our pages are grouped in categories, it would have been better to create mockups of the different categories of pages for just one ethnic group. Then, before extensive work had been done, we could have presented them to the group for comment and review. After we went through the tedious process of revising several files many times to implement changes and make them consistent with each other, the team decided to develop the Cambodian file, for which we had the most information, until it represented what we wanted. Then we could stabilize our format and build the other files to correspond to this model.

A project computer account under a University of Washington campus public Web service was used as a construction site, and then completed documents were moved to the public site on HealthLinks, the University of Washington Health Sciences Web site. We soon plan to have both the construction and public sites on HealthLinks.

We also found it important to provide some members of the group with paper copies so that they could review and revise documents in their spare moments and mark changes they wanted made. Having both paper and electronic copies available also helped bridge the gap within the group between those with extensive computer access and skills and computer novices.

Initially, considerable time went into raising the levels of computer access and skills within the group. The librarians played a crucial role in this learning phase. The librarians documented the technical details of file preparation; taught group members how to do HTML editing using Windows-based and UNIX computers, to move files electronically, and to navigate complicated file structures; gave advice about software; converted Mac files to Windows files; found helpful books and documents; and gave advice about the control of computer viruses. Later, the librarians developed editorial and HTML standards for all files, and instigated more efficient ways to prepare and search a large Web site with the use of templates and a search engine. The IAIMS staff provided technical assistance regarding ways of introducing efficient file management and search options. For example, "server side includes," or ssis, are the HTML coding used at the top and bottom of each Web page. This coding tells browsers, such as Netscape, where to find files that contain repetitive information, such as copyright information. This information is stored in a separate file and is automatically inserted in the Web page when the document is viewed with a browser. If any of this repetitive information needs to be altered, it only needs to be changed in the one file. Then this change shows up automatically in all the Web pages that have the coding to pull up that ssi. Including ssis in the files initially requires additional work, but their use results in more efficient file management.

Because many of our potential users may use text-based access, we designed EthnoMed files so that either a graphics browser such as Netscape, or a text browser such as Lynx, can be used to look at the documents on the Web. This also helps maintain transmission speed. We have kept the graphics to a minimum, although we did need to incorporate scanned documents in order to handle patient education documents in non-Roman scripts.

An ongoing technical problem concerns the materials in non-Roman script, such as Cambodian. We received many of these documents in paper form, and viewing them on the Web requires scanned GIF images. This created a problem because most of the documents require multiple images, so they load very slowly and sometimes crash Netscape. Additionally, Web documents are not read in a page format as paper-based documents are. As a result there can be problems with page breaks when the document is printed from the Web site. We are currently working to solve these scanning problems so that we can mount patient education documents more efficiently and effectively. This aspect of our project has great potential for sharing materials that are difficult and expensive to produce and disseminate.

Several challenges were created because the members of the team were spread out geographically in Seattle and many people were working on various aspects of the project. Although we hold monthly in-person team meetings, connection via e-mail was very helpful for intrateam communication. To manage the documents, we designated one person as the central repository of the working documents and files—a person who would know who had what at what stage of development. An office assistant for pediatrics at Harborview assumed this responsibility and took over the long-term HTML editing and support which freed a librarian from that level of detail. It helped that the assistant was in close proximity with the lead physicians who were generating and reviewing files; this made it easier to transmit and revise documents. She was well-organized, understood the project, and was excited about learning all the technical aspects of Web site development. The HSLIC librarian taught her most of the technical information, answered her questions by e-mail, and arranged occasional on-site meetings. The Harborview librarian took technical materials to her from the HSLIC librarian. This level of close communication is crucial to the development of such a project especially in the formative phase when there are many changes at many levels.

An ongoing problem is the control of computer viruses. The two librarians involved in the project have played a significant role in educating the group about this problem. Because the EthnoMed documents originate from and are reviewed and revised at many different workstations, computer disks have to be treated as potential sources of computer viruses. We have very current antivirus software on our computers, and whenever possible we exchange material via computer networks or e-mail.

TECHNICAL DETAILS

All the members of the project use the e-mail program, Pine, developed at the University of Washington. Pine makes it is easy to send messages to the whole team, subgroups of team members, or individuals.

When we get materials from authors, we can accommodate electronic text from Macintosh or Windows-based computers. We do ask authors to label the disks they submit as to the type of computer and word processing program used so that we can quickly convert the information.

Most of our work was done using Windows-based computers that run Microsoft Word for Windows and simple text editors like Write, Notebook, or Wordpad. While it is more efficient if the people working on a project of this kind all have the same version of Windows, it is not crucial. Windows 95 has some especially useful features: for example, a file can be given names ending with .html, a requirement of the UNIX server where we have our public Web files, or long file names can be used which makes it easier to identify the contents of the large number of HTML files we are generating.

We did much of our HTML editing by hand, with micros, with templates, or with the help of an HTML toolbar developed at the library. In addition, we stored our files on a UNIX computer and used the UNIX text editor, Pico. To load any EthnoMed files into our public site, validation criteria must be met, including spell checking, link checking, and HTML tagging.

The EthnoMed team members who do technical jobs have 486-level PCs with Windows 95 for multitasking; this is important in Web page development since it is not unusual to have four or five windows open at once (e.g., a window for a word processing file, an e-mail session, a window to the UNIX computer where the files are stored, and two Netscape windows).

One book that was particularly helpful because of its many useful examples was *Teach Yourself Web Publishing with HTML in a Week* by Laura Lemay (Indianapolis: Sams Publishing, 1995). We also use a number of the UNIX handouts from the University of Washington's Computing and Communications division.

We are fortunate here in at the University of Washington Health Sciences Libraries and Information Center to have considerable in-house expertise. We received help from support staff, other librarians, and computer programmers in the IAIMS project. Indeed, we chose to have our public site and construction site on the UW Health Sciences Libraries and Information Center server so that we would have ready access to the technical knowledge and skills that its staff possesses, as well as access to the software which is installed on the HSLIC computers.

HOW THE PROJECT AFFECTED RELATIONSHIPS

At the UW, EthnoMed has drawn attention to the library staff and new roles that might be assumed by the library in the field of information management. The librarians directly involved in EthnoMed have developed new working relationships with departments at Harborview, becoming partners in a project rather than a peripheral resource to be drawn upon as needed. The administration at Harborview sees us as involved in a project that directly helps to support the mission of the hospital in a way that draws favorable attention and comment from internal and external groups. The UW libraries recognized the potential of the project for creating and disseminating original material which would support university goals by providing partial funding via the Kenneth S. Allen Library Endowment for 1995/96.

In the Seattle/King County area, the project has attracted the attention of many groups who would like to make translated patient education materials more available. This common interest will probably result in a collaborative effort which will include the UW, public health departments, public libraries, and various local hospitals.

Nationally, we have received positive comments from health care workers, in other parts of the country, who have found the information useful—but often want more information and additional groups covered. When the site has been demonstrated at various meetings, attendees immediately see what could be done with the site, and several groups wish to collaborate with us so that we can expand and enrich the content of EthnoMed. One group, the Institute for Ethnic Studies in the United States, has supported a grant to gather information on fever and dizziness from Cambodians in Seattle via focus groups, for example (see Figure 16.2).

MARKETING

We have not systematically marketed EthnoMed. It is a part of the Community House Calls Program, which has gained the attention of health care providers dealing with diverse culture groups in many cities. Various team members have presented EthnoMed at regional and national programs. Since we want the project to be useful to both clinicians and community members, the Pediatric resident currently involved with EthnoMed has been going to clinics, community centers, and branches of the Seattle Public Library to investigate access issues. He has also contacted groups of individuals within and outside the university to encourage participation and use of the site. Repeatedly we have been asked, "Can community members really look at the files on the Web?"

To date we have not been concerned with how often the file is accessed because it remains a far cry from what we envision. It is still in the developmental stage. However, we do get several comments or questions a month via

---

EthnoMed

Ethnic Medicine Guide
Harborview Medical Center, University of Washington

Cambodian

Select any of the following: <u>Cultural</u> or Medical Topics. Medical Topics include both <u>Symptoms</u> and <u>Health and Illness</u>. For additional information, select <u>References and Further Reading</u> or <u>Patient Education Materials</u>.

Cultural Topics

Country of Origin: <u>Cambodia</u>
    <u>Geography</u>
    <u>History and Politics</u>
<u>Language</u>
<u>Etiquette</u>
    <u>Greetings</u>
    <u>Social Distance</u>
    <u>Displays of Respect</u>
<u>Family Life</u>
    <u>Family and Kinship Structure</u>
    Naming
    <u>Child Rearing Practices</u>
    Rites of Passage and Life Stages
    <u>Gender, Status, and Age Relationships</u>
<u>Nutrition and Food</u>
<u>Religious Life</u>
<u>Traditional Medical Practices</u>
<u>Experience with Western Medicine in Home Country</u>
<u>Experience with Western Medicine in the United States</u>
<u>Seattle Community Life</u>
    <u>Community Organization</u>
    <u>Cambodian (Khmer) Resources</u>
    <u>Neighborhoods</u>
    <u>Common Acculturation Issues</u>

Symptoms

  ⊓ Abdominal Pain
  ⊓ Back Pain
  ⊓ Chest Pain
  ⊓ Constipation
  ⊓ Diarrhea
  ⊓ Dizziness
  ⊓ Fever
  ⊓ Headache
  ⊓ Hematuria
  ⊓ Jaundice
  ⊓ Joint Pain
  ⊓ Too Much Cold/Hot
  ⊓ Too Much Wind
  ⊓ Weakness
  ⊓ Wheezing

Figure 16.2. How an ethnic group is broken down

the e-mail address on the site. We are getting so many communications that are not directly related to the material in EthnoMed that in the future we shall have to place restrictions on the types of questions to which we will respond.

MAINTENANCE

To continue to develop and maintain EthnoMed for the next few years we will need a technical support person who can work fifteen to twenty hours a week and a librarian who can work at least one day a week on the project. These team members need time to concentrate on the detailed tasks as well as keep the whole project together as it grows. Additionally, they need to keep up with and evaluate new technological developments. But a beautifully designed site without content serves no purpose. We must find a way to recruit and train writers and editors so that there is "more meat on the bones." Doing that may mean clarifying issues related to copyright and tenure.

HINDSIGHT

We did not realize how time-consuming this undertaking would prove to be. In some ways it seemed that it would be like merely writing/editing chapters in book. However, each team member had to deal with a learning curve regarding new computer technology that related to the aspects of the project with which she/he was involved. This learning curve was especially steep because it often had to do with seemingly endless details in an extremely dynamic field. As a team we had to work out the details of the design, content, and function of the site so that it would meet the standards of the UW as well as those of each member. Working with voluntary and changing team members under such conditions means that it takes longer to produce a quality product.

Based upon our experiences, we should have initially developed a section for only one ethnic group with a model of each type of page within that section available for team approval. Ideally, the technical support would be provided by permanent staff, already familiar with Web site creation, and the writing would be done by health care professionals who could devote a significant amount of time to writing documents for the site. However, had we waited for this the project would probably still be merely a concept.

THE FUTURE

EthnoMed will continue to be developed over time, and we will collaborate with others so that we can cover more ethnic groups. We shall need to decide whether it is best to have collaborators supply information to us or for them to develop parallel sites, perhaps using templates provided by us. Staffing issues and software/server accessibility may help determine the road best followed.

Chapter 17

DEVELOPING A LOCAL LIBRARY ASSOCIATION WEB PAGE

Frank M. Campbell
campbell@pobox.upenn.edu
Barbara Bernoff Cavanaugh
Biomedical Library
University of Pennsylvania
bbc@pobox.upenn.edu
Randall A. Lowe
University Libraries
Allegheny University of the Health Sciences
lowe@allegheny.edu

BACKGROUND

The Philadelphia Regional Chapter, Inc. of the Medical Library Association (MLA) serves the eastern portion of Pennsylvania and all of Delaware. It is one of fourteen regional groups affiliated with the national MLA organization. The local chapter was created in 1951, and as of 1996 has a membership of approximately 250.

According to the Philadelphia Regional Chapter's bylaws, its purpose is "to promote health sciences libraries by fostering the educational and professional growth of health sciences librarians and information specialists in the Philadelphia region." MLANET, the Medical Library Association's Web page, describes MLA as "a professional organization of approximately 5,000 individuals and institutions in the health information field." MLA "is dedicated to improving excellence and leadership of the health information professional to foster the art and science of health information services. The association also serves as an advocate for the profession and for all health sciences libraries and librarians."

OUR CHARGE

With the explosion of Web access during the last few years, the chapter decided to begin developing a Web site of its own. The chapter Web Design Team was created as a subcommittee of the chapter's Communications Committee. The initial goal of creating a chapter Web has been to provide access to general chapter information and to use the Web site to promote our organization. Future Web additions will promote the chapter's educational activities. The Web Design Team currently consists of three chapter members, representing two chapter institutions.

DEVELOPING A POLICY/GUIDELINES STATEMENT

The policy/guidelines statement is developing as the project progresses. The process of designing the Web site and preparing the policy/guidelines statement began when the Web design chair attended a chapter board meeting to discuss what the board envisioned in a chapter Web site and to enlighten board members as to various Web design options. During the discussion it became clear that the board had several preferences. The following were decided upon:

- images would be included on the Web pages, but not to the point where Lynx users would lose functionality or become frustrated
- horizontal lists would be avoided, primarily for the convenience of Lynx users
- the chapter's letterhead logo would be used on each Web page to denote ownership and to remind the user "where they are" on the Internet
- navigational buttons would be incorporated into the Web site
- the chapter's official colors, buff and dark green would be used
- the chapter's newsletter would become part of the Web site
- specific links were targeted for inclusion

As the Web site takes shape, more standards are being developed. For example, it was decided that a "mailto" link would be placed at the bottom of all Web pages to allow the user to easily send questions and comments to the Web Design Team. It became clear that all images chosen to display on the chapter's Web site should load relatively quickly. Thus it was decided that image size would be limited. Finally, because maintenance was a concern, it was decided that the standing Web Design Team would continue to exist as part of the chapter's Communications Committee. This subcommittee will maintain the chapter Web, adding and updating Web documents and interfacing with the Web server provider.

TECHNICAL ISSUES

The Server

Fortunately, the chapter chose to purchase space on an existing server. The Health Sciences Libraries Consortium (HSLC), a not-for-profit organization, offers a Web page service to member institutions. For a minimal fee the consortium maintains the server, allowing the chapter Web team to focus on designing and organizing the Web pages.

Because the chair of the Web Design Team has an HSLC account, members of the team were able to develop the Web pages in a segment of the HSLC server. This was extremely helpful because it allowed the team members to familiarize themselves with the server and get comfortable with HTML code.

Software

The majority of the Web pages produced were created on a desktop and then moved to the HSLC server. Macintosh HTML editing software called *HTML Editor* was used to create most of the Web pages. After a majority of the pages were tested on the desktop, FTP software called *Fetch* was used to transfer the files onto the server. Revisions were made using the desktop files and then those files were uploaded onto the server.

Because HSLC separates personal Web sites from institutional sites, all of the Web pages had to be copied into the chapter's official Web location. This transfer can only be done by HSLC staff. After creating the Web documents, editing them, and finally placing them in a personal Web location on the HSLC server, an e-mail notification was sent to HSLC. Staff there would then copy the Web files from the personal account and move them to the chapter segment of the server.

CREATING THE HOME PAGE

After the initial input from the chapter board, the Web Design Team began meeting to lay out how the Web documents would be developed. The initial goal was to focus only on developing text and links within the chapter's Web and move on to images later. The team chose six main topics to display on the initial Web page. This was a concerted effort to make the home page simple, clean and short. Keeping the home page short would allow Lynx users and individuals with small monitors to see the home page all at once without moving to a second screen. Following are the six main topics selected to be listed on the home page (see Figure 17.1):

- About the Chapter
- How Do I Join
- Continuing Education and Other Events
- Professional Associations
- MLA National Organization
- *The Chronicle* (the chapter's newsletter)

A seventh link remained available during beta testing. This link pointed to the meeting minutes of the Web Design Team for easy access. When the Web site went live, this administrative link was removed.

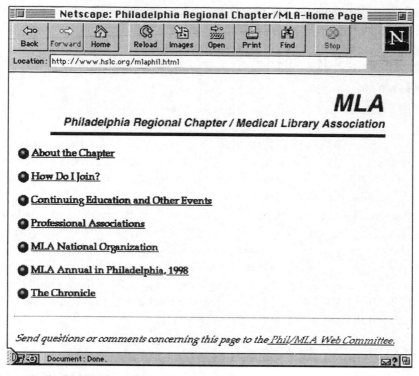

Figure 17.1 The Philadelphia Regional Chapter's home page

About the Chapter

Much of the material already available in print form was placed in the "About the Chapter" section of the Web. This material included chapter history, past and present officers, committee information, bylaws, awards, listserv information, and a map of the chapter region. Because much of this material is included in the chapter's *Membership Directory and Handbook*, a print resource which is maintained electronically, it was relatively easy to take the electronic text and convert it into HTML format using HTML Editor software.

How Do I Join

At present, the "How Do I Join" link points to a membership application form. The user is required to print out the form and mail or fax it to an address listed at the bottom of the Web page. However, the Web Design Team is interested in creating an electronic "Membership Application" form that would allow the user to type in the pertinent information using a graphical Web browser and send the data electronically. When our knowledge of CGIs (common gateway interfaces) is more developed, no doubt, we will attempt to offer this service.

Continuing Education and Other Events

The "Continuing Education and Other Events" link points to chapter events currently planned, as well as events scheduled by other library-related organizations. Later, the team chose to include information about the Education and Credentialing Committee. This committee is responsible for continuing education events for the chapter.

Professional Associations

The "Professional Associations" link points to national, international, and regional library-related professional associations. In addition, library and informatics-related Web search tools, such as Yahoo and MedWeb, were included on this page.

MLA National Organization

The national MLA home page provides extensive information about the association, and the design team felt that the "MLA National Organization" link should be placed on the chapter's Web home page. The national MLA home page points to all chapter home pages as they are created, including ours.

The Chronicle

Finally, *The Chronicle*, the chapter's newsletter, was selected as a link on the home page. It would have required a vast amount of staff time to convert the chapter's newsletter into HTML, so the Web team chose to offer access as a "portable document format" (PDF) file. This format, developed by Adobe Systems, allows you to present material on the Web regardless of the application, hardware, or operating system used to create the material. In order to view PDF files, users must access them using a graphical Web browser and have installed Adobe's free software, Acrobat Reader, onto their computer. To facilitate access to Acrobat Reader, links to Adobe Systems (http://www. adobe.com/) and an FTP site for Acrobat Reader (http://www.adobe. com/acrobat/) were included on *The Chronicle* Web page. In order to convert the newsletter into a PDF file, Adobe software called Acrobat Pro was purchased. This software allows you to easily convert a document from any word-processing or desktop publishing software into a PDF file. After conversion, this same software allows you to manipulate the PDF file in order to make it more user-friendly. Bookmarks and articles were defined within the file.

Images

Early in the Web Design Team's meetings it was decided to use the chapter's official letterhead as the Web sites logo image. The image is quite simple, made up of text and a straight line, both in dark green. This image did not exist as an electronic file; therefore, an electronic image was created using the print image as a guide. Adobe Photoshop (software which happened to be owned by the library of the team's chair) was used to create the image. Because the GIF format is a standard format for simple images on the Web, the chapter's Web logo was saved as a GIF file. After tweaking the file several times, its final size turned out to be 3K. In order to service Lynx users, alternate text was included with the image HTML code so that the text, "Philadelphia Regional Chapter/MLA," would appear if the image was unable to load into the user's Web browser. In addition, an "align=right" code was placed within the HTML document. Netscape Navigator reads this code and aligns the image to the right. Other graphical browsers ignore the code all together.

In addition to the Web's logo, it was suggested that the team create maps displaying the chapter's region. A map of the United States found on the Web was used as the basis of the final image. The map was manipulated using Adobe Photoshop to add text, color, and a rudimentary three-dimensional effect. As time allows, additional maps will be developed zeroing in on the region.

The Web Design Team has moved slowly in developing additional images for the chapter's Web site. This has been a conscious decision in order to keep the Web site clean-looking and to allow for quick loading of Web pages. As we see the need, additional images will be included. In addition, designing images takes a great deal of time. An important need for an image must arise before time would be allotted for the task.

Backgrounds and Colors

Because the chapter's official colors are dark green and buff, the Web Design Team tried using a background color for all the Web pages. A background color code was included within the body code on all Web pages to display the color buff. In addition, unfollowed links on the home page were coded to display as green text, followed links as black text, and active links as goldenrod text. The actual code that creates this effect is <body bgcolor="faf7c0" link="006400" vlink="05083f" alink="daa520">. The six alpha/numeric elements enclosed in quotation marks makeup the hexadecimal code which describes the RGB (red/green/blue) values that represent a color. There are several Web sites that can help Web designers with background color selection. The Web Design Team used ColorMaker (available at http://www.missouri.edu/~c588349/colormaker.HTML) to choose appropriate colors and retrieve the corresponding hexadecimal codes.

Buttons

Button images were created using Adobe Photoshop software. While not displayed on the home page, they appear on all other chapter Web pages. There was some concern about including button images on every page, but once the images load the first time in a graphical browser such as Netscape, they are stored in cache and load almost immediately when additional Web pages are displayed. Each button is approximately 3.5K. The buttons themselves represent several of the links available from the Web home page. They act as a quick navigational tool to important sites on the chapter Web. Like the logo image, the HTML code that displays the button image also includes alternate text which will display when a user accesses the Web site using a Web browser that can not display images.

MAINTENANCE ISSUES

Our Web site, as of this publication, is still extremely young. However, maintenance has been discussed. The current Web Design Team will continue to exist as part of the chapter's Communications Committee. This subcommittee will maintain the chapter Web site, adding and updating Web documents, and interfacing with HSLC, the server administrators. HSLC produces "traffic analysis" reports that track the number of hits a specific Web page receives. We look forward to using these numbers to improve our Web site in the future. Currently, users are asked to send comments and suggestions concerning the chapter Web to the Web Design Team chair. This can be accomplished by using the "mailto" links available at the bottom of every chapter Web page.

The initial material for the Web site was obtained from printed sources or by asking chapter committee chairs for information. Future plans call for committee chairs to submit updates in a systematic fashion. This will enable the Web Design Team to focus on the technical appearance issues of the page.

PROMOTING/ADVERTISING OUR WEB PAGE

The chapter's Web was introduced to chapter members at a recent annual meeting. To demonstrate the Web site at the meeting, the HTML files that makeup the Web were copied onto a portable Mac. Using *Netscape Navigator* software installed on the Mac, and an LCD/projector, we showcased the Web site without requiring a live network connection. Since the Web site is still relatively small, copying the HTML files onto the portable Mac was not problematic.

The Web site has also been promoted on the Chapter's local listserv, MLA-PHIL@SHRSYS.HSLC.ORG, and the Web site is a link on the national MLA home page. The Web Design Team chair has been appointed as the chapter liaison to MLANET, the national MLA's home page.

The Web has been well-received. We are just beginning to receive suggestions and comments regarding additional links and information.

CONCLUSIONS

The process of designing the page went smoothly. This was in part due to the fact that the Web Design Team was small, and there was usually complete agreement on the various design decisions. We saved time by using text that already existed for some of the links on the home page, instead of creating everything from scratch, and maintenance should not prove to be problematic if updates are submitted in a timely fashion.

The Web site plays an integral role in chapter communications. The chapter's newsletter editor doubles as Communications Committee chair, and coordinates the activities of all three of the chapter's vehicles for communication: the newsletter, the listserv, and the Web site. The Communications Committee works as a team, so the three modes of communication complement each other rather than compete. For example, the committee member who prepares the calendar of the events for the newsletter also posts the events on the listserv. The Web Team chair then copies the events from the listserv to include on the Web site.

NOTES

The following are URLs relevant to this chapter:

Philadelphia Regional Chapter/Medical Library Association
    http://www.hslc.org/mlaphil.html
Medical Library Association (MLANET)
    http://www.kumc.edu/MLA/
The Health Sciences Library Consortium (HSLC)
    http://www.hslc.org/
Adobe
    http://www.adobe.com/
Adobe Acrobat
    http://www.adobe.com/acrobat/readstep.html
Adobe Photoshop
    http://www.adobe.com/prodindex/photoshop/main.html
ColorMaker
    http://www.missouri.edu/~c588349/colormaker.HTML
HTML Editor
    http://dragon.acadiau.ca/~giles/HTML_Editor/Documentation.html

Chapter 18

BRINGING THE BRAZORIA COUNTY HISTORICAL MUSEUM TO THE WEB

Kevin C. Marsh, Executive Director

Information Access Institute
KMarsh@Information.org

Brazoria County Historical Museum (http://www.bchm.org) is a regional local-history museum located in Angleton, Texas, in the heart of the original Anglo colony in Texas. Their award-winning Austin Colony exhibit chronicles the birth of Texas as an independent nation. By early 1995 the museum director, Mr. Robert Handy, was watching the development of the Internet and the Web with interest. He made contact with some Web experts from a local university for advice and investigated funding sources. He also enrolled in a continuing education course on Internet servers for libraries, museums, and archives. The course was sponsored by the University of Texas Graduate School of Library and Information Science and presented by Information Access Institute (IAI).

After the class Mr. Handy contacted IAI and asked us to put together a proposal to provide staff training and project planning in order to help the Brazoria County Historical Museum prepare to serve its collections on the Internet (see Figure 18.1). We also provided him with some suggestions for appropriate wording to include in his grant proposal. In mid-June the museum had obtained an Institute of Museum Services technical assistance grant and we were ready to begin.

TRAINING AND PLANNING

We used a series of four weekly half-day training sessions to introduce the museum staff to the Internet, to explain how the various protocols worked to share information, and to coach them in their first HTML authoring efforts. They had some delays in obtaining sufficient Internet accounts for each of the staff members to connect from their desks; in retrospect, the training might

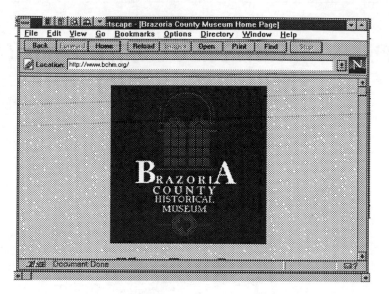

Figure 18.1 Brazoria County Historical Museum home page

have been more productive if each staff member had been given their own account and their own set of software before the training began. Despite this setback the training was very helpful in getting the staff up to speed on the Internet, enthusiastic about the possibilities, and actively involved in the Brazoria County Historical Museum Internet server project.

During that same period we worked with the museum director to establish goals and priorities for their Internet project, to assess the scope of the project, and to prepare a project plan. This planning process cannot be overemphasized. Too often organizations get caught up in the excitement of new technology without pausing to reflect on how that technology can best be harnessed to serve their organizational goals. In this case the Brazoria County Historical Museum wanted to go beyond a simple informational site to provide networked access to digital representations of the majority of the museum's holdings. The specific goals were to provide to users

1. The images and text of the Austin Colony exhibit to students, educators, and the general public on the Internet
2. The Genealogy Database on the Internet through a searchable interface
3. The Documents Catalog on the Internet through a searchable interface
4. The Photographic Collection and Catalog on the Internet at a resolution suitable for on-screen viewing and intersearchability between the Exhibit, Genealogy, Documents, and Photographic collections

5. Kiosks on each floor of the museum for access to the museum's Internet server and other related Internet sites

Note that while goal number 4 only specifies intersearchability among the Brazoria County Historical Museum collections, there was much discussion and interest in the possibility of expanding that capability to include other related museum collections across the state.

For each of these goals we identified appropriate standards for file formats, image resolution, and user interfaces. We also assessed the hardware, software, and manpower needed to meet each goal and evaluated both in-house and outsourcing options. At the end of this process we provided a written project plan with clearly identified options and cost estimates. The museum director presented this plan to the board of directors and obtained authorization to proceed. If additional funding had been required at this point, the project plan would have served as the basis for a grant proposal.

WHAT SHOULD BE MADE INTERNET-ACCESSIBLE

The typical institutional Web site on the Internet provides basic information about the location, hours, services, and unique features along with contact names, phone numbers, and e-mail addresses for requesting more information. In addition to these basics many libraries, museums, archives, and other information organizations are now loading the catalogs and content of their collections onto the Internet. For Brazoria County Historical Museum this was a high priority. The educational mission of the museum could best be served by widespread public access. Texas middle school students in particular are required to study Texas history, and networked access to the Austin Colony exhibit was seen as a valuable tool to enrich that study.

The Austin Colony exhibit is composed of sixty-eight large (4 x 8 foot) panels of text, documents, photographs, and maps interspersed with cases of artifacts and dioramas. While most of this material is owned by the museum, a few images had been borrowed or copied from other sources. The staff had to obtain copyright clearance from the owners of these images before publishing them on the Internet. Brazoria County Historical Museum decided to load digital versions of the entire exhibit onto the Internet, including digital images of the artifacts and digital video panning through the dioramas and zooming in on points of interest.

The museum's genealogy database includes records for nearly 3,000 individuals who are the ancestors or descendants of the "Old 300" original families in Steven F. Austin's Texas colony. These records are maintained by the museum staff in a commercial genealogy software package and updated regularly as new information becomes available. Brazoria County Historical Museum chose to offer this information on the Internet for the benefit of genealogists and Texas history scholars.

The Documents Collection is somewhat misleadingly named, since it contains both documents and artifacts ranging from personal letters and financial records of early settlers to cannonballs and clothing. This collection is currently being recataloged with text descriptions and subject terms for each item. The catalog for this collection will be available on the Internet to help scholars locate materials, but only selected items will be photographed and digitized.

The Photography Collection contains approximately the following items:

Black and White Positive Prints	2,500
Color Positive Prints	100
Oversize Positives	200
Black and White Film Negatives	500
Total	**3,300** images

Since the goal of this project is merely to provide adequate image quality for on-screen viewing, we advised Brazoria County Historical Museum to scan the images at approximately 640 pixels in width. This will allow the image to display on most monitors without scrolling side-to-side. Since the negatives are such a small portion of the collection it will be less expensive to have prints made than to purchase a transparency adapter for the scanner. The oversize images (maps, etc.) will either be photographed in order to make an image small enough to fit on the scanner be or sent out to a local facility with a large-format scanner. All images will be scanned and linked to catalog data to provide the best possible access for scholars.

If the scanned images had been intended for archival preservation of the image content they would have needed to scan at much higher resolution (roughly 2,000 by 3,000 pixels). These high-resolution files could be stored on recordable CDs and stored off-line, with lower resolution versions used for online access. Even then, I would advise making every effort to preserve the original film or prints because they contain a level of detail that cannot be captured with current equipment.

INDEXES AND STANDARDS

There are a multitude of search engines available for use in conjunction with a Web site, ranging from text indexes like AltaVista or Harvest to relational databases like Oracle or Microsoft Access. While these products are certainly appropriate for stand-alone applications such as a vendor's product catalog or a university's list of course offerings, they are less suitable for library or museum collections. An individual library or museum can usually collect only a portion of the available material in any given subject area, so it is often useful to be able to conduct a single search against multiple related collections. This is possible and even easy over the Internet, but only if the related collections use a standard method for receiving and answering searches.

Fortunately the ANSI/NISO Z39.50 standard for information retrieval provides an open, nonproprietary standard to accomplish this task. By using a Z39.50-compliant search engine, the Brazoria County Historical Museum not only established a simple mechanism for simultaneously searching two or more of its collections, it also opened the door to intersearchability with other Texas history collections as they become available online.

The specific software chosen for this project was freeWAIS-sf, developed by researchers at the University of Dortmund, Germany. Although this package is based on the older WAIS version of the Z39.50 standard, it was chosen because of the following reasons:

1. It can be installed and used with minimal system administrator support and no programmer support.
2. The University of Dortmund provides excellent on-line documentation and user support
3. It supports structured fields of data and field-specific searching.
4. It is free. (Commercial WAIS meets the above criteria but costs $15,000 for a network license.)
5. It has free software utilities to provide access to a WAIS database from a Web page.

The ISITE package available from the Center for Networked Information Discovery and Retrieval was also considered, in part because of its support for the current version of the Z39.50 standard. Unfortunately, we determined that ISITE, at that time, required more initial and ongoing programmer support than the museum would be able to provide. We will continue to assess ISITE and other current Z39.50 implementations for a possible upgrade to the Brazoria County Historical Museum site and for use in future projects.

WHERE DO WE PUT IT ALL?

Another critical decision was the nature and location of the Internet server. Although a Web server can be configured using any major operating system (Windows, Macintosh, OS/2, UNIX, etc.) this server needed to run some version of UNIX in order to support the searching software. In addition, it needed to provide about 200 megabytes of server space for network access and a fast network connection to support multiple simultaneous users downloading images and other large files. Three options were considered.

The first was to purchase a Pentium PC and configure it as a server at the Brazoria County Historical Museum site, with an ISDN Internet connection. This option gives the best local control, but incurs the highest cost because of the need for a UNIX system administrator. The cost of the ISDN connection is also considerable and it provides only marginally acceptable connectivity for an image-intensive server. Faster connections are available but only at significantly higher cost.

The second option was to purchase a Pentium PC and configure it as a server at an Internet service provider's site with an Ethernet connection to their Internet backbone. The service provider would not only set up a network connection, but also provide basic system maintenance support. This avoids the staffing and connection speed problems of option 1, but still incurs a considerable cost for hardware, initial system setup, and on-going support.

The final option, leasing space on an existing server at an Internet service provider's site, proved to be the least expensive and most attractive option. Many Internet service providers (ISPs) offer Web space for a monthly fee and provide discounts for large volume users or for nonprofit organizations. Fewer ISPs support a Z39.50 search engine, but we located one willing to install our chosen software for a moderate fee.

GETTING THE JOB DONE

With the staff trained, project plan in place, and the Internet server space procured, the Brazoria County Historical Museum was ready to proceed. They again contracted IAI to assist with their Web site design and initial implementation. For the Austin Colony exhibit, museum staff provided the text in WordPerfect format, shot video of the dioramas, photographed the artifacts, and scanned all of the images using an inexpensive flat-bed scanner. IAI staff then formatted the text as HTML, resized and retouched the images as needed, converted images to GIF format, digitized the video, created custom graphics, and loaded the resulting files onto the server.

Museum staff exported the genealogy data from their commercial PC-based system in a standard GEDCOM file format and loaded this file onto the server. IAI developed and documented a procedure to convert this data into HTML using freeware utilities downloaded from the Internet: Lifelines by Thomas Wetmore and dump_html by Scott McGee. While it is possible to use Lifelines as a Web-accessible genealogy database, we chose to export the data in HTML format and index it in freeWAIS-sf instead. This was essential to allow intersearchability with other collections. For example, a search for "Durazno Plantation" now retrieves both exhibit panels about the plantation and genealogical records for individuals who were born there.

Prior to this project the museum had begun work on cataloging their documents and artifacts collection in a commercial PC-based relational database. IAI developed and documented a procedure to export data from this database as HTML. This same procedure will be used for the photo collection database, with the addition of in-line GIF images (small images that appear on screen when the HTML documents are displayed) and links to the full-screen images in JPEG format. Museum staff are currently working on enhancing the documents and artifacts catalog data before loading it on the Internet.

The photo collection will be the last to be loaded on-line. Museum staff and volunteers will need to scan all 3,300 photos and save them as image files. Each image will be saved as a full-screen image in JPEG format with a compression ratio of roughly 20-1 to minimize file storage space requirements and network transmission times. A small GIF file (roughly 80x80 pixels) of each image will also be created for use on that image's Web page as a preview of the full-screen image. The museum staff will enter the existing catalog data into the museum's database so that it can be exported to HTML documents which will be loaded onto the server and indexed just like the other collections. This index will be built so that searching provides a list of titles, selecting a title from the list returns the page of catalog data with the small GIF image, and clicking on the image returns a full-screen JPEG version of the image which the users can save or print on their own computers.

Each of these collections has a unique structure or format to its HTML files. In freeWAIS-sf this structure is identified in a special file for each collection that defines which data will be included in individual fields like Title, Date, Subject Terms, and Description. IAI prepared and tested format files for each collection to ensure proper indexing and produced detailed instructions for the museum staff to ensure successful collection maintenance.

Getting the search engine up and running proved to be an unexpected challenge. Despite consistent success in other locations, the freeWAIS-sf indexing software would not execute without crashing on the ISP's server. After several attempts and much consultation among the ISP's technical staff, the computer support staff at IAI, and the authors of the software, this problem has not been resolved. We were forced to develop a work-around solution, so we copied the entire site to IAI's own Internet server and built the indexes there. We configured the Web site so the end user does not know (or care) that the indexes being searched actually reside on a separate machine in a different part of the state. Hopefully this problem will be resolved soon and IAI will be able to use this server space for other projects.

FUTURE PLANS

The museum is still working to procure and install kiosks which will provide access to a small selection of Texas history Web sites. Meanwhile the director is working to encourage other Texas history museums to load their collections onto the Internet with standard compliant search capability. This will provide students, scholars, and the general public with unprecedented access to these resources and harness, at least within this subject area, the full potential of the Internet to provide information.

WEBLIOGRAPHY

Brazoria County Historical Museum: http://www.bchm.org

FreeWAIS-sf: http://ls6-www.informatik.uni-dortmund.de/freeWAIS-sf/

Information Access Institute: http://Information.org

Intersearchability with WAIS: http://ls6-www.informatik.unidortmund.de/ir/projects/SFgate/demo.html

Intersearchability with Z39.50: http://europagate.dtv.dk/cgi-bin/egwcgi/egwirtcl/mtargets.egw

Lifelines software: http://www.shore.net/~ttw/lines/lines.html

Lifelines dump-html utility: ftp://ftp.cac.psu.edu/pub/genealogy/lines/reports/smcgee/

WAIS Usenet Group: comp.infosystems.wais

Worldwide Web "How-To" Resources and Guides: http://lcweb.loc.gov/global/www.html

Z39.50 and the World Wide Web, Sebastian Hammer: http://www.indexdata.dk/webz.html

Z39.50 resources—a pointer page: http://ds.internic.net/z3950/z3950.html

Isite Z39.50 server: http://vinca.cnidr.org/software/Isite/Isite.html

Recommended File Formats for WWW Documents, Ken Jenks: http://sd-www.jsc.nasa.gov/web_formats.html

Chapter 19

FREELANCE WEB DESIGNER

Juleigh Muirhead Clark

Golden Retriever Research Service
Williamsburg, Virginia
librarian@widowmaker.com

GOING FREELANCE

For the past eighteen years I have worked in a variety of capacities in public and academic libraries. Although primarily in public services, I have also worked in administration, cataloging, and collection development. During these experiences I have learned much about the interrelationships of public and behind-the-scenes work and staff that are fundamental to a growing library. Among other things, this work has required creativity, independent thinking, perseverance, and humor, and I have always found it challenging and intensely absorbing. So, why go freelance? A favorite aspect of my previous jobs in public and academic reference had always been in-depth research, and it seemed that the intrusion of other responsibilities left little time for using the reference skills that I had worked so hard to develop. The fun of the search and the exhilaration of following through to the end of the hunt has been one of the greatest benefits of my new endeavor. Generally, I have marketed my skills to the academic community and do bibliographic research on topics in the social sciences and humanities and find my sources in public and academic libraries and online. Most recently I have added Web design to my repertoire.

My "alternative" worklife has also allowed me to add teaching—as an adjunct lecturer with a nearby library and information science graduate program—to my professional life. I find in teaching that I reiterate all those ideals that began my career not only to my students, but to myself. Now, however, I have experience which gives those ideals meaning and balance.

Consequently, I find myself working still in public and academic libraries as well as in my home-office as I serve both my clients and my students. Yes, the hours are more flexible and allow for added dimensions in my life. On the other hand, when a urgent commission comes in, my careful plans are shuffled while this new work takes precedence. Now I really know what flexibility means!

RESEARCHER TO WEB SITE DESIGNER

I became involved with the Internet through curiosity and timing. I took a temporary position with the Swem Library Reference Department at the College of William and Mary in 1993, at which time the campus was presenting its own gopher. Swem Library took a leading role in introducing it to faculty, staff, and students, and in a naive effort to thoroughly understand the Internet, I began reviewing recommended sites and investigating search strategy using the "Internet Hunt," which used the traditional method of the treasure hunt to teach Internet conventions. (For more information, see "The Virtual Reference Library," Gord Nickerson, *Computers in Libraries*, May 1993, pp. 37–40).

Because of my fascination with things electronic and my extensive bibliographic instruction background, I was employed in 1994-95 on a grant to coordinate students, faculty, and staff at the College of William and Mary to evaluate and design user instruction for a government system of Internet databases (Global Change Data and Information System, "GCDIS", http://www.gcdis.usgcrp.gov/). I soon realized that most of the academic community had never previously accessed the Internet either by gopher, which had been available on campus for only a year, or through the World Wide Web, which was widely available with a text browser (Lynx), but only accessible in the library with Netscape. Therefore, before I could find people to evaluate the user-friendliness of one specific system, it was clear that I would need to engage their interest in the Internet. The media had recently discovered the "Information Superhighway," so most of my potential users had unrealistic ideas as to what the Internet could do and no idea whatsoever how to navigate it.

It became apparent that the most positive way for neophytes to deal meaningfully with the enormous system was through the traditional library pathfinder. I had developed pathfinders on a variety of topics over the years, and this was a method of research familiar to most students which helped them in their approach to a bewildering new world of information (both in libraries and on the Internet). While following the paths to specific information I outlined on their pathfinders, the students could serendipitously find other information. Perhaps guiding students to a good experience somewhat affected their evaluations of the system, but like all good librarians, I wanted the students to leave the Internet (and the library) with positive impressions. After having good results with the printed pathfinders, I placed one on the Internet ("Finding Information on Ozone Depletion in GCDIS"— http://janus.swem.wm.edu/gcdis. html) to globally assist new users of GCDIS.

This no-frills home page improves on the traditional pathfinder in that the destination is hotlinked. Therefore, the user can follow the Internet path if they choose, or link directly to the source.

BECOMING A WEBMASTER

After over 200 hours of browsing, critiquing, and demonstrating GCDIS myself, I was highly sensitized to the possibilities offered by the WWW and ready to build on my experience. I received preliminary instruction on HTML conventions and a "cheat sheet" of basic HTML commands by another librarian and felt ready to experiment. The HTML authoring tool I used was HTML Assistant, a software package available at the college. This software is relatively simple to use, but its template and command buttons do not include several basic options (like "mailto" for hotlinking email addresses). Whenever I wanted to do something not obviously available in HTML Assistant, I tried several options with varying success. Checking the books available in the library on HTML was not helpful. Either I was not able to phrase my question in a way that was recognizable in the book's table of contents or index, or the books were theoretical while my current need was practical. Looking at the HTML WWW help guides on Yahoo (Yahoo: Computers and the Internet / WWW / HTML: Guides and Tutorials) gave me more help. But my favorite way of trying something new was to follow the steps of other Web page authors. I would search for a page that contained elements or formats I wanted, then use the Netscape software to select "VIEW DOCUMENT SOURCE." I could then copy their strategy.

CASE STUDY: SWEM LIBRARY DEPARTMENTAL HOME PAGES

While I was involved in the GCDIS grant, Swem Library formed a committee to design a library home page, and this committee subsequently mounted a library Web site. The Internet was becoming more and more useful to the library staff, and library department heads expressed interest in departmental home pages to further expedite library work. But while the library Web page progressed, the departmental home pages remained wistful discussion. I spoke to the department heads for Reference and Acquisitions and ascertained that they lacked time to locate and organize the data which they felt could be used frequently by their staff. They responded positively when I suggested the possibility of an independent librarian designing their Web pages, so I drew up a formal proposal, generally outlining the kinds of information, the basic design of each Web page, and the cost of such work, which I submitted to the library's administration. The following aspects were considered in formulating my proposal:

- What original information needed to be loaded and how was it formatted? For example, was the information available as a WordPerfect file?
- What were the estimated known links that should be included? For instance, what links did they already use?
- What would be the general arrangement/amount/format of the data? How many levels of information or separate files of information would be loaded?
- How should the Web page be refined? The Web pages needed to be efficient—no extraneous links should be established and the information that is linked or loaded should be high-use. Choices made by me and the department head and staff evaluation let us know whether this goal was met.
- What would not be included, such as slow-loading graphics or excess verbiage? These pages were to be worker aids, not library marketing material or Internet teaching tools.

The reaction from Swem Library administration was generally positive. I was asked to rewrite my proposal to include home pages for the Cataloging and Circulation Departments. However, my proposal for updating (all but one of) the home pages was rejected. It was decided that each department could find the personnel to update each Web site. I was retained to periodically update the extensive home page designed by the Government Documents librarian.

DESIGNING THE WEB PAGES

As you can imagine, the Web pages for each department vary widely. While the Reference Department page is an electronic ready reference collection, linking them to Internet search mechanisms, databases, neighboring libraries, and ready reference texts, the Circulation page is primarily Swem Library policies. The Acquisitions page combines departmental information with publishing business links, and serials check-in sites, while the Cataloging Web page connects them to bibliographic utilities and databases, with no local policies added at this time.

I began each Web page after I conducted an in-depth interview with the department head, reviewed his/her bookmarks, and examined other libraries' departmental home pages. Then with this data I proceeded to draft a Web page for the department to review for relevancy, arrangement, and textual correctness and FTPed the Web page to the library's Unix computer. After two to three weeks of review, I met again with the department head to find out what changes needed to be made, and then I made them. The time spent on each home page varied, with the Circulation Department's taking about ten hours, while the Acquisitions Department's more complex requirements took over twenty-five hours. Devising staff evaluations, compiling the results and meeting with the departments (within two months of the Web page's appearance) took over seventy hours.

The order of work that I followed was established by the library administration. Using that order, I will describe in more detail the types of decisions that had to be made in designing each home page and the evaluation of staff members.

REFERENCE: http://janus.swem.wm.edu/Depts/Ref/ref.html

Format

Initial arrangement was by the link's perceived importance to the reference process. It was determined that the major reference use of the Internet was for searching for specific bits of information and that Internet search tools should be at the top of the page—much as index areas and CD-ROMs are often located near the reference desk! However, once I realized how long the home page was growing, I placed a Table of Contents at the beginning of the page (see Figure 19.1). Hotlinks from the Table of Contents meant that all the links were equally close. This became the rule in all of the departmental home pages. Following the search engines are bibliographic search tools—links to FirstSearch, RLIN, and to most frequently accessed library catalogs. Textual resources follow—favorite resources such as "Project Vote Smart," or the "Richmond (VA) Times Dispatch." Finally, reference librarians can quickly link to other Swem Library home pages should they need to check on information about a circulation policy, a government document, or a publisher's catalog, for example.

Content

This depended partly on staff experience with the Internet, partly on known user needs, and Internet strengths. Bibliographic resources for searching the "Net" and other online databases were the first links requested by the department. The staff had observed that Netscape's Net Search was often difficult or slow to access and wanted to go directly to available search tools without the Netscape intermediary. Therefore, direct links to search engines were a first priority.

Next, easy access to FirstSearch and to the resources offered through the Virginia academic library consortium, "Virtual Library of Virginia" (VIVA), was required so several links to that system were added. While this access is also available from the public Swem Library Web page, it requires navigating through several levels. Now with one click of the mouse on the Reference Department home page, the librarian can connect into the desired database provider.

Catalogs of neighboring libraries have been consulted by reference librarians for several years, but the procedure had taken precious time to effect, either through telneting directly, or navigating the Internet with gopher and Web hierarchy. Now with two clicks (Table of Contents to Library Catalogs to

---

Electronic Ready Reference

Earl Gregg Swem Library

College of William and Mary

The following links have been chosen potential high use by reference staff and for ease of access.

TABLE OF CONTENTS

[ ] Search Engines
[ ] FirstSearch
[ ] Virginia Library Catalogs and Homepages
   [ ] VIVA
[ ] Library / Library Assns Homepages: National and International
[ ] Other Bibliographic Sources
[ ] Current Events
[ ] Directories
[ ] Encyclopedias
[ ] Geographical Sources
[ ] Weather
[ ] Other Reference Sources
[ ] Local Homepages
[ ] Index of Links

SEARCH ENGINES

[ ] Understanding WWW Search Tools -- *brief explanation of features offered by popular search engines*
   --also hyperlinks for searching
[ ] All-In-One Search
[ ] Altavista-- *allows boolean searching & nesting*
[ ] Excite -- *searches Websites & Usenet Newsgroups*
[ ] Lycos -- *searches 91 % of the WWW*
[ ] Metacrawler
[ ] Open Text Index -- *searches over 1 million Web pages*
[ ] Internet Sleuth
[ ] WebCrawler
[ ] Yahoo

FIRSTSEARCH

[ ] FirstSearch -- *authorization/password required*
[ ] OCLC Reference Services Home Page
   -- includes links to both OCLC Electronic Journals Online and to FirstSearch Web

VIRGINIA LIBRARY CATALOGS AND HOMEPAGES *selected*

College of William and Mary
[ ] LION Webcat
[ ] LION -- *telnet*
[ ] Swem Library Homepage

Library of Virginia
[ ] Catalog: Cavalier
Enter: hello gopher,user.clas52
[ ] Homepage

Figure 19.1 Home page of the Earl Gregg Swem Library Reference Department

specific catalog), the reference librarian will find him/herself logging into the neighboring library's catalog.

Political science and government students are ardent library users who frequently have questions about events too current to be easily located through traditional reference sources. Therefore, the largest number of textual links on the home page deal with local, national, and international sources for current events.

Problems/Issues

The first issue to confront was that of databases requiring passwords. The VIVA databases are already accessible to the IP addresses of consortium members, so that was not a problem. However, other databases systems such as the Latin America Database, RLIN, or the Electronic Telegraph required passwords. Therefore, these passwords were kept separate from the home page to ensure security.

Initially, the machines were not loaded with tn3270 software and one of the library sites we needed to access required it. I consulted with one of the library systems staff and with his help downloaded a copy of this freeware from the WWW and onto the Reference Desk machines, but it was up the individual librarian to see that it was added to their office computer. How did we find it? A net search for "tn3270" brought up another library, which not only used this software, but also made the software available for downloading.

Evaluation

Six weeks after the completion of the home page, I met with the Reference Department. Their initial reaction was that a complete academic year must pass before they would be able to comment meaningfully about their new home page. However, they did ask for an additional access point to their homepage: an alphabetical index of sites, the addition of some telephone/address directory sites, such as "800 Numbers" and "The Switchboard," and additional links to the VIVA-provided databases from IAC and Chadwick-Healey.

ACQUISITIONS: http://janus.swem.wm.edu/Depts/Acq/acq.html

Format

Much discussion ensued on how to arrange the content for a department that includes monographs and serials acquisitions. Initially, I divided the information by "serials" and "monographs," but found that there was too much repetition in the two lists on the home page. Mindful that I had not been engaged to update this home page, the department head decided that rearrangement and deletion of double links would be necessary. We considered alphabetical order before finally opting for estimated frequency of staff use. Local information is first, so staff can check on current assignments, fund codes, and policies. Publishing sites are next—general publishing sites first, and specific companies and formats (audiovisual, microform) following. Then general professional sites connect staff to useful associations, other libraries' accquisitions pages, or listserv archives.

Content

The Acquisitions librarian had a clear conception of how he expected his department to use the Web page. Therefore, the general publishing trade links were based on his bookmarks, while the individual company Web sites reflect the companies with whom the library does business. The publisher links are to serials, monographs, and audiovisual sites, as the acquisitions department includes the purchasing of all kinds of materials. However, information of special interest to the serials acquisitions staff is provided through links to back issues sources and to library catalogs with online serials check-in. In providing the links to these catalogs I reviewed the Hytelnet lists of library catalogs by type and ascertained that Innopac, VTLS, GEAC, and Melvyl all offer this feature. I printed out a list of the libraries similar in collection size or subject content to Swem Library and consulted with the department head to further limit the list. Eight catalogs were included in the home page with login instructions when needed.

Current reference resources—especially currency exchange and directories—were requested for a "virtual reference corner," and so I identified possible links through viewing other acquisitions home pages and through Net directories such as Yahoo or Internet Sleuth.

Problems/Issues

How much text to place on the home page? Although the Acquisitions Department home page contains eighty links, only three links to text pages are maintained locally. For convenience when updating, the acquisitions librarian opted to have as few separate Web pages as possible. Therefore, the lists of staff members and librarian liaisons appear on the home page. A second level of Web pages were developed for the lengthier policy section and the tables, which were digitized in separate files.

Evaluation

I distributed survey forms several weeks after the Acquisitions home page was completed. Again staff felt that a full fiscal year was needed to test the efficacy of the Web site, but in the short period they had used it, local information and currency exchange information were cited as most useful.

CIRCULATION: http://janus.swem.wm.edu/Depts/Circ/circ.html

Format

The main question was how to index the list of forty-five special borrower groups: should there be three hotlinks to alphabetical categories which would link the staff member to either the borrower groups listed under A-K, L-R, or S-Z; or should there be an alphabetical list of all forty-five special borrower groups, with hypertext links to the information about these groups? The first option would make the home page more concise, but new staff members unfamiliar with the many groups might have trouble locating the one they need (for instance would the Christopher Wren Society be under "C" or "W"?) The department head chose the second option, so in the appropriate place in the borrowers policy, hotlinks to each group exist, and the two policy notebooks shelved behind the circulation desk are now seamlessly integrated and accessible from computers all over the library.

Content

Borrowers and reserve policies make up the body of this Web page. Previously contained in notebooks at the circulation desk, the data is now easily accessible by library staff at any service desk. Furthermore, mail-links were established to staff supervising the various activities described in the policies.

Evaluation

Staff felt that an academic year would be needed to evaluate effectively, but they generally approved content and arrangement.

CATALOGING: http://janus.swem.wm.edu/Depts/Cat/cat.html

Format

The department head and I were able to formulate an arrangement combining two goals which were that there was an need for an alphabetical list and that the most important sites should appear first. Contents are as follows:

- Library of Congress
- OCLC
- Online Catalogs
- Other Resources of Interest to Catalogers
- Virtual Reference Corner
- William and Mary Home Pages

Content

Links have been established to policy, standards, and format-setting organizations such as LC and OCLC, to library online catalogs which display MARC records (VTLS, Innovative Interfaces, and MELVYL), to SIRSI sites other than the College of William and Mary, and to lengthier cataloging Web sites. Future plans for this home page are to add local policies.

Evaluation

Staff was pleased with the organization of the home page, but not accustomed to the idea of using the Internet in their daily work. It will probably take some time for them to get into the habit of using this resource.

OUTCOMES

For a Freelancer

I found this to be an absorbing and multifaceted experience. Working with the department heads was very enjoyable—learning about their perspectives on the WWW and its uses added to my knowledge gained from examining the scientific uses with GCDIS. My interaction with these people was also very positive; of course, they all knew me from my earlier work with the library, but now, working as an independent contractor, I was able to establish a different level of rapport. Upon reflection, I perceive that my consultant position, outside the usual lines of library authority and departmental conventions, allowed department heads the luxury of a client relationship: they told me what they wanted, and blending my knowledge of the Internet and the library world, I put it together. At most, each supervisor spent three hours in initial interviews, in evaluation of the product, and in consultation with me during development.

I wildly underestimated the extensiveness of the home pages desired. Initially, the Reference and Acquisitions department heads requested a Web page of about twenty-five links to maintain. This turned out to be unrealistic, and their home pages have seventy to eighty links each. The Cataloging home page is over fifty links long. The work of reference and technical services librarians requires access to a wide variety of resources, and while I expect that several of the links will be dropped within twelve months, others will probably be added.

Locating information, adding and discarding links, and arranging the data on the home pages took the bulk of my time, while reformating a WordPerfect policy document to HTML was comparatively fast and easy. Addresses to useful Web sites changed even within the two-week period I worked on each homepage, and in my efforts to tailor these home pages and in the pure fun of designing them, I worked a total of about twenty more hours than I had estimated (originally about forty-five hours) for the four home pages. Since I was being paid by the job and not the hours, this was not desirable economically. However, since I was looking at this as an experiment for my business, I was expecting some inaccuracy in my estimates.

I would say that the department head's interest in the Internet and commitment to using the home pages contributes greatly to their success as staff aids. While I offered to set the home page default on Netscape to each department's page on each staff computer, no department head took up my offer. Only one department head did make sure that all staff's Web-browers home destination was the departmental Web page. When you are an independent agent, you do not have the power to ensure people use your product in quite the same way a department head can!

For a Webmaster

While surfing the Web, notice the content and style of home pages. In questioning the clarity of the headings, one might point to my Cataloging Department home page and quibble with "Resources of Interest to Catalogers" which is the catch-all miscellaneous heading for items that do not fit elsewhere. Yes, *all* the resources on the page are of interest to catalogers, but we chose this heading because we wanted the entry to come after OCLC in the alphabetic arrangement. So, while it may puzzle the outsider, those for whom the home page was developed understand the heading. The reality check which I use came from one library's home page which labeled a local link as "Answers to All Your Questions." Will this URL connect us to a divine being? No, just a reference department suffering from hubris.

Notice, too, the formats that work on other home pages, and when you see one with useful elements, bookmark it. This practice helped me when trying to figure out how to put a long list of short items into columns. Even though I found instructions on how to do this, my efforts did not meet with success. However, I combined these instructions with a real world example of column format (called "Tables" in HTML) and finally accomplished the task.

Maintenance of these pages is an issue that the department heads will have to face. While the work is not difficult, most staff members have a full job description already, and adding this duty will mean cutting back on something else—a difficulty for a library which has been dealing with staff cuts. Yet the worldwide access that the Internet offers to the inside workings of your library demands that you keep it current. Librarians around the world who previously could only laugh at your cataloging input in OCLC can now chortle about the accuracy and clarity of your departmental home page. Candidates deciding whether or not to accept a position at your library will be checking out your home page as well as contacting colleagues for the inside word about your library. A sloppy, dead-linked home page will not impress the library world.

The experience of reviewing the WWW for library work-related information was enlightening. I became aware of the Internet's practical uses and learned how the electronic world can bring the work of the library department together— beyond the usual lines. The Acquisitions Department's sources can enhance a reference librarian's work while all public desks can improve their service due to quick access to circulation policies. A public services view of online catalogs can assist catalogers to construct the library's database. Reviewing electronic cheat-sheets and newsletters designed for catalogers can help librarians understand the unique structure of their catalog, and improve their reference effectiveness.

We are only beginning to realize the differences that the Internet can make in our workflow. The huge amount of information on the Internet may never be tamed to our satisfaction, and in the meantime, engaging an intermediary who can dedicate time to the exploration of emerging resources to put together an electronic pathfinder/home page tailored to a librarian's activities will become a necessity, not a luxury.

INDEX

Other Books of Interest from Information Today, Inc.